IRREGULAR UNIONS

IRREGULAR UNIONS

CLANDESTINE MARRIAGE IN EARLY MODERN ENGLISH LITERATURE

KATHARINE CLELAND

CORNELL UNIVERSITY PRESS
Ithaca and London

Publication of this open monograph was the result of
Virginia Tech's participation in TOME (Toward an Open
Monograph Ecosystem), a collaboration of the
Association of American Universities, the Association of
University Presses, and the Association of Research
Libraries. TOME aims to expand the reach of long-form
humanities and social science scholarship including digital
scholarship. Additionally, the program looks to ensure the
sustainability of university press monograph publishing
by supporting the highest quality scholarship and
promoting a new ecology of scholarly publishing in
which authors' institutions bear the publication costs.

Funding from Virginia Tech made it possible to open this
publication to the world.

www.openmonographs.org

Library of Congress Cataloging-in-Publication Data

Names: Cleland, Katharine, 1982– author.
Title: Irregular unions : clandestine marriage in early
    modern English literature / Katharine Cleland.
Description: Ithaca [New York] : Cornell University Press,
    [2021] | Includes bibliographical references and index.
Identifiers: LCCN 2020015143 (print) | LCCN 2020015144
    (ebook) | ISBN 9781501753473 (paperback) |
    ISBN 9781501753497 (pdf) |
    ISBN 9781501753480 (epub)
Subjects: LCSH: Marriage in literature. | Clandestinity
    (Canon law) | English literature—Early modern,
    1500–1700—History and criticism.
Classification: LCC PN56.M28 C58 2021 (print) |
    LCC PN56.M28 (ebook) | DDC 820.9/3543—dc23
LC record available at https://lccn.loc.gov/2020015143
LC ebook record available at https://lccn.loc.gov
    /2020015144

For Hattie and Alice

Contents

Acknowledgments

All scholarly books have long histories, and I would like to start at the very beginning. I am grateful for wonderful teachers and mentors at early stages in my education. First, I would like to thank Kristopher H. Koechling. I would also like to thank Megan Matchinske and Larry Goldberg at the University of North Carolina at Chapel Hill. In particular, I would like to thank Jessica Wolfe, who introduced me not only to Spenser's *Faerie Queene* but also to the jouissance of scholarship.

As a graduate student at the Pennsylvania State University, I benefited from the stellar early period faculty in both the English and History departments. I would like to thank Robert R. Edwards, Ronnie Hsia, Joan B. Landes, Marcy North, and Linda Woodbridge. A special thanks to Laura L. Knoppers for her continued advice and friendship. Furthermore, I would like to thank the following members of the Early Period Studies Group for their conversation and friendship: Ryan Croft, Gabriel Ford, Ryan Hackenbracht, Giuseppina Iacono Lobo, Niamh O'Leary, Chad Schrock, Paul Dustin Stegner, Catherine Thomas, Sarah Breckenridge Wright, and Paul Zajac.

I cannot adequately express my gratitude to Patrick Cheney and Garrett A. Sullivan, Jr. for their advice, encouragement, and mentorship throughout the writing of this book. Each of them read multiple drafts of several chapters, and always with the same interest and enthusiasm as though approaching the project for the first time. I am deeply indebted to them both.

I am grateful for my colleagues and students at my current institution, Virginia Tech. My department heads, Joseph Eska and Bernice Hausman, have been exemplary in their support. Ernie Sullivan was an excellent mentor when I first arrived in the English department. I never would have finished the manuscript without the help and support of Katy Powell. Peter Potter and Elizabeth Spiller provided advice and encouragement along the way. I would also like to thank my two graduate research assistants: Rachel Wurster and Anna Merz.

At Cornell University Press, Mahinder Kingra has been the ideal editor, and I am grateful that he saw the potential in my project. I am particularly indebted to the reviewers, Sarah Beckwith and an anonymous reviewer, who read the manuscript closely and wrote highly detailed reports. The final manuscript greatly benefited from their insightful comments and suggestions, as well as from suggestions by Cornell University Press's faculty and editorial review boards.

This project had financial support from a number of sources. At Penn State, I received funding from the Humanities Institute and the Rock Ethics Institute. The Folger Institute funded a short-term fellowship at the Folger Shakespeare Library. The project benefited from my conversation with other fellows, particularly Jay Zysk and Kat Lecky. At Virginia Tech, I also received funding from a Niles Research Grant and the Center for Humanities.

Parts of this book have already appeared in print. Portions of chapter 1 appeared as "English National Identity and the Reformation Problem of Clandestine Marriage in Spenser's *Faerie Queene*, Book I," in *Spenser Studies* 29 (2014): 75–103. Copyright © 2014 by the University of Chicago Press. Used by permission of the publisher. https://press.uchicago.edu.

Portions of chapter 2 first appeared as "'Wanton Loves, and Yong Desires': Clandestine Marriage in Marlowe's *Hero and Leander* and Chapman's Continuation," in *Studies in Philology* 108, no. 2 (2011): 215–237. Copyright © 2011 by the University of North Carolina Press. Used by permission of the publisher. https://www.uncpress.org

I have saved the most important people in my life for the end. My parents, John and Pam, and sister, Elizabeth, have been patient, loving, and supportive through these long years. My husband, James, always maintained confidence that I would finish the book, and I am happy to acknowledge officially in print: he was right. I would like to thank my parents-in-law, Jon and Kathy, for their help during the COVID-19 crisis. While I was completing this book, my two daughters—Harriet Elizabeth and Alice Helen—were born. They have brought more joy to my life than I could have ever thought possible. I dedicate the book to them.

IRREGULAR UNIONS

Introduction

Making a Clandestine Match in Early Modern English Literature

In Shakespeare's *As You Like It*, Touchstone, the fool, attempts to marry Audrey, a poor country girl, in a clandestine ceremony in the forest of Arden. Sir Oliver Mar-Text, the would-be officiate of the wedding, insists that Audrey "must be given, or the marriage is not lawful" (3.3.69–70).[1] What no one in this scene realizes is that this statement is not technically true: witnesses or participants of any kind were not required to make a legal marriage in early modern England. Sir Oliver's ineptitude, however, can be forgiven. His misstatement reflects the widespread confusion concerning the making of a match during the period, even on the part of the clergy. Many early modern audience members probably would have nodded along in agreement. Since the *Book of Common Prayer* does call for witnesses, those not familiar with the law could easily assume that they were necessary for a legal union. The *Book of Common Prayer* also dictates the types of witnesses: a couple's "frendes and neighbours."[2] Even more specifically, a woman's "father or frendes" should be the ones to present her to the minister.[3] An eavesdropper who happens to be lurking in the bushes nearby (in this case, the melancholy Jaques) would not seem to fall into one of these recommended categories. Jaques, who obligingly offers to give the bride away, also persuades Touchstone to delay the wedding to a more appropriate time and venue:

> And will you (being a man of your breeding) be married under a bush like a beggar? Get you to church, and have a good priest that can tell you what marriage is. This fellow will but join you together as they join wainscot; then one of you will prove a shrunk panel, and like green timber warp, warp.
>
> (3.3.83–89)

By ordering Touchstone to "get . . . to church," Jaques informs the fool that a nuptial ceremony with an officiate and a stranger giving away the bride does not fulfill the proper requirements. Even more tellingly, he insists that the marriage be performed by a more qualified minister, "a *good* priest who can tell you what marriage is," so that the union does not "warp" over time. Performing the appropriate rituals is just as important as thoroughly understanding the duties and responsibilities associated with marriage. Couples who participate in clandestine marriages, Jaques suggests, may not learn marriage's true purpose or how to foster that marriage after a wedding has occurred. Touchstone, of course, indicates that he has no desire for his marriage to be a success. In an aside, he admits that he is aware of the minister's shortcomings: "I am not in the mind but I were better to be married of him than of another, for he is not like to marry me well; and not being well married, it will be a good excuse for me hereafter to leave my wife" (3.3.90–94). By employing a minister not well versed in the law or the appropriate rituals, Touchstone anticipates that he might be able to finagle his way out of the marriage later. Happily, Jaques's chiding spoils this plan. His meddling legitimates the potential benefits of constant communal surveillance: he rescues Audrey from being left in the lurch by an unscrupulous groom.

Shakespeare thus stages the confusion surrounding the proper making of a marriage in early modern England. The officiate himself does not understand the lawful requirements of marriage, but everyone involved seems to agree that a witness is necessary to give away the bride. There is also such a thing as a good officiate and a bad officiate: one who can "tell you what marriage is" as opposed to one who might "mar the text" of the marriage ceremony as Sir Oliver's name implies. Furthermore, the *proper* way to make a match may not be entirely the same as the *legal* way. A proper minister and witnesses may not be necessary for a legal union, that is, but they may be necessary for a good one that will not "warp." Throughout his works, Shakespeare famously portrays an array of marriage rituals and oaths—none of which adhere exactly (or, in most cases, remotely) to the *Book of Common Prayer*. On the one hand, Shakespeare takes advantage of his role as artist. He manipulates rituals and customs to suit his story and purpose (and to escape the

Master of the Revels' censorship).[4] On the other, Shakespeare's varying approaches evince the range of marital practices during the early modern period. Shakespeare could portray marriage making in such a variety of ways because they were all within the realm of legal possibility, even if some of them were not always very likely.

The practice of clandestine marriage, however, was far more than one of Shakespeare's favorite plot devices. As this book demonstrates, a range of other early modern authors, including Edmund Spenser, Christopher Marlowe, and George Chapman, incorporate clandestine marriages into their works, underscoring the widespread interest in irregular unions and their impact. The issue of clandestine marriage was also at the heart of theological, political, and social controversies that permeated all levels of early modern society. In theological terms, clandestine marriages undermined the rituals of the *Book of Common Prayer*, destabilizing the state's desire for religious uniformity. The practice also created possibilities for political maneuvering, allowing members of noble families to strengthen their claims to the throne through intermarriage. From a social perspective, clandestine marriages had the potential to create general unrest, resulting in single mothers, for instance, who struggled to provide for their children (the hapless Audrey's conceivable fate if not for Jaques's interference). Often, these differing controversies entangled with one another. This book reveals how taking the complexities of these controversies into consideration can inform and even change our reading of clandestine marriage in early modern literature, including—but not limited to—Shakespeare's plays.

Irregular Unions: Clandestine Marriage in Early Modern English Literature thus constitutes the first literary history of clandestine marriage in early modern England. R. B. Outhwaite has already provided a historical account, while other historians have recognized the importance of the practice.[5] Considering the long-standing general interest in early modern marital practices, however, it is surprising how infrequently literary scholars have considered the subject of clandestine marriage specifically. Most of the literary scholarship on irregular unions has been confined to chapters in monographs devoted to marriage and Shakespeare more generally.[6] In this book, I look beyond descriptions of discrete rituals or practices in Shakespeare's plays to call for a wider cultural view on clandestine marriage and its literary significance.

In doing so, I not only uncover instances of neglected marital practices in early modern literature but also explore how attention to these practices and the controversies surrounding them can influence how we read individual works as a whole. We can thus see how the controversies surrounding clandestine marriage inform and collide with one another, sometimes in a single work. Historical documents often tell only one side of the story. Court depositions, for instance, may include only questions asked or evidence provided. Protestant reformers may condemn the theological basis for clandestine vows when championing their cause, while ignoring real-life practicalities. Works of literature show that attitudes toward irregular unions did not remain stagnant after the Reformation or change overnight. Literary genres allow authors to look at clandestine marriage from different angles, portraying it as troubling the foundations of nation in the epic or allowing for sexual liberty in the epyllion or being the reason for psychological torment in the complaint. Furthermore, by foregrounding irregular unions, this book's chapters illuminate difficult aspects of familiar works that have long puzzled readers and scholars alike, such as the imbroglio between the Redcrosse Knight and Duessa in Spenser's *Faerie Queene*, book I, and Jessica's seeming discomfort when entering the Belmont community in Shakespeare's *Merchant of Venice*.

In reading fictions of clandestine marriage, I argue that early modern authors use irregular unions to explore the intersection between the self and the marriage ritual in post-Reformation England. The texts that I consider—Spenser's *Faerie Queene*, Marlowe's *Hero and Leander* and Chapman's continuation, Shakespeare's *A Lover's Complaint*, *The Merchant of Venice*, and *Othello*—all display a strong link between clandestine marriage and the transformation of identity. Early modern theologians, preachers, and moralists frequently dwell on the transformative nature of the marriage ritual, which turns a couple into a husband and a wife, as well as into householders and citizens. Since the public solemnization became a vehicle through which couples confirmed their commitment to the nation's new rituals and ideals, participating in a clandestine marriage called a couple's intentions and even their very identities into question. On the one hand, clandestine marriage allowed couples complete freedom of choice when transforming their identities through marriage. On the other, these transformations could fail if the couple's families and communities did not accept their new identities as husband and wife. This book explores how early modern authors exploit and interrogate this potential contradiction.

Defining Clandestine Marriage

What made a marriage "clandestine" in early modern England? In an affirmation of the importance of the practice to the period, the *Oxford English Dictionary* cites a letter describing the clandestine marriage between the Earl of Hertford and the Lady Katherine Grey in 1562 when defining the term as "secret, private, concealed; usually in a bad sense, implying craft or deception; underhand, surreptitious."[7] Clandestine marriages certainly could be "secret" in the literal sense. Canon law, deriving from the Middle Ages, dictated that consent alone was all that was necessary to make a legally binding match even in the absence of witnesses.[8] In his *Treatise of Spousals, or Matrimonial Contracts*, Henry Swinburne explains the meaning and significance of spousal vows that could result in legal marriage.[9] A *de praesenti* contract, or marital vows spoken in the present tense, resulted in an immediate marital union, while *de futuro* vows indicated the promise of a future marriage (a kind of high-stakes betrothal).[10] Swinburne elucidates: "Spousals *de praesenti* are a mutual Promise or Contract of present Matrimony . . . as when the man doth say to the Woman [*I do take thee to my Wife*] and she then answereth [*I do take thee to my Husband*]."[11] While Swinburne acknowledges "that man and that woman, which do contract Spousals *de futuro* as [*I will take thee to my Wife; I will take thee to my Husband*] are not very Husband and Wife," he does warn that *de futuro* spousal vows can be dissolved only by "mutual agreement."[12] Otherwise, any relationship or contract made later would be adulterous or even bigamous. Furthermore, the sexual consummation of a *de futuro* contract automatically resulted in a legally binding contract. While Swinburne urges couples to use the language he recommends, spousal contracts did not have to follow an exact formula. A variety of verbal and nonverbal expressions could result in, or at least be confused for, a promise of marriage. As Martin Ingram, Ralph Houlbrooke, and Loreen L. Giese have all shown, church court records are full of depositions between couples where one member clearly thought that a marriage had been contracted via spousal vows and the other, quite simply, did not.[13]

While clandestine marriages could be secret or even "underhanded," this was not always the case. The term "clandestine" also operated in a more technical legal sense. The ecclesiastical courts considered any marriage that violated the other canons relating to marriage to be "clandestine."[14] The church courts, therefore, could punish couples that married clandestinely (as well as ministers who officiated clandestine weddings and their witnesses), but they could not invalidate irregular unions.[15] Ingram explains: "A marriage ceremony was regarded as 'clandestine' when it neglected one or more of the canonical regulations governing the solemnization of matrimony. . . . This meant a marriage without the threefold publication of banns or the issue of a valid license, a ceremony conducted outside the diocese in which the couple dwelt, or a marriage performed during certain prohibited seasons or outside certain set hours, or in any circumstances save within a lawful church or chapel and in the presence of a proper constituted minister of the church of England."[16]

According to Outhwaite, "Some irregular unions might have involved only minor breaches of the ecclesiastical code. . . . Such a union was irregular but not necessarily a hole-in-the-corner affair. Nevertheless it was technically clandestine."[17] Outhwaite's useful categorization of the varying levels of clandestinity further illustrates the range of possible irregular unions:[18]

1. Handfastings or trothplights (marriages without church or priest)
2. Marriages by priest but without church
3. Marriages by priest in church but without banns or license
4. Marriages in the "lawless" churches or in prison churches
5. Licensed clandestinity

Handfastings or trothplights were supposed to be performed via the spousal vows described above. Since these unions did not require witnesses to form a legal union, they were the locus of much anxiety. In actual practice, however, many early modern couples who did not have the resources for a public celebration would cement their marital bond with a trothplight before participating in a public solemnization when they could better afford it. The second and third options became more frequent in the late sixteenth and early seventeenth centuries. It is well known, for instance, that Shakespeare married his wife, Anne Hathaway, after the banns had been called only once instead of the requisite three times.[19] "Lawless" churches, including the Fleet prison chapels, enjoyed the most notoriety during the mid to late seventeenth century, though they were in operation by the mid-sixteenth century.[20] In these churches, unordained ministers operated a kind of black market in weddings, willingly marrying couples without banns or licenses. Couples could also buy licenses to marry without banns or during the restricted seasons (or to marry underage as Shakespeare did)—these licenses were the only way to avoid potential punishment in the church courts for marrying irregularly. So, while canon law dictated that consent alone was all that was necessary to make a legal match, it also dictated that, ideally, marriages should be performed during certain seasons and at certain times (clocks in the Fleet prison chapels were always set to the canonical hour to ensure compliance), and properly solemnized in a church with witnesses only after the banns had been called three times.[21] Clandestine marriages, therefore, were *transgressive* since they violated societal and religious norms, but they were not *illegal*.

The popularity of marriage manuals further illustrates the confusion surrounding the making of a match, since it required so much elucidation. Heinrich Bullinger's *Der Christlich Eestand*, or *The Christen State of Matrymonye*, for instance, was published more than any other continental Protestant work during the reigns of Henry VIII and Edward VI.[22] Bullinger's emphasis on love and mutuality between spouses was especially popular. English moralists and preachers, such as William Gouge and Robert Cleaver, borrow heavily from *The Christen State of Matrymonye* in their own domestic treatises.[23] In *Of Domesticall Duties*, Gouge confirms the broad definition of clandestine marriage while unequivocally condemning the practice. "Contrary are clandestine marriages," he proclaims disapprovingly, "such as are made in priuate houses, or other secret places, or in Churches without a sufficient number of witnesses, or in the night time, or without a lawfull Minister of the word."[24] Gouge admits that clandestine marriages did not necessarily have to be surreptitious affairs as the dictionary definition suggests. They could have been performed in a church with witnesses, simply without a "sufficient" amount. Or without a "lawfull Minister," such as Sir Oliver Mar-Text.

As Shakespeare's Jaques insists, a "good" or "lawfull Minister" is necessary to learn "what marriage is." The *Book of Common Prayer* not only dictated types of witnesses for marriage ceremonies but also added a new reason for entering into wedlock. After the Reformation, sexual desire alone no longer constituted a valid reason to enter into a marriage. In addition to the previously accepted goals of matrimony, "the procreation of children" and a "remedy agaynste synne and to avoide fornication," the prayer book adds a new goal stressing companionship: "the mutual societie, help, and comfort, that the one ought to have of the other, bothe in prosperitye, and adversitye."[25] Social historians have argued over whether the period actually resulted in the "companionate" marriages that the third ordinance describes (and that moralists like Bullinger and his English counterparts champion).[26] Investigating fictions of clandestine marriage contributes to our understanding of this evolving marital paradigm.

In doing so, this book arrives at a counterintuitive conclusion. The Reformation's emphasis on marital companionship would seem to encourage a couple's agency within the matchmaking process, perhaps even encouraging clandestine marriage so as to foster the ideal of wedded love. This book demonstrates that clandestine marriages, and their association with desire rather than companionship, undermined the perceived purpose of the marital bond. Arranged marriages, particularly the contracting of children and infants, did become increasingly rare.[27] Preachers and moralists, however, associated clandestine marriages' catering to matrimony's second ordinance (sexual desire) as undermining the other goals of marriage that benefited not just the couple but society as a whole. Bullinger, for instance, claims that those who "layed together" without participating in a public church ceremony "sekest nothyng but carnall desyre" in wedlock.[28] To avoid suspicion surrounding their reasons for marrying, couples relied on both familial and communal approval for their marriages to go forward. Literary fictions, therefore, often portray the negative consequences of desire, or must defuse the connotations of desire associated with a clandestine marriage, for that union to be successful.

The aforementioned clandestine marriage between Lady Katherine Grey and the Earl of Hertford exemplifies how the fear of unruly desire could serve as a scapegoat when calling irregular unions into question. In 1564, Lady Katherine—Queen Elizabeth's cousin—created scandal when she claimed that she was secretly married to Edward Seymour, the Earl of Hertford. The secret came out when the heavily pregnant Lady Katherine, alone and desperate at the time (the earl was abroad finishing his education), sought the help of Lord Robert Dudley. This was ill advised. A loyal and dutiful subject (at least in this instance), Dudley informed his sovereign; the infuriated queen promptly threw her cousin in the tower. After the hapless Seymour returned from Paris, the couple was accused of "carnall copulation."[29] A commission, formed especially for the purpose, interrogated the lovers separately at length to determine if a marriage had actually taken place. Questions about minute details, such as "what did youe weare upon y[our] hedd at the tyme you lay in bedd with the said Erle," were obviously intended to catch the couple in conflicting stories.[30] The commission did not uncover any egregious conflicts, but the lack of witnesses meant that there was no way to prove a legal union. (Jane Seymour, the marriage's only witness, had died the previous year, and the officiating minister, a real-life Sir Oliver Mar-Text, could not be found.) After the commission pronounced that the marriage had never taken place, Lady Katherine never saw the earl again. Today, no one doubts that the Lady Katherine Grey and the Earl of Hertford had a clandestine marriage, and it is likely the commissioners felt the same way. Queen Elizabeth's underlying fear that the marriage constituted a plot to strengthen Lady Katherine's claim to the throne, however, necessitated that the commission find the couple guilty of fornication rather than of marrying clandestinely.[31]

The length of the commission's deposition on the Hertford marriage provides fascinating insight into the kinds of details that could legitimate (or illegitimate) clandestine marriages. The commissioners were keen to determine whether a minister performed a religious ceremony and according to what rituals. As Lady Katherine recalls, a minister did preside over the solemnization, but he "ware noe surples."[32] He also read from "the booke of service," from which he took "the wordes of matrimony they both spake one to thother."[33] Lady Katherine showed the examiners a wedding ring from the earl "conteyneinge five links of Gold" as evidence that a marriage had taken place.[34] Perhaps less obviously, the commission asked about aspects of the wedding day that might have connoted the sincerity of the proceedings. They asked, for instance, how long Lady Katherine spent "dressing & tyringe" herself (one can only wonder how long the commissioners expected a bride to spend on her clothing).[35] They also discussed the practical matters surrounding marriage, such as whether the couple made wills and discussed financial concerns. Even though consent alone technically created a legal union, the commissioners clearly believed that there should be more to making a marriage: a ceremony conducted by a "lawfull Minister," expressions of mutual love and affection, and even financial transactions. High-profile clandestine marriages such as this one naturally captured the imagination of early modern readers and audience members, making excellent fodder for both the page and stage.

John Webster caters to the fascination with courtly intrigue surrounding clandestine marriage in *The Duchess of Malfi*. The play portrays the actual clandestine marriage of the historical Duchess of Amalfi, Giovanna d'Aragona, while also capitalizing on the scandal in the Jacobean court surrounding Arbella Stuart's clandestine marriage to William Seymour.[36] One cannot find a more textbook example of a marriage via spousal vows in early modern literature. After proposing to her steward, Antonio, the Duchess states: "I have heard lawyers say a contract in a chamber, / *Per verba presenti* is absolute marriage" (1.2.385–386).[37] She is clearly savvy to the legal language that legitimated marriages in an early modern court. During the contracting of the marriage, the Duchess and Antonio discuss the nature of their marital bond:

> *Antonio:* That we may imitate the loving palms,
> Best emblem of a peaceful marriage,
> That ne'er bore fruit divided.
> *Duchess:*   What can the church force more?
> *Antonio:* That fortune may not know an accident,
> Either of joy or sorrow, to divide
> Our fixed wishes.
> *Duchess:*   How can the church build faster?
> We now are man and wife, and 'tis the church
> That must but echo this.
>
> *(1.2.392–399)*

The Duchess's repeated references to the church ("what can the church force more?"; "how can the church build faster?") serve to stress the legality of the marriage while hinting at the Duchess's anxiety underlying the secret contract's religious context. One does not ask such questions if one is absolutely certain. Indeed, the Duchess indicates that their legal marriage vows will strong-arm the church, which "must but echo" their personal choice, rather than necessarily garner its approval. In this scene, Webster underscores the tension between the legal requirements for making a marriage and the ecclesiastical ones.

Not all stories of clandestine marriage were ripped from the headlines, however, or even about the nobility. Clandestine marriage was a controversial practice at all levels of society—not just where large sums of money, titles, and the governance of the realm were at stake. When authors portray clandestine marriage, therefore, they may be catering to the demand for juicy stories about courtly intrigue, or addressing the more plebian concerns of day-to-day life: What should a father do if a daughter runs off with a suitor her family has not approved? Does the clandestine marriage of one's neighbors indicate that they are secretly adhering to Catholic traditions? Is there recourse for a pregnant woman whose husband has abandoned her and denies that a marriage took place? How can such occurrences be prevented? Early modern authors and their readers had to navigate these issues surrounding irregular unions in their own everyday lives.

In 1601, for example, the then little-known John Donne married the seventeen-year-old Ann More in a clandestine service. The couple met while Ann was staying with her uncle, Sir Thomas Egerton, who also happened to be the twenty-nine-year-old Donne's employer. In a clear effort to lend legitimacy to the proceedings, Donne's friend Christopher Brooke gave the bride away, while his brother, Samuel Brooke, an ordained minister, performed the ceremony.[38] Despite these efforts, however, Ann's father, Sir George More, was not happy when he learned of the union. Doubtless, Donne's "poverty and obscurity" did not make his daughter's choice a pleasant surprise.[39] The poet's Catholic background did not help smooth things over. Donne, however, had clearly anticipated More's anger, obtaining "expert legal advice" in advance to ensure that the marriage could not be invalidated.[40] Cunningly, he preemptively hired lawyers to argue the validity of the marriage in the ecclesiastical Court of Audience. By the time his father-in-law found out about his daughter's marriage, Donne was already anticipating a ruling in his favor. While the church courts could not invalidate the marriage, they did (temporarily) excommunicate Donne—a common punishment that the courts inflicted on those who married irregularly. The irregular union also had dire financial consequences for the young couple. While More's father could not dissolve the marriage as he had hoped, he punished the couple personally by initially withholding Ann's inheritance and ensuring that Donne was not able to return to his former employment. Donne's hopes for a prestigious public career were dashed, and, while he clearly cared deeply for his wife and children, the au-

thor wrestled with suicidal thoughts during the years that followed as he struggled to provide for his rapidly growing family.[41]

Of course, since the canons relating to marriage existed relatively un-
changed since the Middle Ages, clandestine marriage did not suddenly become a problem in the Renaissance whereas it had not been one before.
Children have always married secretly against the wishes of their parents. In
his *Concordance of Discordant Canons*, Gratian begrudgingly agrees that clandestine marriages cannot be dissolved while also claiming that they should be
considered "infected."[42] Henry Ansgar Kelly demonstrates that some medieval
works of literature that have been traditionally associated with illicit sexual
desire or the practice of "courtly-love," most notably Chaucer's *Troilus and Criseyde*, actually depict clandestine marriages.[43] *Irregular Unions* builds on Kelly's
work by revealing some early modern literary portrayals of clandestine marriage that go unnoticed by modern readers. As a testament to the fascination
with the practice in the early modern period as opposed to the medieval one,
however, even the casual reader of Shakespeare can probably name several
plays that feature a clandestine marriage.

The Elizabethan Religious Settlement's groundbreaking standardization of
the marriage ritual makes the period an important one in the history of clandestine marriage. Before the widespread implementation of the *Book of Common Prayer*, there was not a uniform solemnization of matrimony. The Sarum
Missal provided the most commonly used marriage rite in pre-Reformation
England, but it was not the only option. Brian Cummings informs, "There was
more variation among the medieval English uses (such as Hereford and York)
on matrimony than for other services."[44] The *Book of Common Prayer's* "The
Fourme of Solempnizacion of Matrimonye" does borrow heavily from pre-
Reformation marriage rituals, particularly from the Sarum rite.[45] As in medieval marriage rituals, the calling of the banns provides an important safeguard
against clandestine marriage. The prayer book, however, incorporates more
severe language warning against impediments or improper solemnization.
This language reflects a new "attempt to use the church service to regulate
social practice."[46] The 1559 Religious Settlement, which reestablished the Act
of Supremacy and set in place the Act of Uniformity, therefore, standardized
the marriage ritual for the first time by *requiring* ministers and their constituents to adhere to the prayers and rituals set forth in the *Book of Common Prayer*.
Theoretically, this standardization should have eliminated the problem of clandestine marriage since it legally obligated couples to adhere to every aspect
of the reformed ritual (including the calling of the banns). Instead, an uneasy
tension arose between the Act of Uniformity's stance that all marriages should

take place in a public ceremony according to the prescribed rituals and the canon stating that consent alone was all that was necessary to make a legal match.

An increased emphasis on the marital bond after the Reformation, as evidenced by the prayer book's new ordinance on companionship, also naturally resulted in an increasing public concern over the prevalence of clandestine marriage. As chapter 1 will explore in further detail, the Elizabethan regime relied on communities to report violators of the new prayer book's rituals to the ecclesiastical courts, creating an atmosphere of marital surveillance. Furthermore, social problems that had always been associated with clandestine marriage, such as poverty, bigamy, and matters of inheritance, were now viewed as destabilizing the Protestant nation, which counted on strong households to foster domestic and economic tranquility. Beginning in the Elizabethan period, therefore, the ecclesiastical courts worked not just to enforce canon law but also to enforce the new rituals laid out in the *Book of Common Prayer*. Any marriage that did not conform to the official Solemnization of Matrimony could be deemed "clandestine."

Becoming "One Flesh"

The practice of clandestine marriage called into question which rituals, words, and actions resulted in a man and woman transforming into husband and wife. While Swinburne insists that vows spoken in present tense result in the transformation, the *Book of Common Prayer* indicates that more is necessary for the transformation to occur. Before the ceremony can even begin, the prayer book lists requirements:

> First, the bannes must be asked thre severall Sondaies or holy daies, in the tyme of service, the people beyng present, after the accustomed maner.
> And yf the persons that would be maryed dwell in diverse Paryshes, the bannes must be asked in both Parishes and the Curate of the one Paryshe shall not solempnyze matrimonye betwyxt them, wythout a certifycate of the bannes bying thryse asked, from the Curate of the other Parysh. At the date appoincted for solempnizacyon of Matrimonye, the persones to be maryed shal come into the body of the Churche, wyth theyr frendes and neighbours.[47]

Only after these prerequisites does the priest begin the marriage ceremony with the familiar words: "Dearely beloved frendes, we are gathered together here in the sight of God, and in the face of his congregacion, to joyne together this man and this woman in holy matrimony, which is an honorable state, instytuted of God in Paradise, in the time of mannes innocencie, signifiyng unto us the mistical union that is betwixt Christ and his Churche."[48] This statement indicates that marriages occur only "in the sight of God" when couples are in their own parish churches, surrounded by their own friends and congregations. Only then can their union mimic the "mistical" one between Christ and church. The officiate pronounces the couple to be "man and wife together" immediately after their spousal vows, emphasizing the significance of these expressions of mutual consent for the transformation.[49] Even after this pronouncement, however, he goes on to add a blessing and preach a sermon, elaborating on "what marriage is." This is a long way from simply stating vows, which is all the law requires. If couples were supposed to abide by the *Book of Common Prayer*, then, one might ask, are the couples that do not abide by the rituals actually married? Or is their marriage, to use Jaques's terminology, "warped" in some way? Is the transformation into husband and wife somehow incomplete if all of the rituals have not been followed? Should a community feel uncomfortable accepting couples who married clandestinely into their midst for these reasons? As Gouge explains, the *Book of Common Prayer* leaves absolutely nothing to chance when it comes to marriage making:

> There are declared the grounds, ends, and vses of mariage. There open proclamation is made whether any can except against the intended mariage. There each partie is solemnly charged, that if either of them doe know any impediment, why they may not lawfully be maried, to disclose it. There also each partie is openly demanded if freely and willingly they will take one another for man and wife. There the duties of maried persons are declared, and they seuerally asked whether they will subiect themselues thereto or no. All which being openly professed, the parent or some in his stead is called forth to giue the Bride to the Bridegroome. Then they two actually taking each other to be man and wife, and testifying the same by expresse words, and by mutuall pledges, the Minister in Gods name ioyneth them together, pronounceth them to be lawfull husband and wife, and by prayer craueth Gods blessing vpon the action, and vpon their persons. Thus is the mariage consecrated, and they two made one flesh, that is, lawfully ioyned together by the inuiolable bond of marriage.[50]

By providing such a thorough summary of the prayer book's marriage ceremony, Gouge implies that couples who do not abide by *all* of the prescribed guidelines may not actually be "one flesh." They may have a bond, but it may not be "inuiolable." In his discussion of clandestine marriages, the preacher admonishes: "There is little hope that such mariages should have any good successe."[51]

Perhaps surprisingly considering his own relationship with clandestine marriage, John Donne makes a similar assertion in a marriage sermon in 1621. He explains how marriages should properly take place in Protestant England:

> As mariage is a civill Contract, it must be so done in publick, as that it may have the testimony of men; As mariage is a religious Contract, it must be so done, as that it may have the benediction of the Priest: In a mariage without testimony of men they cannot claim any benefit by the Law; In a marriage without the benediction of the Priest they cannot claim any benefit of the Church: for how Matrimonially soever such persons as have maried themselves may pretend to love, and live together, yet all that love, and all that life is but a regulated Adultery, it is not mariage.[52]

Donne would have been keenly aware that couples who participate in clandestine marriages cannot "claim any benefit by the Law" after he struggled to obtain financial support from his father-in-law, but his proclamation that clandestine marriages amount to "regulated Adultery" is astonishing. A church court might rule that a marriage has taken place, but, according to Donne, the marriage is indeed tainted, or even sinful, as the accusation of adultery implies. Couples who marry clandestinely, Donne explains, do not enter into marriage at all. It seems unlikely that Donne considered his own clandestine marriage to be "regulated Adultery." What we do know, however, is that, as a popular and influential preacher, he encouraged his congregation to think along these lines.

Couples who married clandestinely thus cast suspicion on their new identities as husband and wife. Perhaps the transformation was not complete: warped. "As such seeking of secrecie taketh much from the honour and dignitie of mariage," Gouge warns ominously, "so it implieth some evill cleaving thereto: *For euery man that evill doth hateth the light*."[53] Marrying clandestinely cast doubts on a couple's intentions, suggesting that they have something to hide, something that they do not want to bring into "the light," such as Touchstone's own self-professed ill intentions toward Audrey. These ill intentions did not even have to be true to be problematic. The Earl of Hertford and the Lady Katherine Grey hid their own marriage because they knew it would transform them into traitors in Queen Elizabeth's eyes. Though it seems unlikely that the couple intended to use their marriage as a means to seize the throne, they could not escape the presumption: their vows transformed them into traitors despite their intentions. In *The Duchess of Malfi*, the Duchess's secret vows result in her subjects calling her a "strumpet" (3.1.26) because they do not realize that she is married to the father of her children. They do not realize that she has undergone a marital transformation. In *As You Like It*, Jaques also counts on the relationship between marriage and identity when persuading Touchstone to marry Audrey in a proper ceremony. By flattering the fool as a "man of breeding," Jaques implies that a true gentleman would never marry clandestinely, and the vain Touchstone agrees to a public marriage at the comedy's end. Touchstone's desire to be viewed as a "man of breeding" overcomes his desire to abandon his wife.

Fictions of Clandestine Marriage

Not all literary instances of clandestine marriage are as obvious as Touchstone's abortive attempt or the Duchess's contract with Antonio. Due to the myriad of possibilities through which couples could contract marriages, modern readers unfamiliar with early modern marriage practices may not recognize unions that an early modern reader would interpret as constituting (or potentially constituting) a marriage. In both reality and fiction, whether a couple had transformed into husband and wife could, at least under some circumstances, be up for debate. This becomes even more evident in works of fiction that trade in such ambiguity to drive their narrative. In this book, I am also interested in literary portrayals of irregular unions where transformations of identity beyond simply becoming husband and wife are at stake. Does entering into a contract with a Catholic undermine one's Protestantism? Can a Jew convert to Christianity through marriage if no one sees the ritual performed? The ways in which authors grapple with such questions suggest that narratives of clandestine marriage were far more than interesting plot devices on the early modern stage or scandalous stories ripped from the headlines. Instead, fictions of clandestine marriage allow early modern authors to explore topics of identity formation within post-Reformation England.

The following chapters particularly focus on fictions of clandestine marriage written during the late Elizabethan or early Jacobean periods—periods impacted by the Religious Settlement and yet before the turmoil of the Caroline period and the civil wars that drastically changed the nature of marriage in England, at least temporarily. I have divided the chapters into two sections. In the first three chapters, I focus on poetic representations of clandestine marriage that the modern reader not familiar with the practice might easily overlook. In chapter 1, I look to the role that clandestine marriage plays in the

English nationalism of Spenser's *Faerie Queene*, book I. The following two chapters on Marlowe's *Hero and Leander* and Chapman's continuation, and on Spenser's *Epithalamion* and Shakespeare's *A Lover's Complaint*, focus on literary dialogues about clandestine marriage that either directly or indirectly respond to Spenser's project. As these chapters reveal, clandestine marriage was such an important and controversial issue that early modern authors engage with, revise, and even correct each other's portrayals of the practice. In the final two chapters, I look to Shakespeare's representations of elopement in his Venetian plays. In these plays, Shakespeare compellingly explores how clandestine marriage creates opportunities for racial and / or religious outsiders to enter into white, Christian society, underscoring the importance of the marriage ritual to identity in the early modern period. In the conclusion, I briefly look to the Caroline period by examining John Ford's appropriation of Shakespeare's *Romeo and Juliet* in his tale of incestuous clandestine marriage: *'Tis Pity She's a Whore*. The conclusion thus explores the escalating disputes about irregular unions in the period leading up to the English Revolution. Ultimately, readers will leave the book with an understanding of how widespread controversies surrounding clandestine marriage made a profound impact on early modern English literature and culture, and will be better able to identify and interpret irregular unions in other early modern works for themselves.

CHAPTER 1

Reforming Clandestine Marriage in Spenser's *Faerie Queene*, Book I

In this chapter, I establish how clandestine marriage plays an important role both in the English Reformation and in one of the period's most defining texts, Spenser's *Faerie Queene*, book I. Spenser embroils the patron of holiness, the Redcrosse Knight, with the morally suspect Duessa. In doing so, he associates the practice of clandestine marriage with a religious outsider, revealing its potential to destabilize the Protestant English nation. Since Redcrosse contracts himself to Duessa in book I's second canto, the knight's marital mishap haunts him throughout his quest. Of course, romantic entanglements are inherent to the genre of epic romance. Romance digressions from an epic's true narrative enable authors to explore topics of identity and virtue.[1] An early modern reader, however, would not have been able to dismiss a marital contract—even a clandestine one—as a simple bump along the road of a knightly journey, a mere digression that can be left behind when the actual quest resumes. By entering into an irregular union with Duessa, Redcrosse participates in a romance digression to which he is legally bound. The clandestine marriage threatens Redcrosse's attempt to transform himself into the epitome of English national identity: St. George.

Spenser thus uses the *Legend of Holiness* to enter into both the Reformation discourse concerning clandestine marriage generally and the English discourse on the subject specifically. The practice of clandestine marriage was at the center of the theological debates on the reformation of the marriage ritual.

The issue joins such religious disputes concerning Reformation doctrine as the relationship between good works and grace, the topic of predestination, and the use of iconography, all of which Spenser is well known to explore in book I.[2] Especially since Spenser places marriage at the heart of his epic, irregular unions formed according to the dictates of Roman canon law are particularly threatening, undermining the Protestant rituals that his epic romance espouses as the foundation of a developing English identity. Indeed, Timothy Rosendale reveals how the language and rituals of the *Book of Common Prayer* served as a cornerstone for a new English national identity.[3] He explains: "On the morning of 9 June 1549, for the first time in history, the common parishioner attending services at St. Paul's or St. Giles' Cripplegate could know that, at least in theory, there were people in Yorkshire and Kent, in Exeter and Colchester and Gloucester and Coventry and Norwich—but not in Frankfurt or Paris or Rome—who were participating in precisely the same services, *English* services, and quite likely at the same time."[4] In addition to regular church services, the occasional services, such as the ceremony of matrimony, "encouraged a sense of both temporal and spatial community: the . . . wedding . . . attend[ed] today is being replicated elsewhere, and has occurred innumerable times in the past, and will in the future."[5] Even if the participants of a clandestine marriage did not have ulterior motives, their failure to publicize their union appropriately could cast suspicion on their commitment to England's Protestant national project.

Scholars have overlooked the issue of clandestine marriage in book I. Usually, they consider issues of love and marriage in books III and IV. C. S. Lewis started this trend when speaking of books III and IV as "a single book . . . of love," and other critics interested in Spenser's discourses on love and marriage have mainly followed suit by focusing on these two particular books.[6] Most scholars view Spenser's commitment to wedded love and companionate marriage in these books as a hallmark of his Protestantism.[7] However, Andrew Zurcher and Andrew Hadfield have re-called attention to Spenser's indebtedness to the medieval tradition. When observing that Spenser portrays few wedding ceremonies, Zurcher claims that marriage's manifestation in *The Faerie Queene* as "a more general preoccupation with social bonds and contract" owes more to the medieval tradition than to the Protestant one.[8] Hadfield looks to Redcrosse and Una's halting path to marriage in book I, including Redcrosse's problematic departure after their betrothal, as Spenser's acknowledgment that the "impact of the Reformation has not yet been absorbed" in early modern England.[9] This chapter demonstrates that Spenser, rather than simply acquiescing in England's continued adherence to medieval tradition, suggests a way to speed up the English Reformation in book I.

In the *Legend of Holiness*, Spenser proposes that England's next step in so-lidifying its identity as a Protestant nation is to eliminate the Roman canon law that condoned religious deviance within the marriage ritual, allowing couples to bypass some or even all of the rituals in the *Book of Common Prayer*. In doing so, he focuses on clandestine marriage as a deceptive practice associated with Catholicism, a practice that he rejects when dismissing Redcrosse's marriage with Duessa in canto xii. This dismissal of Roman canon law in book I, however, conflicts with Spenser's emphasis on wedded love in later books of *The Faerie Queene*, especially books IV and VI, where clandestine marriage becomes a romanticized, rather than a merely deceptive, practice. By taking these complexities into account, we can also better understand how the Reformation context surrounding clandestine marriage intersects with the related issues of companionate marriage and wedded love in Spenser's Protestant epic. Before turning to these matters, however, let us consider the role that clandestine marriage played in the development of an English national identity based on the *Book of Common Prayer*.

Clandestine Marriage and the English Reformation

In January 1533, the English Reformation began with a clandestine marriage. On or around January 23, Henry VIII married Anne Boleyn in a secret ceremony (we do not know the exact date due to the secrecy surrounding the event). E. W. Ives informs that, even before this ceremony, Anne and Henry probably "exchange[d] . . . vows before witnesses."[10] "A procedure which was irregular," Ives adds, "but nevertheless canonically valid."[11] Once Henry VIII achieved his desire of marrying Anne, however, he used public ritual later that year to test his subjects' approval of the marriage through a coronation ceremony. Archbishop Thomas Cranmer officially declared Henry and Catherine's marriage to be null and void in May, days before the coronation. The secret ceremony thus forced the invalidation of the marriage with Catherine of Aragon to avoid the awkwardness of bigamy, while the public coronation ceremony served to legitimate the marriage in the eyes of the people. Even though Henry VIII and Anne were legally married, the king could not expect his subjects to accept Anne as queen without a lavish and royal display. He also used the ceremony as a way to test his courtiers' support for his new marriage—Sir Thomas More was notably absent. This historical moment captures the paradox of the marriage ritual during the English Renaissance. On the one hand, consent alone was all that was necessary to make a legally binding contract; on the other, a public ceremony legitimated a marriage in the eyes of the community and doubled as an opportunity to support the crown's religious reforms. Not participating called one's commitment to the reforms—and to the crown—into question.

Reforming the marriage ritual was a driving force of the Protestant Reformation on the continent. Continental reformers viewed marriage's sacramental status as part of the Catholic Church's tyrannical inclination to control its constituents through Roman canon law. In his "Open Letter to the Christian Nobility," Martin Luther proclaims, "The canon law has arisen in the devil's name, let it fall in the name of God."[12] He urged his followers to join him in dramatizing their disdain for the papacy by throwing books of canon law into bonfires.[13] In his *Institutes*, John Calvin further elaborates on the "Oppressive Consequences of the Roman Doctrine" concerning marriage: "They sought nothing but a den of abominations when they made a sacrament out of marriage. For when they once obtained this, they took over the hearing of matrimonial cases; as it was a spiritual matter, it was not to be handled by secular judges. Then they passed laws by which they strengthened their tyranny, laws in part openly impious toward God, in part most unfair toward men."[14] According to Calvin, canon law's allowance for clandestine contracts undermined marriage as a divine ordinance designed for "fellowship" and "companionship."[15] In his *De Regno Christi*, Martin Bucer confirms this opinion when declaring that the "supremely godless dogma" of canon law allowed couples to satisfy "the desire of the flesh" by marrying clandestinely.[16] As these reformers demonstrate, clandestine marriage was at the center of the theological debates on the reformation of the marriage ritual.

Despite his seeming ambivalence toward the marital bond, Henry VIII was hesitant to desacramentalize marriage as the continental reformers urged. When the Ten Articles first dropped marriage as a sacrament in 1536, his fears were confirmed: some ministers took marriage's absence as a sign that the institution had ceased to exist.[17] Henry VIII's handwritten corrections to *The Bishop's Book* (1537) indicate that he thought marriage should remain a sacrament.[18] It did not. To clarify marriage's new nonsacramental role, Thomas Cromwell explicitly directed the clergy to emphasize the importance and dignity of the institution instead. England, however, did not follow its continental counterparts by abolishing Roman canon law after its desacramentalization of marriage. Instead, mutual consent alone remained the only standard for a legal marriage.

To solve the problems associated with clandestine marriage, the Catholic Church itself discarded the idea that consent alone created a marital union. R. H. Helmholz explains that "after debate and hesitation, the Council of Trent cut th[e] gordian knot of medieval marriage law; its decree *Tametsi* declared the presence of the parish priest a requirement for contracting a valid and enforceable marriage."[19] (Importantly, Catholics living in England were exempted from the *Tametsi* decree.) England did come close to eliminating canon law—and clandestine marriage—under Edward VI. The *Reformatio Legum Ecclesiasticarum* (1552) proposed radical changes to canon law that would have followed those of the continental reformers by requiring a church ceremony for a valid marriage.[20] The law, however, was never put into place.

Despite her very different experience with matrimony, Queen Elizabeth maintained her father's conservative approach to marriage reform: when she came to the throne, she did not abolish canon law. She did, however, institute the first widespread implementation of the *Book of Common Prayer*. The drop in the number of clandestine marriage cases in the ecclesiastical courts from the medieval to the early modern period is partly due to the success of the Elizabethan Religious Settlement. Martin Ingram informs that marriage contract contestations did not constitute the overwhelming amount of church court business during the early modern period as they did during the Middle Ages.[21] The lower numbers of court contestations indicate young people's internalization of the social pressures that encouraged them to participate in publicly sanctioned wedding ceremonies.

Furthermore, by the late Elizabethan era, clandestine marriages were usually marriages performed, paradoxically, according to the rituals of the *Book of Common Prayer*—yet simply without a sufficient number of witnesses or at an inappropriate time or place.[22] The Elizabethan settlement had succeeded in convincing much of the population that the state-sanctioned rituals were the only means through which to have a legitimate marriage, even if the medieval practice of handfasting remained technically legal. Another reason why clandestine marriages appear less frequently in court records, however, derives from the harsh penalties instituted under the Elizabethan regime. Unlike during the medieval period, the Elizabethan church courts punished witnesses, as well as participants, of clandestine marriages.[23] One bishop of London even forbade the giving of evidence by witnesses of a clandestine marriage because doing so made them *"ipso facto* excommunicate."[24] This discouragement of witnesses made clandestine marriages much harder to prove, and must have contributed to fewer cases being brought to trial. Due to this concerted effort to suppress the practice, clandestine marriages became increasingly significant and controversial. People who married clandestinely could be suspected of not believing in the reformed religion. Perhaps they did not, as the Act of Uniformity suggests, have "due reverence" of God.[25]

Particularly during the paranoia surrounding Catholic infiltration in the late Elizabethan period, concerned citizens worried that the practice of clandestine marriage allowed Catholics to proliferate and form familial alliances. They were right. The presence of Jesuit monks, such as William Weston and John Gerard, who roamed the countryside performing Mass and other rituals for Catholic recusants, confirms that these fears were justified.[26] In 1590, for instance, Anglican priests in the county of Lancashire reported with alarm that "divers [were] married in private houses without any banns asked, or any intelligence thereof given to the minister."[27] They suspected that "massing priests" were marrying recusants in an effort to keep "the old religion alive."[28] York ecclesiastical archives also contain many instances of clandestine weddings performed by Catholic priests. In 1590, a Catholic priest secretly conducted a marriage ceremony in a chamber in the Inner Temple while a "Marian priest" married Henry Warwick of Ripon under a tree in 1598.[29] As Eric Josef Carlson observes, "Anyone whose marriage was even remotely unconventional fell under suspicion of recusancy."[30] To make a "Catholic-trap," the Elizabethan High Commission increasingly oversaw cases of clandestine marriages.[31] By 1599, irregular marriages had become a "standard feature of each meeting."[32] The commission also examined cases brought against those baptized in a "Popish manner" or for simple recusancy. The purpose of the court, therefore, was not simply to solve the problem of clandestine marriage in general but specifically to enforce conformity to the Church of England in an effort to find people who did not agree with the Elizabethan settlement.[33] The fact that clandestine marriages could be interpreted in this way could be anxiety-producing for the general population. Naturally, many people had perfectly legitimate reasons for having an irregular union—Catholic recusants were not the only people who had clandestine marriages. The High Commission, for instance, questioned William and Margaret Pickhaver because they married late at night, only to discover that they married at the unconventional time because their parish minister was at a conference of preachers that day and could not marry them earlier.[34]

Clandestine marriage's potential for political transgression also makes the prevalence of the phenomenon in Queen Elizabeth's court weightier than has been previously believed. Indeed, much to the queen's ire, clandestine marriages proliferated among her favorite courtiers, both male and female alike. In the introduction, we saw how the Lady Katherine Grey's clandestine marriage to the Earl of Hertford created political controversy. Lady Katherine's own sister, Mary, made the same mistake. She secretly married the queen's sergeant porter, Thomas Keyes, infuriating Elizabeth so much that Keyes tried to have the marriage annulled after being thrown in the Fleet (the Court of Arches proclaimed the marriage to be valid).[35] Many of Elizabeth's male courtiers, including Sir Walter Ralegh, Robert Dudley, Earl of Leicester, and Robert

Devereux, Earl of Essex, participated in clandestine marriages because courtly love games in which Elizabeth played the role of the ultimate unattainable mistress were an "inherent part of [the] court's identity."[36] Johanna Rickman explores how secret marriages increased during the later years of Queen Elizabeth's reign.[37] Particularly since Elizabeth founded her rule on her virtuous identity as the Virgin Queen, she was invested in the idea that her courtiers should adhere to a similar standard. As Rickman observes, "Elizabeth considered illicit sexual behavior at her court as contempt for her princely authority."[38] The queen was so annoyed by Elizabeth Vernon's secret marriage to the Earl of Southampton, for instance, that she "threatened to throw every person who had been involved in the secret marriage in the Tower."[39] Refusing to abide by the state-sanctioned rituals also could be considered a serious affront to one of her rule's main agendas to establish a uniform religious practice. Elizabeth's harsh reaction to the clandestine marriages of her courtiers, therefore, does not indicate simple caprice or jealousy, as it has been sometimes portrayed. After all, her father had even proclaimed that clandestine marriages that strengthened a person's claim to the throne constituted an act of treason.[40] In Queen Elizabeth's day, clandestine marriages in the court continued to be potentially political—even treasonous—acts.

Elizabeth did not confine her concerns about clandestine marriage to its presence in her court. She also fretted over the lax rules pertaining to marriage licenses, which allowed people to legitimately bypass some aspects of Roman canon law and/or the rituals of the *Book of Common Prayer*. In 1598, regulations were put in place to make these licenses more difficult to obtain, as Archbishop Whitgift explained: "The Ordinary's Power was limited in granting of licences for celebrating marriage within a competent time fit for so holy an action; namely, betwixt the hours of eight and twelve in the forenoon; and to a prescript place, that is, in the parish church, where the parties to be married, or their parents or governors, dwelt."[41] The language of this decree confirms the marriage ceremony as a public, holy action rather than a mere social contract. The attempt to control marriage both in the court and in the population at large was thus one of the central concerns of Elizabethan rule. Participating in the appropriate rituals demonstrated one's commitment to the Protestant state, and doing so in a public ceremony meant that one had nothing to hide.

As a poet invested in marriage, Spenser was well versed in these discourses. Hadfield goes so far as to claim that Spenser's general interest in marriage derives from his familiarity with the works of John Calvin: "Calvin's understanding of theological issues and problems engages Spenser's creative imagination and, in particular, determines the allegorical development of the first edition of *The Faerie Queene*."[42] Considering Calvin's contempt for Roman canon law, therefore, Spenser would have been acutely aware that England's continued adherence to canon law was out of step with the Reformation on the continent. Even if the participants of a clandestine marriage did not have ulterior motives, their failure to publicize their union cast suspicion on their commitment to the Protestant national project. When taking this anomaly into account, we find that the marital landscape in book I of *The Faerie Queene* becomes a treacherous one, providing the Redcrosse Knight with a variety of avenues to enter into marriage matches that could either confirm or deny his virtuous identity.

Clandestine Contracts and the False Church in Book I

Scholars usually refer to the Redcrosse Knight's relationship with Duessa as a dalliance. The euphemistic "dalliance," however, does not account for the gravity of Redcrosse's vows of faith. Their dalliance amounts to, or at the very least could be mistaken for, a clandestine marriage. When Redcrosse first meets Duessa (masquerading as Fidessa) in canto ii, he states: "Henceforth in safe *assuraunce* may ye rest, / Hauing both found a new friend you to aid, / And lost an old foe, that did you molest" (I.ii.27.1–3; emphasis mine).[43] "Assuraunce" means a "formal engagement, pledge or guarantee," specifically an "engagement guaranteeing peace and safety"—not the kind of language one would associate with a passing flirtation.[44] Even more evocatively, the term also means "betrothal" or "marriage engagement."[45] In his editorial note, A. C. Hamilton references this secondary meaning, observing that the term later foreshadows Duessa's claim that they are "affyaunced" (xii.27.2). Even if Redcrosse only considers himself to be offering Duessa safe passage, his language gives her reason to believe they are entering into a betrothal. Referring to himself as Duessa's "new friend" further suggests that Redcrosse understands that their relationship will be romantically charged. In canto vii, he sends Duessa more marital signals by making "goodly court" (I.vii.7.1) to her as "his Dame." He then substantiates the marital implications of their spoken contract and courtship by consummating the match: he "pourd out in loosnesse on the grassy grownd, / Both carelesse of his health, and of his fame" (I.vii.7.2–3). The discrete reference to the sexual act is significant since a consummation of a betrothal constituted an irrevocable pact. Redcrosse provides Duessa (or any other early modern woman) with at least enough evidence to *claim* that they have entered into an irregular union, even if it was not necessarily the knight's

original intent. If the exchange of ambiguous vows followed by the sponta-
neous fulfillment of sexual desire does not seem weighty enough to carry marital meaning to a modern reader, many Protestant reformers would have
agreed. Abolishing Roman canon law and insisting that marriages be publicly
solemnized to be valid was supposed to disambiguate the marital process.

Of course, as Zurcher shows, the making of private contracts does play an
important role in the makeup of Faeryland's social fabric. Not all social contracts, however, are equal. The ability to enter into such a social contract so
easily—speaking vaguely ritualized words, exchanging gifts, grasping hands—
takes on a different significance when that contract is a marital one. After
Prince Arthur rescues Redcrosse from Orgoglio's dungeon, for instance, the
future St. George plights himself to the prince in a way similar to that in which
he plights himself to Duessa:

> Then those two knights, fast frendship for to bynd,
> And loue establish each to other trew,
> Gaue goodly gifts, the signes of gratefull mynd,
> And eke as pledges firme, right hands together ioynd.
>
> *(I.ix.18.6–9)*

By joining their right hands (especially after making pledges and exchanging
gifts), the two knights participate in a textbook example of a handfasting, a
symbol of a marital contract when performed between a man and a woman.
One can assume, however, that Redcrosse's pledge of friendship to Prince Arthur does not hinder his ability to make similar pledges with other knights
that he meets on his journeys. The sexual nature of a marital contract requires
an exclusivity not necessary to friendship. Contracting oneself to more than
one knight might be an early modern form of social networking; contracting
oneself to more than one woman is bigamy.

Redcrosse's infamous lustiness makes him susceptible to the trap of clandestine marriage. In the very first canto, Archimago's ruse that separates the
knight from Una establishes the connection between clandestine marriage and
the fulfillment of sexual desire. To make Redcrosse more susceptible to the
temptation of an irregular union, Archimago arouses the knight by having him
"dreame of loues and lustfull play" (I.i.47.4). In one of these dreams, Redcrosse
sees Una come to his bed:

> And she her selfe of beautie soueraigne Queene,
> Fayre *Venus* seemde vnto his bed to bring
> Her, whom he waking euermore did weene,
> To bee the chastest flowre, that aye did spring

On earthly braunch, the daughter of a king,
Now a loose Leman to vile seruice bound:
And eke the *Graces* seemed all to sing,
Hymen iõ Hymen, dauncing all around,
Whylst freshest *Flora* her with Yuie girlond crownd.

(I.i.48)

The *"Hymen iõ Hymen"* refrain, a convention of classical epithalamia, gives the episode a distinct marital undertone.[46] The dream implies that Redcrosse will enter into a marriage with Una if he sleeps with her. Rather than assuaging his fears of sexual desire, these marital implications enhance Redcrosse's "wonted feare of doing ought amis" (I.i.49.2). His "feare" derives from his understanding that he will be committing a marital transgression, in addition to a sexual transgression, if he enters into an irregular union with his beloved. Even though Redcrosse is destined to marry Una, his reaction to the anti-epithalamic dream vision stresses his understanding that there is a right—and wrong—way to do so.[47] Entering into a clandestine marriage binds one to the "vile seruice" of sexual desire.

Just as clandestine marriage served as a sign of the participants' possible Catholicism in early modern England, the practice alludes to religious deviance in Spenser's Faeryland as well. Scholars have long recognized that Duessa's background and accoutrements associate her with the papacy.[48] Her ability to trick Redcrosse into contracting himself to her by preying on his good intentions and sexual frustrations not only allegorizes the duplicitous nature of Catholicism in general but also further associates Catholicism with the deceptive practice of clandestine marriage specifically. Even as the practice of making matches through handfasting began to wane during the Elizabethan period, it remained prevalent in northern England—a Catholic stronghold. If Gouge insists that the "seeking of secrecie [in marriage] . . . implieth some euill cleauing thereto," then, according to book I's theological allegory, Redcrosse cleaves himself to evil quite literally when entering into a contract with Duessa.[49]

Taking the historical allegory into consideration, we can also connect Duessa not just with the papacy in book I but also with the Catholic identity she takes on in book V: Mary, Queen of Scots.[50] Duessa's penchant for clandestine marital contracts in book I, for instance, associates her with the Norfolk affair in a way that has gone hitherto unnoticed. In 1569, Thomas Howard, Duke of Norfolk, quite ill advisedly agreed to pursue a secret marriage match with the imprisoned Mary.[51] The ultimate goal was to restore Mary to the Scottish throne and name her Queen Elizabeth's successor, using a marriage with a high-ranking member of the English nobility to pave the way. It is unclear if the duke was a crypto-Catholic (something he denied) or simply vain and naive (much more likely). During the Northern Rebellion, the rebel leaders championed Norfolk's cause despite his attempts to distance himself from the uprising. Even though Norfolk knew that a match with Mary would be considered treasonous, he continued to exchange letters and tokens with Mary even after the rebellion failed. Queen Elizabeth was not amused by his continued insubordination and Norfolk was indeed executed for treason in 1572. Duessa's attempt to entangle the Redcrosse Knight in an irregular union shadows the threat that Mary, Queen of Scots, posed to the Elizabethan regime through her potential ability to marry clandestinely.

Redcrosse's relationship with Duessa thus threatens his identity as the distinctly Protestant Knight of Holiness. After he defeats Sansfoy, Duessa bestows on him the "*Sarazins* shield" (I.ii.20.7). The shield becomes a token of their union, a dowry of sorts. The fact that Redcrosse later fights Sansjoy to maintain possession of the shield evinces his investment in the token, suggesting his tacit acknowledgment of the marital bond. The shield's implication that its owner is "without faith" emphasizes the spiritual emptiness of marriages made through contracts without the blessing of the church. Furthermore, when fulfilling his sexual desire with Duessa in canto vii, Redcrosse gives up his knightly identity completely by taking off his armor. He confirms the subsuming of his identity into Duessa's transgressive one at the moment the consummation makes their union final.

Redcrosse's unholy liaison with Duessa warns readers that an inability to control sexual desires could result in an irregular union, which could then be interpreted as a need to disguise transgressive religious (and/or political) beliefs. Whether this interpretation is correct is not necessarily the issue—what matters is how one's actions are perceived. Indeed, Spenser must insist that Redcrosse is the "true *Saint George*" (I.ii.12.2) even when the knight carries the Sarazin's faithless shield. Otherwise, the reader may believe that Redcrosse really has become an infidel. This insistence calls the clandestine marriage into question. If Redcrosse remains the "true *Saint George*," then perhaps he and Duessa have not literally become "one flesh." Duessa, however, has the kind of evidence that would back up a claim of clandestine marriage in the church courts. In the end, Redcrosse's fate rests on whether Una's father and community are willing to accept him as the "true *Saint George*" at the betrothal ceremony after learning of his relationship with Duessa. In light of the relationship's marital undertones, Redcrosse's failure to mention Duessa in his "poynt to poynt" (I.xii.15.8) account of his adventures now seems a matter of expedience, indicating his belief that he might not be able to marry Una if he does.[52]

Even though Redcrosse performs the iconic deed of defeating the dragon in canto xi, the revelation of his contract with Duessa in canto xii calls his identity into question at the moment he is about to plight himself to Una. Archimago's dramatic arrival in a "breathlesse hasty mood" (I.xii.25.3) to reveal the impediment that Redcrosse conveniently omitted from his own narrative, and with a letter as evidence, exemplifies the purpose of public marital banns. Referring to Redcrosse as "that new vnknowen guest" (I.xii.26.7), Archimago claims that the knight has "already plighted his right hand / Vnto another loue, and to another land" (8–9). In short, to the King of Eden's astonishment, Archimago's letter claims that Redcrosse cannot marry Una because he is married *"already."* The calling of the banns allowed community members to express impediments, such as a previous clandestine contract, to a marriage before it took place. In the age before computerized record keeping, the fact that someone could marry secretly, leave his spouse, and then remarry in a different location where his actions were "vnknowen" was a distinct possibility—one that could keep any potential father-in-law up at night. Una's father would not be fulfilling his paternal duty if, after reading the letter, he did not look upon Redcrosse with "doubtfull eyes" (I.xii.29.6), in addition to demanding a full explanation before he could marry "his onely daughter, and his only hayre" (I.xii.21.3) with a "conscience cleare" (I.xii.30.5). At this moment, Redcrosse finds himself teetering on the verge of an embarrassment of (quite literally) epic proportions. One could certainly not expect a dismissed bridegroom to be accepted as England's national hero.

Previous scholarship has not dwelled on Archimago's attempt to forbid the banns because, in allegorical terms, Redcrosse is obviously supposed to marry Una, the "one true church"—not Duessa, the figure of duplicity and Catholicism. In early modern terms, though, the claim that Redcrosse is already married is a serious charge, especially since even a pre-contract would illegitimate his impending marriage to Una. A closer look at Duessa's letter underscores the import of her allegations:

> To me sad mayd, or rather widow sad,
>   He was affyaunced long time before,
>   And sacred pledges he both gaue, and had,
>   False erraunt knight, infamous, and forswore:
>   Witnesse the burning Altars, which he swore,
>   And guilty heauens of his bold periury,
>   Which though he hath polluted oft of yore,
>   Yet I to them for iudgement iust doe fly,
> And them coniure t'auenge this shamefull iniury.
>
>   *(I.xii.27)*

Duessa (writing under the guise of Fidessa) is clearly savvy to the kind of terminology that legitimates her claim. Both the words "affiance" and "pledge" appear on Zurcher's comprehensive list of early modern legal terms in *The Faerie Queene*.[53] The legal language would carry little weight if it was not true. Considering Duessa's role as the personification of falsehood, we are not obliged to believe her testimony. However, we also know that Duessa's letter contains an element of truthfulness. Redcrosse cannot deny that he has given her "sacred pledges," even if the "burning Altars" were not physically present at the time (one can only expect a bit of artistic flair from a woman who dresses like the Whore of Babylon).

By allowing Redcrosse's marital mishap to trouble his identity at the moment of his triumph, Spenser refuses to gloss over the classical episode that Redcrosse and Duessa's relationship shadows: Aeneas's secret union with Dido in the *Aeneid*.[54] In the classical epic, the vindictive Juno arranges a clandestine marriage between Dido and Aeneas in conjunction with the well-meaning but naive Venus. Juno schemes to join the couple in matrimony after they seek refuge in a cave during a rainstorm: "Adero et, tua si mihi certa voluntas, / *conubio iungam stabili propriamque dicabo*; / hic hymenaeus erit" (I will be there and, if certain of thy good will, will link them in sure wedlock, sealing her for his own; this shall be their bridal).[55] Juno's description of the scenario is unequivocal: Dido and Aeneas enter into a marriage when plighting themselves to one another and consummating the match. When Virgil states that Dido "coniugium vocat; hoc praetexit nomine culpam" (calls it marriage and with that name veils her sin), however, he muddies the marital language.[56] If Dido only "calls" the union a marriage, then perhaps it is not a union at all. "Culpam" also could be interpreted in a variety of ways. The Christianized Loeb translation implies that Dido has committed a sexual "sin" by breaking her chastity and sleeping with Aeneas, but the word could also mean simply that she has committed an "error in judgment" by marrying Aeneas in such a clandestine manner.[57] Aeneas, apparently, does not believe that he is married to Dido the way she believes she is married to him, anticipating the kind of confusion that accompanied clandestine contracts in early modern England. As Colin Burrow observes, Virgil presents the Dido episode as a triumph of Aeneas's *pietas* as he abandons her to marry Lavinia and found the Roman Empire.[58] St. Augustine later allegorizes this episode, proving his need to turn away from his youthful sympathies for Dido and toward the church.[59] Considering these precedents, Spenser could easily dismiss Redcrosse's relationship with Duessa in a similar fashion, portraying the Knight of Holiness's abandonment of Duessa as a matter of course (as most scholarship has done) as he turns from the Catholic to the Protestant Church.

Complicating matters, both the medieval and classical traditions offer alternatives to this interpretation of Aeneas's treatment of the Carthaginian queen. In his *Heroides*, Ovid counters Virgil's rejection of romance digressions by portraying Dido as the victim and Aeneas as a faithless husband. In her complaint, Dido wishes "mihi concubitus fama sepulta foret" (that the story of our union were buried).[60] Dido laments that since she publicized her marriage, she cannot back away from the match, even though she realizes that Aeneas will marry "altera Dido" (a second Dido) when he founds Rome.[61] In this way, Ovid suggests that if she and Aeneas had been lovers alone—not husband and wife—perhaps the tragedy of her suicide would not have taken place. Ovid's arresting depiction of Dido's interiority remained popular throughout the medieval and early modern periods. Even though Spenser portrays Chaucer as England's first Virgil in *The Shepheardes Calender*, Chaucer takes an Ovidian approach to the Dido story in his *Legend of Good Women*. With these alternative precedents, Spenser cannot dismiss his own hero's suspect marital behavior by simply condemning an inconvenient wife to suicide. Redcrosse's irregular union, however, threatens the epic's ability to fulfill the distinctly Protestant theme of "fierce warres and faithfull loues" (I.Proem.1.9).[62] As a result, Spenser seizes the opportunity to solve the problem of Virgil's Dido—not just for Redcrosse but for England as a whole.

In early modern terms, the most incontrovertible way to exonerate Redcrosse from his marital mishap with Duessa is to prove that he already has a preexisting contract with Una. Duessa's marriage would then be the unlawful one. Una does indeed claim that this is the case. After Redcrosse fails to come up with a good excuse for his transgression, Una explains Duessa's behavior:

> And now it seemes, that she suborned hath
>   This crafty messenger with letters vaine,
>   To worke new woe and improuided scath,
>   *By breaking of the band betwixt vs twaine.*
>   (I.xii.34.1–4; emphasis mine)

By claiming that they are "band[ed]" together before the ceremony has even taken place, Una insists that she and Redcrosse had a preexisting contract. Una thus asserts that she and Redcrosse are married already, or at least are betrothed to the point that they have a contract invalidating any others: the high-stakes betrothals that derived out of private contracts invalidated any marriage that could come after. Gouge explains the benefit of such contracts:

> It may preuent many plots and practises of inueigling, or stealing away
> maids and widowes. For it oft falleth out, that when parents or other

REFORMING CLANDESTINE MARRIAGE

friends haue prouided a good match for their daughter, or for some other vnder their gouernment, and all things on all parts well concluded, the wedding day appointed, and all things fitted and prepared for the sol-emnizing of the wedding, some desirous to forestall that mariage, by secret and cunning deuices get the bride away a few daies before, if not on the very morning of the intended wedding day, and mary her out of hand to another. That which maketh men so bold is, that they know a clandestine mariage being consummate shall stand firme in law. But a legall contract preventeth such mischiefes, because it maketh such a fur-tiue mariage vtterly void.[63]

Una suggests that her pre-contract with Redcrosse makes his "furtiue mariage" with Duessa "vtterly void." The case, however, is not straightforward. When looking to the *Letter to Raleigh* for guidance, we find that Redcrosse was "well liked of the Lady" (717) after he made his transformation from "rusti[c] . . . clownishe younge man" to knightly champion when he put on her armor. There is no further evidence (besides Una's insistence) to suggest that they are betrothed until the public ceremony in the final canto. The case, therefore, devolves into one of she said–she said (as did many clandestine marriage cases during the period). Early modern readers would have recognized this kind of marital confusion to be an inherent problem of Roman canon law's allowance for clandestine marriages.

By choosing Una over Duessa as Redcrosse's bride, the King of Eden makes an important intervention into early modern marital discourse. Naturally, he is inclined to side with his prostrate daughter, after being "greatly moued" (I.xii.35.1) by her pleadings. For her part, Andrew Hadfield observes, Duessa "is dismissed without a proper consideration of her legal rights."[64] This dis-missal, however, is profound. Without considering the evidence of whether Redcrosse entered into a marital contract with Duessa or Una first, the king sides with the validating effects of the impending public ceremony over Red-crosse's sexual consummation of his union with Duessa. Since Redcrosse and Duessa do not participate in a public solemnization, the king does not con-sider the match to be valid. Spenser thus announces how easily such marital mishaps could be solved—by refusing to recognize any marriage that does not take place publicly according to the proper rituals. By abolishing Roman canon law, troublemakers like Archimago could be dismissed without a hearing.

Taking the issue of clandestine marriage into account also elucidates book I's allegory of English church history. In allegorical terms, Redcrosse's mis-guided contract with Duessa mirrors England's own centuries-long contract with the Roman church. England, however, had not always been wedded to the papacy before the Reformation. In his *Actes and Monuments* (1563), John Foxe's tracing of church history demonstrates how the false Roman church undermined and usurped the existing true church during the Middle Ages. As Hadfield reminds us, Una's ancestry derives "from the true Catholic Church that Protestants claimed had been *re-established* in Britain after the Reformation."[65] According to this history, just as England was initially contracted to the "true Catholic Church," Redcrosse was also contracted to Una, invalidating the contract with Duessa and the false church. The need for Una and Redcrosse to undergo a public betrothal, however, suggests that any concrete evidence of their pre-contract appears to be lost, or needs to be reasserted, in order to avoid any future claims to the contrary. The public betrothal ensures that England's relationship with the "true Catholic Church" cannot be questioned again. One way that England can reestablish this connection is by eliminating the canon law that maintains a lingering relationship with the papacy and that calls England's initial contract with the true church into question.

Back in canto viii, Una reveals herself to be Redcrosse's true bride because of her willingness to carry out the vows that accompany the public solemnization of the marriage ritual. Upon seeing Redcrosse after their long separation, she greets him by saying, "But welcome now my Lord, in wele or woe" (I.viii.43.1). Her words echo the language of the wedding vows in the *Book of Common Prayer* requiring the bride and groom to take one another "in sickenes, and in healthe."[66] This language, of course, is not unique to the reformed ritual—the Sarum also calls for spouses to take one another "in sykenesse" and "in hele."[67] In book I, however, the public ceremony becomes associated with the "one true church." The ambiguous clandestine contract that elides proper ritual (including ritualized language) becomes associated with the false church. The fact that the emaciated Redcrosse has cheated on Una certainly indicates her willingness to take the "wele" with the "woe." Spenser emphasizes the importance of the vows affiliated with the public solemnization rather than the legal contract alone.

In canto xii, the marital language surrounding Redcrosse's betrothal to Una gives the event the weight of an actual wedding. Spenser deploys elements from classical epithalamia as well as from the medieval Sarum rite, such as the sprinkling of holy water, when depicting the public betrothal ceremony:[68]

> His owne two hands the holy knotts did knitt,
>   That none but death for euer can diuide;
>   His owne two hands, for such a turne most fitt,
>   The housling fire did kindle and prouide,
>   And holy water thereon sprinckled wide;

> At which the bushy Teade a groome did light,
> And sacred lamp in secret chamber hide,
> Where it should not be quenched day nor night,
> For feare of euill fates, but burnen euer bright.
>
> *(I.xii.37)*

The doubling of the betrothal ceremony for the wedding ceremony highlights the importance of the ritual as being the true affirmation of a marriage. Protestant preachers advocated a formal betrothal ceremony such as Redcrosse and Una's, since it gave couples more time to prepare for the responsibilities of marriage and disallowed the possibility of any later confusion regarding previous contracts. A formal betrothal, Gouge further explains, "putteth a difference betwixt such as intend mariage in the feare of the Lord, for such holy ends as are warranted in the word, and such as intend it only to satisfie their lust, or for other like carnall ends."[69] Spenser thus demonstrates that Redcrosse and Una's marriage will be for "holy ends," while dismissing the "carnall ends" that made up the false marriage with Duessa. Proper marriages do not derive out of private contracts followed by sexual consummations but rather out of public affirmations of love, faith, and goodwill. Despite the episode's religious syncretism, Spenser's insistence that only public marriages are valid marriages follows in the footsteps of the Protestant reformers.

Spenser returns to this model in book IV, emphasizing the importance of ceremony over private contract, with his description of the marriage of the Thames and Medway. Scholars hail the river marriage as allegorizing the virtue of friendship through concord, and as representing the "proper and healthy relationships between parents and offspring, proper and healthy relationships between old and young, and proper relationships between male and female."[70] Spenser describes the wedding feast:

> It fortun'd then, a solemne feast was there
> To all the Sea-gods and their fruitfull seede,
> In honour of the spousalls, which then were
> Betwixt the *Medway* and the *Thames* agreed.
>
> *(IV.xi.8.1–4)*

The term "spousalls" evokes the spousal contract, but the spousals are legitimated by the "solemne feast" to which, apparently, everyone is invited. Spenser's catalog of the rivers from the British Isles and around the world in attendance at the feast suggests that weddings are a place to celebrate not only individual unions but also communal and national harmony. As Rachel E. Hile observes, the wedding of the Thames and Medway is "a social bond endorsed by authority and enforced by ritual."[71] The episode exemplifies the ideal Spenserian marriage as one that brings together family, community, and nation.

The triumph of holiness in book I through a public marriage ceremony translates into a triumph over Roman canon law. By making Redcrosse's public betrothal to Una the final moment in the book, rather than the slaying of the dragon, Spenser insists that the marriage ritual confirms Redcrosse's English identity as St. George once and for all. To do so, he releases Redcrosse from the stranglehold of his irregular union with Duessa, allowing the public wedding of the English nation to the Protestant church to move forward. By staging Redcrosse's betrothal in this way, Spenser indicates that England must be willing to dismiss Roman canon law if it is to finalize its commitment to the Reformation. Otherwise, clandestine marriages will continue to infect the realm with Duessa-like deception.

Romanticizing Clandestine Marriage in *The Faerie Queene*

Yet the public ceremony in book I, canto xii, must be a betrothal ceremony rather than a wedding ceremony because Redcrosse cannot fulfill his duties as both husband and knight at the same time. Within the tradition of medieval romance, only the knights of the Round Table go out on quests—King Arthur stays at home with Guinevere. While feminist scholars are quick to point out that Britomart will have to retire once she marries Arthegall and bears children, it is easy to forget that husbands were expected to attend to domestic responsibilities as well. Lisa Celovsky observes that the young male knights in *The Faerie Queene* appear distressed by the patriarchal pressure to settle down.[72] For Redcrosse, however, his inability to stay at home does not derive from a personal desire to engage in youthful pursuits but from a need to serve his sovereign.

Indeed, Redcrosse reveals in canto xii that he does have a preexisting contract—and not to Una. Rather, he has already contracted to the epic's eponymous ruler: the Faery Queen herself. Before the betrothal ceremony takes place, Redcrosse admits:

> Of ease or rest I may not yet deuize;
> For by the faith, which I to armes haue plight,
> I bownden am streight after this emprize,
> As that your daughter can ye well aduize,

> Backe to retourne to that great Faery Queene,
> And her to serue six yeares in warlike wize.
>
> *(I.xii.18.2–7)*

His six-year contract with the Faery Queen precludes any other contracts that he makes—even a marital one. When Redcrosse leaves Una behind at the end of book I, his actions suggest that a knight's duty to his sovereign must come before all other relationships. Redcrosse has already attempted to prepare Una for this moment when establishing an uneasy love triangle with the Faery Queen in canto ix. After Arthur rescues him from Orgoglio's dungeon, Redcrosse admits his own love for Arthur's beloved:

> Thine, O then, said the gentle *Redcrosse* knight,
>   Next to that Ladies loue, shalbe the place,
>   O fayrest virgin, full of heauenly light,
>   Whose wondrous faith, exceeding earthly race,
>   Was firmest fixt in myne extremest case.
>
> *(I.ix.17.1–5)*

Since Una has just spoken, it seems likely that she is the object of the "thine" in this passage, and that Redcrosse's love for her will be "next." The ambiguous language highlights the difficulties inherent in having two beloveds in the form of a sovereign and wife—difficulties with which many of Queen Elizabeth's own courtiers were familiar.

Insisting that a couple wait for years to finalize a marriage is cruel by anyone's standards. Of course, in terms of the religious allegory, Redcrosse cannot marry the "one true church" within regular history—that marriage is for the end of time, necessitating what one can only assume will be an incredibly long wait. As a literary character rather than simply an allegorical one, however, Una certainly does not seem happy with the arrangement to wait six years since Redcrosse leaves her to "mourne" his absence (rather than to patiently await his return) (I.xii.41.9). The six-year waiting period would have been an alarmingly long time for an early modern betrothal, which were ideally brief lest "Satan take occasion to tempt [the couple] for their incontinencie."[73] Bullinger agrees: "After the handefastynge and makyng of the contract, the churche goynge and weddynge should not be differred to longe."[74] The Redcrosse Knight does seem to struggle with temptation. When we meet him again at the beginning of book III, he is valiantly fighting Malecasta's six champions because he refuses to disavow his love for Una. While his intentions are good, he puts himself in the uncomfortable situation of becoming Malecasta's lover if he wins: the knights inform that whoever overcomes them will "haue our Ladies loue for his reward" (i.27.9). It is the misguided battle for the Sarazin's shield all over again. Thankfully, Britomart, representing the virtue of married chastity with which Redcrosse struggles, rescues her fellow knight from accidentally entering into another embarrassing contract. The "braue Mayd" (i.42.7) then chastely retains her armor when they attend a dinner party at Castle Joyous. In doing so, she pragmatically maintains her secret female identity while allegorically demonstrating her commitment to matrimonial chastity generally (and thus to Artegall specifically). Una does not receive such a display of fidelity from her own betrothed. Redcrosse happily allows himself to be "disarmed" (III.i.42.6) soon after they are in the castle, implying his continued susceptibility to sexual desire. The six years he must wait to consummate his match with Una are going to feel long indeed.

Spenser's allegorization of the events surrounding Sir Walter Ralegh's clandestine marriage to Elizabeth Throckmorton in book IV reflects the poet's personal investment in the controversy surrounding the phenomenon in Queen Elizabeth's court. In canto vii, Arthur's squire Timias (a figure for Ralegh) rescues Amoret (a figure for Throckmorton) from the monster Lust. Timias's beloved, Belphoebe (an allegorical representation of Queen Elizabeth's private person), kills the beast, but only to return to find Timias kissing and touching his "new louely mate" (IV.vii.35.3) in an attempt to revive her. The incensed Belphoebe's abandonment of Timias illustrates the difficulties courtiers faced serving the Virgin Queen. Arthur Throckmorton, Lady Ralegh's brother, attempted to facilitate Ralegh's reconciliation with the queen by giving her "a ring made for a wedding ring set round with diamonds, and with a ruby like a heart placed in a coronet."[75] This gesture indicates that Elizabeth did not just play the role of a Petrarchan mistress for her courtiers, but literally attempted to play the far less realistic (but perhaps more Protestant) role of a chaste wife. Queen Elizabeth's favorite courtiers thus had to enter into bigamous clandestine marriages with their real wives so that they could maintain their pseudo-marital contracts with the queen. Spenser must have had the uncomfortable realization that Queen Elizabeth's court fostered the proliferation of clandestine marriages that he portrays as so problematic to England's Protestant identity in book I.

Just as the Elizabethan High Commission was wrong about the seemingly inappropriate motives of some couples who participated in clandestine marriages, so does Spenser acknowledge in later books of *The Faerie Queene* that not all clandestine marriages are undertaken for blatantly underhanded reasons. Instead, some of Elizabeth's courtiers who married clandestinely (such as Ralegh) simply wanted to have their own families and serve the queen at the same time. The discomfort that many readers feel when Redcrosse leaves Una to continue fighting for the Faery Queen reflects the uncomfortable atmosphere of Elizabeth's court. In book I, Spenser condones the necessity that knights, or their real-life courtier counterparts, must put service before desire. In the long run, however, this formulation becomes unsustainable.

In book VI, the court's suppression of romantic love becomes so extreme that it deteriorates into a form of tyranny. In canto xii, Spenser revises the genre of Greek pastoral romance when revealing that the foundling Pastorella is the issue of a clandestine marriage between Bellamour and Claribell.[76] Like many early modern patriarchs, Claribell's father desired his daughter to make a strategic alliance. He "thought in wedlocke to haue bound" (VI.xii.4.5) his daughter with the neighboring "Prince of *Picteland*" (6), most likely with the intention of fostering peace and goodwill between the two realms. Even though she would be doing both her father and her people a valuable service by marrying the prince, Claribell refuses to marry for such pragmatic purposes. Instead, out "of loue to *Bellamoure* . . . [she] shund to match with any forrein fere" (VI.xii.4.8–9). Unlike with Redcrosse and Duessa, Spenser depicts Bellamour and Claribell as having a legitimate and sincere courtship. Bellamour becomes "entyrely seized" (VI.xii.5.3) with love for her after doing her "dayly seruice" (2), which, in turn, "so well her pleased" (1). Knowing that her father would not approve of the match, the couple "closely . . . wed" (VI.xii.5.4). The term "closely" indicates that they married "secretly, covertly," or "privately."[77] "Wed," however, is the same term that Spenser uses to describe the marriage of the Thames and Medway, which suggests that the couple participated in an actual ceremony rather than simply contracting themselves to each other through a handfasting.[78] Furthermore, since the marriage was "knowne to few" (VI.xii.5.4), the ceremony must have had witnesses. Claribell and Bellamour's attempt to follow formal marital guidelines, even if in a clandestine way (as did many couples in early modern England), emphasizes the sincerity of their intentions. This is a love match—not a hasty match for the sake of sexual desire.

Scholars rarely mention the Claribell/Bellamour plotline, perhaps because we only learn of this episode secondhand, and at the end of the book. By overlooking this episode, however, we overlook valuable insight into Spenser's historical allegory.[79] Claribell's father's reaction to the marriage parallels the way in which Queen Elizabeth reacted to the clandestine marriages of her favorite courtiers in the guise of her public persona. In a "great rage" (VI. xii.5.6), he throws "them in dongeon deepe" (6), so that "neither could to company of th'other creepe" (9). After a sympathetic jailer allows them to meet with each other, Bellamour and Claribell's consummation of their marriage (resulting in the birth of Pastorella) is reminiscent of some real-life Elizabethan love stories. The warders of Lady Katherine Grey and Edward Seymour, for instance, allowed the couple to meet while they were imprisoned in the tower, resulting in the birth of their second son.[80] On the one hand, Claribell's father has every right to be angry that she has married behind his back, particularly since he is both her father *and* her sovereign. On the other, Spenser's treatment of the couple is clearly sympathetic. Especially since they become competent rulers after the death of Claribell's father, Spenser forwards the radical idea that personal desire and public duties do not have to be antithetical to one another. The sexual consummation of a marriage does not merely cater to lust but to love.

The denial of romantic love in book VI thus becomes wrapped up in Spenser's association of the court with discourtesy. Even though he insists that courtesy derives from the court, since "it there most vseth to abound" (VI.i.1.2), he reveals that the court is the fountain of rumor and slander spread by the Blatant Beast. Spenser indicates how such rumors can arise in the Belphoebe / Timias episode in book IV when Belphoebe immediately assumes that Timias's love for Amoret precludes his love to herself. We know that this is not the case, but Belphoebe's misreading of the situation damages Timias's reputation, as he deteriorates from a noble squire into something that appears less than human—Prince Arthur does not recognize his squire when he finds Timias living alone in the woods in a disheveled state later in the canto (IV. vii.42–47). The defamation to which Spenser alludes in this episode was another issue within the jurisdiction of the ecclesiastical courts. M. Lindsay Kaplan explains that "since canon law defined defamation as motivated by malice but did not stipulate that it be false, it was conceivable that a malicious, albeit true, accusation could be considered defamatory."[81] In book I, Archimago's attempt to forbid the banns at Redcrosse and Una's betrothal also constitutes a form of defamation, foreshadowing book VI's focus on slander, especially in relation to clandestine marriage, as the locus of discourtesy.[82] One begins to wonder how Claribell's father found out about her marriage, especially since a pregnancy did not give her away.

The theme of clandestine marriage links books I and VI of *The Faerie Queene*.[83] As Isabel G. MacCaffrey observes, "Book VI . . . offers a new perspective on some of the lessons of Book I," and one of those lessons appears to be about clandestine marriage.[84] The romantic undertone of Bellamour and Claribell's marriage anticipates Shakespeare's comedies more than it reflects the moralist undertones of the domestic handbooks that infuse book I. Spenser thus moves from portraying a sovereign's influence on marital affairs as leading to a disappointing delay at the end of book I to being worthy of outright criticism at the end of book VI. Even though Spenser portrays England's need to complete the reformation of the marriage ritual in book I, he reveals in the later books that Queen Elizabeth's insistence on meddling in the affairs of her courtiers' hearts holds England back from making the transition. The abolishment of Roman canon law in regard to marriage will be beneficial only if children and courtiers can marry for love and serve their sovereign at the same time.

By ultimately portraying clandestine marriage in such a conflicting manner, Spenser also acknowledges the uniqueness of English national identity that allowed for the reformed rituals and canon law to coexist. While England championed its Protestant rituals in the *Book of Common Prayer*, it also allowed couples the freedom to bypass the rituals—at their own risk, of course—if they so wished. In this way, *The Faerie Queene* represents the via media of the Elizabethan Religious Settlement, condemning the contracting of clandestine marriages in some instances while tacitly allowing and even celebrating them in others. In the next two chapters, we will explore Spenser's poetic impact on other literary portrayals of clandestine marriage, including Chapman's continuation of Marlowe's *Hero and Leander* and Shakespeare's *A Lover's Complaint*.

CHAPTER 2

"Wanton Loves and Young Desires"

Marlowe's *Hero and Leander* and
Chapman's Continuation

If Spenser identifies clandestine marriage as a
threat to the English nation in *The Faerie Queene*, book I, then George Chapman follows his lead by identifying the threat of a clandestine contract in Christopher Marlowe's *Hero and Leander*. In an early modern reader's imagination, Marlowe's paradigm of the Hero and Leander myth—a secret courtship and consummation—would have translated into a story about clandestine marriage.[1] In his continuation, Chapman concentrates on the marriage ceremony, confirming that marital issues were originally at stake in Marlowe's poem. Just as the issues of love and agency are central to much of the criticism on *Hero and Leander*, so do they lie at the heart of the early modern discourse on clandestine marriage. Entering into a clandestine marriage through a handfasting or trothplight gave couples complete freedom in their marital choice. By neglecting Chapman's continuation, we overlook an early modern literary conversation that sheds light on the Elizabethan debates about clandestine marriage and the practice's ability to transform couples into husband and wife. Whether or not we consider Marlowe's poem to be a "fragment," the difference in the style and tone of Chapman's continuation suggests that he did not so much finish Marlowe's *Hero and Leander* as he responds to it.[2]

To create the conditions for Hero and Leander's clandestine contract, Marlowe must first dispel the Petrarchism at the heart of Elizabethan love poetry. During the Elizabethan period, poetry, particularly sonnets, served as a valuable means for lovers to engage in courtship rituals.[3] Marlowe's evident rejection of the sonnet craze in the 1590s, however, signifies his resistance to the inactive, and thus effeminate, subject position of the Petrarchan lover.[4] Marlowe's seeming disinterest in a courtship that leads to marital love is one reason why M. C. Bradbrook calls *Hero and Leander* an "anti-Spenserian manifesto."[5] Furthermore, as a general rule, sonnet sequences did not result in a male poet fulfilling his sexual desire. Instead, sonnets isolated male agency in courtship to the realm of the discursive, as the female love object dictated whether or not (and usually not) the man fulfilled his desire. Considering Marlowe's rejection of the typical literature of courtship for the more avant-garde Ovidian narrative, his poem unsurprisingly opposes the increasing public surveillance of courtship and marriage under the Elizabethan regime.[6] His blatant rejection of Petrarchan traditions in the poem for an Ovidian framework enables Marlowe to restore agency to Renaissance courtship practices in the realm of the literary, and makes room for Hero and Leander to culminate their courtship through an irregular union.

Chapman's focus on the marriage ritual reveals that what is truly subversive about Marlowe's poem is not its homoerotic undertone or racy extramarital sex as some scholars have suggested, but the lack of a public ritual formalizing a marriage pact.[7] In addition to turning the lesser genre of the "minor epic" into epic, the imposition of Chapman's "sestiads" onto Marlowe's poem reads as a literal attempt to physically constrain its unruly content.[8] Chapman's continuation may seem overly moralistic, but, when he addresses Marlowe in the third sestiad, he does not necessarily condemn the author's immersion in the passions.[9] His depiction of Marlowe as "up to the chin in the Pierian flood" (3.190) associates the author's surplus of poetic inspiration with the myth of Tantalus, or unfulfilled desire.[10] When Chapman sends his muse to inform Marlowe's soul "how much his late desires I tender" (3.195), his use of the word "tender" indicates that he respects Marlowe's poetic project.[11] Acting out of regard for his fellow poet, Chapman does not seem compelled to respond to Marlowe's poem solely for the purpose of strait-laced didacticism but rather reminds the reader that social rituals are in place for a reason. Hence, he inserts a Spenserian emphasis on the marriage ceremony into the myth. What makes Hero and Leander's "wanton loves and young desires" (3.11) so problematic for Chapman is that the lovers participate in transgressive courtship and marriage rituals that put tears in the general social fabric. Considering that Hero and Leander's consummation could be interpreted as the secret formalization of a betrothal, Chapman's arresting portrayal of Hero's despair over her lost virginity warns of the tragic consequences of clandestine contracts for women in particular. Chapman's response to the agency—especially male sexual agency—that drives the action of Marlowe's poem lies in his valuation of female subjectivity.

By recalling Chapman's continuation, we can better understand how Marlowe's own transgressive discourse of desire operates within the Elizabethan discourses surrounding clandestine marriage, and better appreciate the extent of an early modern literary dialogue that has gone largely uninvestigated. In particular, Marlowe's portrayal of Hero and Leander entering into a clandestine contract rejects England's national religious rituals that undermine a couple's liberty when making marital pacts. To trace the trajectory of the literary dialogue with Chapman, I first look to how Marlowe's poem portrays Petrarchan courtship as ineffective in both private and public spaces, and then how Marlowe restores agency to the courtship ritual when Hero and Leander agree to a secret marriage pact. When looking to Chapman's continuation, I demonstrate how his focus on female subjectivity polices clandestine contracts in order to maintain the social bonds created by public courtship and marriage. In this way, Chapman's continuation does not have to "obscure the . . . significance" of Marlowe's achievement, but rather it calls our attention to its original historical context.[12]

"And Thinking on Her Died"

Throughout *Hero and Leander*, Petrarchan conventions impede and defer sexual fulfillment in an epyllion where chastity is not always a virtue. Marlowe critiques the literary methods of Elizabethan courtship by first exposing the limitations of the Petrarchan subject position. The subversion of the Petrarchan blazon at the beginning of the poem underscores the sonneteer's superficial authority when dissecting the female body through verse. Rather than blazoning a female love object, Marlowe openly invites the reader to admire Leander's body. "I could tell ye," he confides:

> How smooth his breast was, and how white his belly,
> And whose immortal fingers did imprint
> That heavenly path with many a curious dint,
> That runs along his back, but my rude pen
> Can hardly blazon forth the loves of men.
>
> *(1.65–70)*

This rare instance of Marlovian humility serves only to heighten the passage's eroticism.[13] If Marlowe "can hardly blazon forth" Leander's body, then who can do better? Marlowe's objectification of Leander's body calls Leander's capabilities as a lover into question. The logic of Petrarchan discourse dictates that the wooer in the relationship should be the one doing the objectifying. Georgia E. Brown points out that here "Marlowe exploits desire not only to undermine the dominant literary mode of Petrarchanism but also to question the nature and even the possibility of literary morality."[14] If Petrarchism privileges the male author's display of his poetical skill over sexual fulfillment, Marlowe seems more interested in demonstrating how to get sexual results. By turning the tables on a man's seeming agency when initiating Petrarchan courtship, the blazon undermines Leander's actual intention to be a desiring subject rather than object.

The naive Leander is not the only one who suffers from Petrarchan impotence. Petrarchan conventions sabotage the courtships of all the other male characters as well. The poem's beginning exposes the male lover's helplessness in Petrarchan courtship in general. Even the classical god Apollo fails to achieve Hero's love through the means of the typical Petrarchan trope of admiring his beloved's hair:

> At Sestos Hero dwelt; Hero the fair,
> Whom young Apollo courted for her hair,
> And offered as a dower his burning throne,
> Where she should sit for men to gaze upon.
>
> *(1.5–8)*

Considering that we never see Hero sitting on Apollo's "burning throne," we can safely assume that she turned Apollo down. Yet, if Apollo had read his Sidney or his Spenser, he would have found that admiring a woman's hair is not the way into her heart.[15] In book III of *The Faerie Queene*, which foregrounds the triumph of sexuality within marital love, Spenser also uses Petrarchan language when introducing Florimel to indicate her status as the unattainable Petrarchan beloved. She treats a group of knights to a conventional Petrarchan display:

> All suddenly out of the thickest brush,
>   Vpon a milkwhite Palfrey all alone,
>   A goodly Lady did foreby them rush,
>   Whose face did seeme as cleare as Christall stone,
>   And eke through feare as white as whales bone:
>   Her garments all were wrought of beaten gold,
>   And all her steed with tinsell trappings shone,
>   Which fledd so fast, that nothing mote him hold,
> And scarse them leasure gaue, her passing to behold.
>
> *(III.i.15)*

As the stupefied knights watch the gleaming stream of her "faire yellow locks" (16.3) disappear behind her as she rides past on her palfrey, even the magnificent Arthur fails to catch up with her. Arthur may be awe-inspired by the Petrarchan beauty of this lady of the court, but he is powerless to satisfy the desire her beauty incites.

Such futility characterizes Petrarchan courtship in *Hero and Leander*. Even though robust men attempt to court Hero, they literally waste away and die when they realize the hopelessness of their prospects. "And many seeing great princes were denied," Marlowe sympathetically imparts, "Pined as they went, and thinking on her died" (1.129–30). Robert Burton's *The Anatomy of Melancholy* documents lovesickness—a fascination in early modern England—as a serious disease that derives from, and causes, a chemical imbalance in the body.[16] When Hero's suitors die from the melancholy that results from Petrarchan courtship, Marlowe draws on the tradition that lovesickness literally makes people physically ill.[17] Another potential and alarming side effect of love melancholy includes its ability to effeminize the men it plagues. The "feare, anxiety, doubt, care, peevishnesse, [and] suspicion" associated with love melancholy "turnes a man into a woman," Burton warns.[18] Leander's deferment of sex in his Petrarchan courtship with Hero does bring out his effeminate characteristics. Men's attempts to turn Leander into a Petrarchan mistress also put them in an effeminate position. This includes the male reader. Men are drawn to Leander just as strongly as they are to Hero. The men do not desire Leander because he is a man but because he looks like a woman: "Some swore he was a maid in man's attire, / For in his looks were all that men desire" (1.83–84). In the humorous descriptions of the men's worshipping of both Hero and Leander as Petrarchan mistresses, Marlowe reminds male readers that the staving off of sexual consummation in Petrarchan love effeminizes men by making them melancholy, impotent lovers. If they wish to cure themselves, they must find a love object willing to give in to sexual temptation. Women may be more open to temptation, the poem reveals, if a promise of marriage is involved.

Indeed, Marlowe's passionate shepherd learns this the hard way in Sir Walter Ralegh's "The Nymph's Reply." In "The Passionate Shepherd to His Love," the shepherd makes no hint of marriage in his sexual overtures. "Come live with me and be my love," he implores, "And we will all the pleasures prove" (1–2).[19] He does promise many gifts as a part of his courtship, ranging from "beds of roses" (9) (a single stem is not enough) to "a gown made of the finest wool" (13) to shoes with "buckles of the purest gold" (16). These gifts, some of them quite significant, could potentially be considered as signs of marital intentions in the ambiguities of Elizabethan courtship practices. Marlowe, however, is careful to keep their context vague. The shepherd does not really want to be stuck with someone forever. As Ralegh makes clear, many early modern women (or their nymph counterparts) know better than to trust a shepherd's purposely vague promises. "If all the world and love were young," the nymph responds:

> And truth in every shepherd's tongue,
> These pretty pleasures might me move
> To live with thee and be thy love.
>
> (1–4)

The nymph knows that the shepherd will not keep his vaguely sounding marital promises just as surely as she knows that winter will always come and flowers will always wither. To be successful, the shepherd will have to offer not just material objects of his affection but also more serious promises of fidelity—promises that could not be reneged on despite the passing of time. Promises, perhaps, of a real marriage with an actual ceremony.

The slippage between courtship and courtiership in Elizabethan England, however, made the possibility of a marriage after Petrarchan courtship even more difficult. Catherine Bates explains that the term "courtship," typically used to describe the practices of a courtier, began to be employed in the rhetoric of romance—blurring the distinction between politics and love.[20] In his seminal discussion of Elizabethan sonnet sequences, Arthur F. Marotti further argues that the male sonneteer's frustrations in love are a code for his frustrations at court.[21] Marlowe's disdain for the kind of courtship rituals that include sonnet writing thus translate into a rejection of the courtiership practiced in Queen Elizabeth's court. The political potency of sonneteering meant that courtship itself could be the purpose of romance rather than the typically desired endpoint of the sexual consummation within marriage. As explained in chapter 1, Queen Elizabeth used this rhetoric to her advantage when encouraging her male courtiers to view her as the ultimate Petrarchan mistress.[22] Her situating of herself in this position also seriously jeopardized her male courtiers' displays of masculine nobility essential to fostering masculine social bonds. As Marlowe indicates, the worshippers of a Petrarchan mistress do not go out and fight battles abroad but rather fight each other at their mistress's feet, as indicated by Hero's clothing spattered by the blood of "wretched lovers slain" (1.16).[23] The incorporation of Petrarchan courtship rituals into the realm of the court meant that men despaired not only of consummating their desire with their Petrarchan mistress but also of participating in the kind of action that distinguished a man of the court in the eyes of his fellow male courtiers.[24]

Hero's dress, which positions her as the Petrarchan love object who invites men to gaze upon her (rather than to have sex with her), also seems reminiscent of Elizabeth's own use of iconography. In her portraits, Elizabeth initiates chaste courtship with her male courtiers by inviting them to gaze not on her body, as is typical of the Petrarchan blazon, but on the artificiality of her iconographic dress. Elizabeth's displays of her chastity were supposed to tantalize male desire through sexual symbolism.[25] Marlowe, however, reveals Hero's seemingly natural dress as a work of artifice: "Her veil was artificial flowers and leaves, / Whose workmanship both man and beast deceives" (1.19–20). This deception is crucial to her role as the unattainable beloved, as she performs her duties in the temple of Venus in order to thwart the advances of her male suitors. The formation of male subjectivity based on a female love object can be superficial only if the object purposely deceives the viewer.[26] If men fail to construct meaningful subjectivities through Petrarchan courtship, Marlowe seems intent on offering an alternative, replacing an emphasis on subjectivity within courtship with an Ovidian emphasis on male agency.

Hero and Leander thus participates in the widespread anxiety that early modern men encountered when under the influence of a powerful woman. This anxiety was not restricted to England. In *The Book of the Courtier*, for instance, Castiglione offers an Italian representation of the same problem when male courtiers of Urbino must fashion themselves after the duchess who presides over their nightly festivities. These festivities include an extended staging of the *querelle des femmes* debates. Harry Berger Jr. points out that even the men who make pro-feminist arguments participate in a shared gyneophobia with the other courtiers due to the effeminizing effects a female ruler has on her male subjects.[27] In Sir Thomas Hoby's translation of *The Courtier* (1561), Count Lewis explains the importance of noble birth through comparison to watching a trial of skill: "Forsomuch as our mindes are very apte to love and hate: as in the sightes of combates and games . . . it is seene that the lookers on many times beare affeccion without any manifest cause why, unto one of the two parties."[28] The twentieth-century editor Walter Raleigh observes that Marlowe's famous line, "It lies not in our power to love or hate" (1.167), echoes Count Lewis's comment, linking Marlowe's critique of Petrarchan courtship with a critique of Petrarchan courtiership.[29] As a result of Petrarchan courtship with their female sovereign, the powerful and noble men of Elizabeth's court become what the men of Urbino's court fear they themselves will become: a group of effeminate losers. Marlowe's goal, therefore, becomes to pull the Petrarchan mistress down off her pedestal, creating room for a more equitable republic within matters of love.

His ability to do so hinges on Hero's own dissatisfaction with her position as the Petrarchan love object. (Florimel is clearly unsatisfied as well since she does not desire to be in the position of Petrarchan mistress to begin with.) Realizing that she is falling in love with Leander, Hero strives "to resist the motions of her heart" (1.364) by praying to Venus. Her eventual encouragement of Leander's advances, however, indicates that she means to do more than just tantalize him. As she runs away from Leander in the temple, she drops her fan so that he has a reason to pursue her. When he does not take the hint and writes her a letter instead to set up a rendezvous, she helpfully leaves her tower door open to allow him easy entry. In the meantime, she turns her bedroom into a place of seduction: "roses strewed the room" (2.21). As she goes on to play hard to get, Hero's clearly conflicted feelings about her sexual desires may provide comic relief for the reader, but they also prove that women can be as frustrated as men by the sexual deferment necessitated by Petrarchan courtship. When overturning Petrarchan convention, Marlowe enables male sexual agency by making room for female agency in matters of love as well. Marlowe's subversion of Petrarchan convention into an Ovidian framework, where even the waves in which Leander swims attempt to become sexual agents, makes the clandestine contract between Hero and Leander possible.

"Quickly Were Affied"

While Marlowe's discourse of desire is distinctly Ovidian, his source text, Musaeus's *Hero and Leander*, makes clear that the story of Hero and Leander is a story of marital love. The poem's first lines are laden with marital language:[30]

> Tell of the lamp, O goddess, the witness of hidden loves,
> And of the one who swam by night, to sea-borne *spousals*,
> And the darkling *marriage-bond*, unseen by deathless Dawn.
> And Sestos and Abydos, where I hear of the midnight *bridals*
> Of Hero, of Leander swimming, and thereto of the lamp,
> The lamp that beaconed forth Aphrodite's ministry,
> Courier of the *night-wed* Hero, furnisher forth of *wedding*,
> The lamp, love's glory.
>
> *(1–8; emphases mine)*

In a moralistic vein of which the Protestant reformers would approve, he also makes sexual desire inseparable from marriage. When the young men watch her going about her duties in the temple, they all wished: "Had I but in my house Hero for my wife" (81).[31] One would think that young men would be more interested in satisfying their desires than taking a wife. Musaeus, however, does not present extramarital sex as an option: sex and marriage go hand in hand. Furthermore, after Hero agrees to place a torch in her window to guide Leander across the Hellespont, Musaeus again uses unequivocal marital language to indicate that a marriage has taken place: "Thus they made their compact to join in secret union, / And pledged their nightly love and the tidings of their bridals" (221–222).[32] Marlowe's source makes clear that Hero and Leander is a story of clandestine marriage. In the *Heroides*, even Ovid's Hero refers to Leander as her "husband from Abydos," lamenting that perhaps he does not visit her because she will "be called no match" for him in his home country (XIX.99–100).[33] Considering the popularity of the Hero and Leander myth, Marlowe's readers would have come to the poem with the assumption that the lovers are married.

The playful tone of Hero and Leander's courtship, however, has masked the couple's clandestine contract in modern readings of the epyllion.[34] One of Marlowe's most prolonged additions to Musaeus occurs when Leander attempts to win over Hero rhetorically. In the second half of a speech bordering on one hundred lines, Leander invokes marital language. He declares:

> One is no number; maids are nothing then,
> Without the sweet society of men.
> Wilt thou live single still? One shalt thou be,
> Though never-singling Hymen couple thee.
> Wild savages, that drink of running springs,
> Think water far excels all earthly things:
> But they that daily taste neat wine, despise it.
> Virginity, albeit some highly prize it,
> Compared with marriage, had you tried them both,
> Differs as much as wine and water doth.
>
> *(1.255–264)*

By inquiring if Hero prefers to live alone, Leander infers that their relationship will be more than a one-night stand. It will be a relationship with living arrangements. By contrasting virginity with marriage, he also borrows the rhetoric of the Protestant moralists who attempted to assuage fears that marriage was not as desirable a state as virginity by redefining chastity to include marital monogamy. Bullinger's *The Christen State of Matrymonye* serves just such a purpose by looking to God's creation of Eve as Adam's helpmate to confirm marriage as a natural and desirable state. Protestantism championed chastity within marriage as just as virtuous as, if not more virtuous than, the state of virginity. When wooing Hero, Leander does not persuade her to ignore virtue entirely, but rather he points to marriage as an alternative to virginity to appeal to her female virtue of chastity. Other marital language, such as his reference to Hymen, gives Hero reason to believe that having sex with Leander will either constitute or, at the least, lead to marriage (just as Redcrosse gives Duessa reason to believe they enter into a clandestine contract in *The Faerie Queene*, book I).

Reading *Hero and Leander* according to the Renaissance belief in chastity's dual nature also helps explain Hero's perplexing status as "Venus' nun" (1.45). After learning that she has vowed chastity to Venus, Leander points out that her (now infamous) job description seems contradictory. William Keach speculates that the phrase could refer to the Neoplatonic tradition of the "Venus-Virgo," or perhaps to the slang meaning of the word "nun," "prostitute."[35] However, married women could exercise the virtue of chastity that nuns practice through virginity, and be followers of the goddess of love as well. In book IV of *The Faerie Queene*, for instance, Spenser illustrates this idea when his allegorical representation of married love, Amoret, resides in Venus's temple until her fiancé Scudamour rescues her from the cold path of virginity favored by her twin sister Belphoebe (IV.x). If Hero's chastity implied only virginity, it seems that she would not sacrifice turtledoves, the popular emblem of married fidelity, when performing her rites to Venus. Similar to Amoret, Hero has apparently misinterpreted her dedication to the goddess of love by devoting herself to virginity rather than practicing chastity within marriage.

Encouraging and aiding nuns to leave their cloisters for marriage was a favorite pastime of the continental reformers. Calvin expresses disdain for the unnatural life of virginity forced on young women in convents:[36]

> How many monsters of crime are produced every day in Popery by that compulsory celibacy of nuns! What barriers does it not deliberately break through! And therefore, although this course had at first appeared to be commendable, yet, taught by experiments so many and so terrible, they ought to have somewhat complied with the counsel of Paul. But they are so far from doing this, that they provoke the wrath of God more and more, from day to day, by their obstinacy . . . disgraceful lusts rage amongst them, so that hardly one in ten lives chastely.

Calvin thus uses the same disapproving language when discussing vows of celibacy as he does when discussing the canon laws pertaining to marriage, proclaiming, "We disapprove of the tyrannical law about celibacy, chiefly for two reasons. First, they pretend that it is meritorious worship before God; and secondly, by rashness in vowing, they plunge souls into destruction."[37] Martin Luther also circulated the pamphlet *Why Nuns May Leave Cloisters with God's Blessing* (1523) after marrying an ex-nun himself. In the pamphlet, he compares the deliverance of women from cloisters to the children of Israel being delivered from Egyptian bondage. Another pamphlet proclaims: "Let the poor virgins be unbound so that none is any longer obligated by such devilish belief [celibacy]. Let them stay in the cloister only so long as they freely chose, and when one wishes no longer to remain, let her follow the example of her friends, take a husband, and serve her neighbors in the world."[38] By rescuing Hero from her role as nun, Leander rescues a woman from a life of sexual dissatisfaction, appearing to side with the Protestant theologians (and Spenser) in the debate over whether virginity or marriage is more virtuous.

Leander thus persuades Hero to sleep with him not by ignoring the accepted moral framework of Renaissance courtship that elevated married chastity, but by suggesting that in doing so they will enter into marriage. His success at the beginning of their first private meeting results in the couple performing what an early modern reader would recognize as a spousal agreement:

> He asked, she gave, and nothing was denied;
> Both to each other quickly were affied.
> Look how their hands, so were their hearts united,
> And what he did she willingly requited.
>
> *(2.25–28)*

Marlowe's use of "affied" is significant here. The term means "engaged to be married," "affianced," or "betrothed."[39] Shakespeare also uses the term "affied" in *The Taming of the Shrew* when Baptista agrees to the pretended marriage settlement with Lucentio's servant, Tranio. When Baptista agrees that the "match is made," Tranio inquires:

> I thank you, sir. Where then do you know best
> We be affied and such assurance ta'en
> As shall with either part's agreement stand?
>
> *(4.4.48–50)*

Here Tranio indicates that he and Bianca will enter into a formal marriage pact when becoming "affied" before participating in a public ceremony later. Spenser also uses the term in *The Faerie Queene*, book IV, when describing Amyas's betrothal to Aemylia (IV.viii.53.1). The term "affied," therefore, indicates a pact of a highly contractual nature—not a pact that someone could easily get out of later. By stating that Hero and Leander are "affied," Marlowe acknowledges that the lovers enter into a contract, or at least a betrothal, of a marital nature.[40] We have already seen how spousals and marital contracts collapsed into each other since spousal vows constituted a kind of high-stakes betrothal. Even though he stresses the public ceremony, Gouge begrudgingly admits that the spousal contracts that occur before a religious solemnization make the marriage legally binding: "A lawfull contract knitteth so firme a knot as cannot be broken: so as a man may conclude that being contracted to a woman she shall be his wife: and so may a woman conclude of a man."[41] When becoming "affied," therefore, Hero and Leander make a marital contract.

The uniting of hands was also a traditional symbol of a marital bond. Bullinger describes betrothed couples as being "handfasted," and Gouge dictates that couples should take one another's hands when plighting their troth.[42] In his discussion of a Nicholas Hilliard miniature, Roy Strong looks to the act of clasping hands as an indication of marriage. "Clasped hands," he informs, "are a common emblem of Concord and plighted faith."[43] When analyzing court depositions pertaining to marriage, Loreen L. Giese further observes, "Almost all depositions which include a description of a marriage mention hand holding . . . at a contract."[44] According to one 1611 deposition that Giese uncovers in the London Consistory Court, the uniting of hands essentially makes the marriage in the eyes of one witness. This witness testified that "Sanders tooke both . . . Newton and Waters hands and ioyned them together and said Thus I make you man and wife."[45] Hero and Leander's uniting of hands at the moment they become "affied," therefore, enhances the scene's marital undertones.

After becoming "affied," Hero gives Leander a significant marital token: a ring. Swinburne confirms that spousal vows did not always even have to include spoken promises, but that *Love Gifts and Tokens of the Parties betroathed . . . [such] as Bracelets, Chains, Jewels,* and namely the *Ring*" could be used to signify an "assured Pledge of a perfect Promise."[46] When Leander departs from her tower, Hero forces the ring upon him: "Nor could the youth abstain, but he must wear / The sacred ring wherewith she was endowed / When first religious chastity she vowed" (2.108–110). The language here implies that Leander did not necessarily want to wear the ring (he *"must* wear" it despite attempting to "abstain"). Perhaps Hero places more significance on their contract than he does (just as Duessa does in her relationship with Redcrosse). Or perhaps Leander's love for Hero compels him to wear the ring despite his seeming reluctance or misgivings. Either way, when putting on the ring after becoming "affied," it becomes an "assured Pledge of a perfect Promise." Of course, the potential ambiguity of their marital contract and the tokens associated with it mirrors the ambiguity that surrounded the practice of spousal contracts in general, anticipating the potential problems with the match that Chapman will explore in his continuation.

Hero and Leander literally seal the deal on their marriage pact through the act of consummation. While unconsummated spousal contracts could be annulled, a sexual consummation resulted in a union that could not be absolved under any circumstance. As Swinburne puts it, "Spousals do become Matrimony by carnal knowledge."[47] Leander's first encounter with Hero in her bedroom, however, proves just how devastating Petrarchan courtship can be for men. After displaying all the appropriate characteristics of a Petrarchan lover, Leander reveals that he knows how to worship his mistress but not how to love her:

> Like Aesop's cock, this jewel he enjoyed,
> And as a brother with his sister toyed,
> Supposing nothing else was to be done,
> Now he her favour and good will had won.
>
> *(2.51–54)*

Only after the lovers struggle physically with each other does Leander come to realize that his marriage has not been solidified, and he seems eager to consummate the match:

>   yet he suspected
> Some amorous rites or other were neglected.
> Therefore unto his body hers he clung;
> She, fearing on the rushes to be flung,
> Strived with redoubled strength; the more she strived,
> The more a gentle pleasing heat revived.
>
> *(2.63–68)*

An Ovidian celebration of sexuality triumphs here, but the term "rites" also suggests that the sexual act carries ceremonial weight.[48] For Marlowe, sex is the ritual through which a marriage is cemented—not the public celebration found in the *Book of Common Prayer* and championed by Spenser.

In *Romeo and Juliet*, Shakespeare associates Marlowe's phrase "amorous rites" with clandestine marriage. After the young lovers participate in a clandestine ceremony in Friar Laurence's cell, Juliet anticipates having sex with her husband later that night:

Spread thy close curtain, love-performing night,
That [th'] runaway's eyes may wink, and Romeo
Leap to these arms untalk'd of and unseen!
Lovers can see to do their *amorous rites*
By their own beauties.

(3.2.5–9; emphasis mine)

Juliet's impassioned expression of sexual desire could easily belong in Marlowe's epyllion. The speech, however, is not in the service of extramarital sex but rather in the service of clandestine marital sex that takes the form of "rites" cementing the nuptials performed earlier that day. In his *A Bride-Bvsh*, William Whately confirms that marriage and "erotic activity" were essentially the same by literally replacing the word "sex" with "marriage" in his advice to married couples: "In a word, marriage must bee vsed as seldome and sparingly, as may stand with the neede of the persons married."[49] For Whately, "marriage . . . becomes the act of making love. Indeed, the marriage bed becomes a synecdoche for marriage itself."[50] After exchanging vows and tokens, grasping hands, and having sex, Hero and Leander easily fulfill the early modern requirements for making a clandestine marriage. The sex scandal that critics often identify in *Hero and Leander*, therefore, derives from sex that takes place within a marriage that has not been solemnized by the church.

Conforming to many other aristocratic marriages, Hero and Leander's courtship and marriage remain transactional, as indicated when Leander describes Hero's virginity as an "inestimable gem" (2.78). As will be explored more thoroughly in the chapter on Shakespeare's *Merchant of Venice*, families could punish unruly children who entered into imprudent clandestine marriages by withholding dowries and inheritance. Marlowe implies that in his ideal courtship the marital transaction in which a woman bestows her virginity on a man will take place privately between the man and woman. The purpose of courtship and marriage for Marlowe lies in the ability for a man to satisfy his sexual appetite—not for a man and a woman to enter into a mutually fulfilling relationship that would benefit their families or community.

By entering into a private, transactional pact concealed from the watchful public eye, Leander eventually gets the upper hand sexually—a position to which the Petrarchan lover can usually only aspire. Marlowe describes Leander in distinctly masculine terms for the first time as the consummation takes place. After being indistinguishable from a maid, Leander transforms into the classical epitome of masculinity when having sex with Hero:

Leander now, like Theban Hercules
Entered the orchard of th' Hesperides,
Whose fruit none rightly can describe but he
That pulls or shakes it from the golden tree.

(2.297–300)

The description of the sexual act is troubling due to its violence.[51] Not only does Leander use force since he "pulls or shakes" (2.300), but he is also like a soldier responding to a "fresh alarm" (2.284). Love makes him "deaf and cruel where he means to prey" (2.288). Hero, meanwhile, is like a bird that Leander has not just captured as his "prey" but means to "wring" (2.289) with his hands. The disturbing nature of the consummation scene perhaps further explains the attempts to regulate private spousal contracts, as it calls the extent of Hero's agency into question. Indeed, Hero's desire to participate in a courtship and consummation with Leander seems outside of her control from the beginning when "Cupid beats down her prayers with his wings" (1.369) as she appeals to Venus for help. While Hero does end up deriving pleasure from the sexual encounter, since she "wished this night were never done" (2.301), she does not give Leander her enthusiastic consent. She may have used only "half [her] strength" (2.296) when attempting to resist Leander, but she still struggles. After the consummation, Leander appears to be the only one completely pleased as he revels in his sexual triumph. While spousal contracts allowed couples to enter into a marriage for love in defiance of their parents' (or monarch's) wishes, Marlowe seems mostly interested in showing men how they can get women to sleep with them by manipulating ecclesiastical law in their favor. Hero may have believed she was entering into a marriage with Leander, but this belief becomes problematic since the contract had no witnesses.

Leander demonstrates his sexual mastery the morning after the consummation takes place. Not entirely certain how to confront Leander after he "took" (2.308) her virginity, Hero hopes to retreat to "some corner secretly" instead (2.311). As she gets up, Leander forcefully detains her, causing her to slide "mermaid-like" (2.315) onto the floor before being able to stand up. Leander thus gains control over his beloved not figuratively by objectifying her through verse but literally by physically constraining her. He further possesses her body as an object of his wealth:

And her all naked to his sight displayed,
Whence his admiring eyes more pleasure took
Than Dis, on heaps of gold fixing his look.

(2.324–326)

Hero's shame at being viewed in this way—betrayed by her "ruddy cheek" (2.323)—reveals that the Petrarchan love object is not a powerful otherworldly mistress but simply a woman who possesses sexual desires and a body that can be mastered. Despite her dissatisfaction with her role as Petrarchan mistress, Hero does not seem entirely satisfied with her new role after giving up this choice either. Even if Marlowe left the poem unfinished, intending eventually to depict Hero grief-stricken over her husband's death as does Musaeus in the original, his depiction of Hero in what has become the poem's final scene would remain problematic. A Petrarchan mistress at least has the ability to accept or reject her courtiers. In the final scene, Hero appears to have no agency left.

Marlowe strips the significance from the Petrarchan love object through one of the most celebrated practices of early modern Protestant England: marriage. In a subversion of accepted societal norms and of the Protestant ideal, but still operating within the legal framework, Marlowe demonstrates how marriage can be a fully private act. In doing so, he directly contradicts Spenser's poetic agenda by insisting that consent alone, as dictated by Roman canon law, remain a possible avenue for marriage. This contradiction also undermines the Calvinist ideology associated with Spenser's religious poetics. Helga Duncan observes that Marlowe's epyllion "presents a 'church' of unpredictable desires that challenge the hardening of doctrine in England's late-sixteenth-century turn toward Calvinism."[52] A hardening that we saw in the last chapter through Spenser's Calvinist rejection of canon law. She directs our attention to the role of English religious identity in *Hero and Leander*, claiming: "The literary trials through which poets sought to fashion an English religious identity were complex and hotly contested. . . . Marlowe's experiment in the fashionable new genre of the epyllion does not firmly belong to the classical, secular domain but is perhaps better understood in the context of Protestant debates about the scope and nature of the Reformation in England."[53] In particular, Marlowe makes clear that some ideologies of the reformed church directly undermine the individual liberty that his epyllion champions. By removing courtship and marriage to the private domain, he gives men the ability to practice their masculinity—both in the bedroom and at court—without constraint. After Leander enters into an irregular union with Hero, he does not seem eager to consider himself married as do the young men in Musaeus's poem. He rather seems eager to satisfy his desire—a clandestine contract is simply the avenue to achieve this goal, not an end in itself. Whether Leander will consider himself to be married the next day, or the next week, for that matter, never comes up. And, conveniently for Leander, it does not have to. In a sense, by not finishing the poem, whether purposely or not, Marlowe lets Leander off the hook.

While Marlowe de-emphasizes the marriage between Hero and Leander in his revision of Musaeus, he does not efface it entirely by completely jettisoning marital language. In the murky context of early modern marital practices, he leaves the door open for the lovers to have a clandestine contract. Chapman seizes on this opening in his continuation, revealing that readers should be attune to the potential of clandestinity. The fact that the contract happens so "quickly" in Marlowe's original, and without much further mention, demonstrates the ease through which couples could enter into handfastings—and leave them. Marlowe's Hero even anticipates this problem. After giving Leander her ring, she tearfully implores him as he departs from her tower: "Let your vows and promises be kept" (2.96). In a way, the modern scholarship that neglects the marriage contract in Marlowe's poem confirms Hero's worst fears.

"How Poor Was Substance without Rites"

If Marlowe rejects the Spenserian ideal of a publicly celebrated marriage for a quick clandestine contract, Chapman writes this ideal back into the poem. In doing so, he confirms that Hero and Leander did participate in a clandestine marriage in the first two Marlovian sestiads. After Leander returns to Abydos, he realizes that he will need to inform the public about his marriage through a ceremony: "And instantly he vowed to celebrate / All rites pertaining to his married state" (3.159–160). By referring to Leander's "married state," Chapman acknowledges that in Marlowe's poem a private contract and a sexual consummation between lovers resulted in a marriage. Leander and Hero's transgression is not that they have had premarital sex but that they have not performed the rituals that garner recognition of their relationship in the public domain. Leander vows to rectify his "neglect of nuptial rites" (3.157) only after he experiences an allegorical vision of the goddess Ceremony, who arrives with other allegorical figures such as Devotion, Order, State, Society, and Policy. These figures highlight marriage not as vows made between two people but as vows that maintain social order, reminding Leander (and the reader) that a ceremony is not a ceremony without a public display. Thus, Ceremony scolds Leander about "how poor was substance without rites" (3.147), and insists that pacts made without civil recognition "but loose and secret, all their glories hide; / Fear fills the chamber, darkness decks the bride" (3.153–154). According to Ceremony, Hero is indeed a bride, but she cannot reap the rewards that come with her new status. And Hero's struggle during the consummation scene in Marlowe's poem literally confirms the belief that sex is

uncomfortable for women when not preceded by a wedding ceremony legitimating the act. Chapman further emphasizes the need for ceremony when
Hero invites two other betrothed lovers to be married in her temple. The Argument of the Fifth Sestiad reveals that Hero performs this service so that
"she covertly might celebrate / With secret joy her own estate" (9–10). Clearly,
Hero believes herself to be in a state of marriage but recognizes that she has
not gone through the public ritual. For Chapman, as for Spenser, the ceremony
is what sanctifies the marriage pact—not the sexual act itself (the "amorous
rites") as portrayed by Marlowe.

Chapman establishes that the people who make these public ceremonies
possible are the patriarchs of the families involved. In the "Epithalamion Teratos," celebrating the marriage of the two lovers, the nymph Teras offers some
advice to future brides:

> Rise, virgins, let fair nuptial loves enfold
> Your fruitless breasts: the maidenheads ye hold
> Are not your own alone, but parted are;
> Part in disposing them your Parents share,
> And that a third part is; so must ye save
> Your loves a third, and you your thirds must have.
>
> *(5.473–478)*

Contrary to what Marlowe would have liked his readers to believe, a virgin
does not have the agency to bestow her maidenhead on a man, and a man does
not have the agency to take it from her: the woman's parents also share in the
ownership of her virginity. After Marlowe has portrayed Hero and Leander's
courtship as transactional, Chapman reminds his readers that this transaction
should take place between families, not couples. Keeping a marriage secret
could result in a man wooing a woman purely for political or personal gain,
as in the case of Sir Walter Ralegh's feigned courtship with Queen Elizabeth
after he secretly married her lady-in-waiting, Elizabeth Throckmorton. Or,
even worse, a clandestine marriage could create the possibility for a man to
unwittingly cuckold another man, which, as Shakespeare humorously makes
evident throughout his plays, was a constant and pervasive fear. Considering
the early modern emphasis on bloodlines, public recognition of marriage miti-
gates social conflict among men. Chapman thus reveals that public rituals
are not just symptoms of female tyranny in matters of love and politics.

In Chapman's continuation, Leander's father realizes the stakes associated
with an early modern marriage. While in Marlowe's poem Leander's father
mildly rebukes his son's sexual activity in a Renaissance version of a "boys will

be boys" mentality, in Chapman's version the father orders his son to swim back across the Hellespont to retrieve Hero for a proper ceremony celebrating their nuptials. The father even arranges for ships to "waft [Hero] safely" (3.168) back to Abydos (why Leander could not be on one of those ships is unclear). Leander's father may be eager to celebrate the marriage (even if in doing so he must risk his son's safety) so that he can defuse any anger felt by Hero's parents when they discover that his son has secretly usurped their daughter's virginity. No matter the reason, he is anxious to solemnize the marriage properly. Since the Fates thwart Leander's attempt to swim the Hellespont, for Chapman the neglect of a public ceremony becomes the reason why Hero and Leander's story ends in tragedy. Not the need to fulfill sexual desire.

Chapman's figures of the malicious Fates echo the curious Mercury interlude where Marlowe anticipates the problems created by a private marriage transaction. In this episode, the courtship between Mercury and the maid is also transactional, since the woman demands that Mercury give her a "draught of flowing Nectar" (1.431) from Jove's cup before she will sleep with him.[54] Mercury agrees. Cupid, however, acting as Jove's avenger, causes the Destinies to fall in love with the messenger god. This event results in Mercury asking the Destinies, in another kind of love transaction, to replace Jove with Saturn. After Mercury spurns his would-be lovers, the vengeful Destinies return Jove to the throne. Mercury's failure to perform his duty to serve Jove for the sake of courtship results in an unsuccessful courtship, and impoverishes academics. Chapman, recognizing that Marlowe wants to restore sexual agency to men, also realizes that Marlowe (like Mercury) is not that interested in marriage. For Marlowe, marriage seems a vow made to be broken. Chapman, however, appreciates that unlimited male agency actually may cause trouble between men (in addition to making patronage difficult for authors in the literary realm), and his continuation absorbs the lessons of the Mercury episode.

While Hero's own parents are notably absent in Marlowe's poem, Chapman writes her father back in to his continuation.[55] The reader may never see Hero's father, but she expresses concern about his displeasure:

> She mused how she could look upon her sire,
> And not show that without, that was intire.
> For as a glass is an inanimate eye,
> And outward forms embraceth inwardly,
> So is the eye an animate glass that shows
> In-forms without us.

(3.233–238)

Hero worries that the physical loss of her virginity, an inner virtue, will register in her outward appearance. In a time when a woman's chastity held immense value for either her father or her husband, the realization that what a woman did with her body was not necessarily physically apparent was fear inducing for men. The goddess Ecte even makes this point to Venus when causing the swan Leucote to ask, "Why may not amorous Hero seem a maid, / Though she be none, as well as you suppress / In modest cheeks your inward wantonness?" (4.277–279). Venus masterfully disguises her own desires. She refuses, however, to allow Hero the same capability of dissemblance. Chapman attempts to regulate female sexuality by reminding the women in his audience that even though their participation in sexual activity may not be immediately obvious, the compromise of their inner virtue could potentially manifest itself.

Claude J. Summers argues that Marlowe portrays social pressures as policing Hero's chastity, but Marlowe also depicts the obvious fragility of these pressures when Hero ignores them.[56] As Marlowe famously declares, sexual desire could strike at any time:

> It lies not in our power to love, or hate,
> For will in us is overruled by fate.
>
> .   .   .   .
>
> The reason no man knows: let it suffice,
> What we behold is censured by our eyes.
> Where both deliberate, the love is slight:
> Who ever loved, that loved not at first sight?
>
> *(1.167–176)*

The power of sight to overcome a person's will implies that if individual women, or men, have agency within courtship, they may make imprudent matches. Both Spenser and Shakespeare also toy with the idea of love at first sight in the initiation of Britomart's courtship with Artegall in *The Faerie Queene* (III.ii.24–26), and in Phoebe's borrowing of Marlowe's line in Shakespeare's *As You Like It* (3.5.82).[57] The crucial difference between Spenser's and Shakespeare's heroines, on the one hand, and Marlowe's Hero, on the other, is that both Britomart and Rosalind move safely through the public domain in masculine disguise, which makes them impervious to the male gaze. Indeed, after Rosalind falls in love with Orlando, her masculine disguise allows her to keep their desires in check while she tests Orlando's virtue. Both Rosalind and Britomart also have watchful female companions to assist them, and Shakespeare stages Rosalind's courtship within her father's jurisdiction in the forest of Arden. Even though Rosalind's father does not initially recognize her, in the end she reveals herself to Orlando under the duke's eye—eliciting her father's approval of the public ceremony that follows.

In Marlowe's *Hero and Leander*, however, Hero is conspicuously alone in her tower, with a nurse who does not accompany her on her visits to the temple when performing her public duties. Here she dangerously invites the gaze of her male suitors, while also exposing herself to temptation. When Leander falls in love with her after seeing her at the festival, he complains, "God knows I cannot force love, as you do" (1.206). While their consummation takes on a violent tone that a modern reader could identify as rape, Leander defensively claims that Hero's physical presence rapes the men who cannot help but look upon her. According to Marlowe, men do not fall in love with women; women make men fall in love with them. To solve this problem, Marlowe allows men the agency to have sex with women rather than worshipping them from afar. Chapman implies that women should remain within the jurisdictions of their fathers and maintain an intense desire to preserve their virginity as a backup for the father's watchful gaze.

Relying on a woman's subjectivity to police her actions thus becomes essential to Chapman's rewriting of Marlowe's transgressive approach to marriage. To protect themselves from the male agents found in Marlowe's portrayal of courtship, women must understand the painful connection between their bodies and their interiorities. Unable to confide in her father as Leander does his, and not realizing Leander's intent to recognize their marriage publicly, Chapman's Hero laments her loss of virginity that comes into conflict with her public duties and violates her parents' wishes in a prolonged interior monologue. Chapman's depiction of the enraged Venus illustrates how clandestine contracts could endanger a person's public position when—despite Hero's sacrifice of her hair—the goddess abandons her. Venus is angered not only by the breaking of Hero's vow to remain a virgin but also by the fact that, unbeknownst to Hero, she made a bet with Diana that one of her followers could live as a maid.[58] Hero's sin in this case is not that she has had sex but that in doing so she has broken a contract with her employer. Hero attempts to efface her loss of virginity by comforting herself with the idea that she and Leander are "one flesh":

> *Hero Leander is, Leander Hero:*
> Such virtue love hath to make one of two.
> If then Leander did my maidenhead get,
> Leander being my self I still retain it.

We break chaste vows when we live loosely ever;
But bound as we are, we live loosely never.
Two constant lovers being joined in one,
Yielding to one another, yield to none.

(3.357–364)

However, Hero cannot dismiss the fact that she had no right to marry in the first place except by rationalizing that she would have killed herself otherwise—thus committing the even greater sin of suicide.

Chapman's allusions to pregnancy foreshadow Hero's potential pregnancy, which would inevitably expose her transgressive behavior. Her guilty conscience literally racks her with the pains of labor: "She was a mother straight, and bore with pain / Thoughts that spake straight, and wished their mother slain" (3.227–228). A possible pregnancy calls attention to another one of the dangers of private spousal contracts when a pregnant woman claimed marriage with a man who denied the bond in the church courts. In 1563, for instance, Ellen Ricroft took Thomas Snelson to court to force him to recognize their marital contract that had resulted in a child.[59] According to the deposition, one witness, Alicia Manwaringe, testifies that Thomas "promysed to marry . . . Eleine bie his faith and trouthe."[60] Thomas then tried to get Ellen to release him from his promise after the child was born by offering her a "piece of mony."[61] Not a woman to be bought off, Ellen refused. Another witness claims that banns had been called "twise or thrise," though Thomas himself insists that the banns were asked "without his consent or knoledge."[62] The case points to the slipperiness between sex and marriage. Thomas readily admits to having "carnall Copulacion" with Ellen but argues that this did not amount to marriage.[63] Ellen, however, believes them to be "man and wife" and is determined to hold him to it. Thankfully for Ellen, some people did seem to know at least something about Thomas's marital promises. Unfortunately for Hero, her own clandestine marriage takes place without witnesses. She may find herself in a position where she not only has broken her obligations to her parents and to Venus but also has difficulty proving herself to be an honest, married woman, as her body betrays her sexual activity. Chapman's continuation suggests the possibility that her relationship with Leander will simply be interpreted as premarital sex, and warns of the dangers of neglecting a public marriage ceremony when performing a spousal contract.

We do not need to return to believing that Marlowe's poem is incomplete without Chapman's continuation to discover the interpretative possibilities that derive from putting the two authors in conversation with each other. To the contrary, we can better understand the social impetus behind Chapman's continuation, which highlights the increasing focus on the public solemnization as the only way to enter into a marriage properly in the wake of the Protestant Reformation. Considering that Chapman also faithfully translated Musaeus's *Hero and Leander* (1616), his elaborate and at times strange interpretation of the myth in his continuation demonstrates that he was responding to (and correcting) the issues he believed to be important in Marlowe's original poem.[64] His focus on the public ceremony and Hero's interiority points to a desire to suppress the ability to make clandestine contracts.

Chapman's and Marlowe's depictions of courtship and marriage, however, may not be as different as they initially appear. While Chapman's continuation seems to be a Spenserian response to Marlowe's poem, his model of marriage remains troubling. His focus on Hero's subjectivity, which Marlowe leaves in a shamed state, also serves as a mechanism for control over the female body. Hero's interiority does not allow her the ability to make her own choices, but rather reminds her of the consequences of her actions—operating as a form of internal surveillance. In *Ovid's Banquet of Sense*, Chapman's Julia operates to spark the imagination of the voyeuristic male author. In a similar fashion, Hero's subjectivity, while operating to keep men from acting on their desires rather than encouraging them, serves to enable the masculine social bonds that kept marriage a transactional practice in early modern England. Both Marlowe and Chapman, therefore, seem to have similar investments in marriage and courtship. Marlowe sets out to remedy the effeminizing practice of Petrarchan courtship popular in the Elizabethan court. To do so, he provides the solution of confining courtship and marriage to the private realm, where men can exercise their sexual agency and preserve their time in the public sphere for more masculine enterprises than wooing. Chapman, however, realizes that this practice may undermine the masculine social bonds that Marlowe actually appears to support. Both authors are more invested in creating and maintaining social bonds between men than in forwarding a more companionate form of marriage that is often celebrated as being at the center of Reformation discourses on marriage. In the next chapter I look to Shakespeare's own Spenserian response to the problem of clandestine marriage in *A Lover's Complaint*.

CHAPTER 3

Sacred Ceremonies and Private Contracts in Spenser's *Epithalamion* and Shakespeare's *A Lover's Complaint*

Similar to Marlowe's *Hero and Leander*, Shakespeare's *A Lover's Complaint* depicts an easily overlooked fiction of clandestine marriage. Early modern readers, however, would have recognized the "fickle maid" (5) as a woman abandoned not just by a lover but by a man she could have considered her husband. As in Marlowe's epyllion, the young man's vows of faith, followed by a consummation, suggest that the couple entered into a private marital contract. The fact that the maid has no recourse but to lament her fate underscores the potential heartache associated with making a match via spousal vows. The exchange of love tokens, such as the ones the maid has received, could indicate a desire to enter into a marriage—or not. The young man clearly did not place the same meaning in his tokens or vows as did his numerous lovers. Participating in the sacred ceremonies of the public solemnization, such as the ones Spenser emphasizes in his *Epithalamion*, disambiguates the marital process. By neglecting these ceremonies, Shakespeare's maid finds herself a victim of early modern marital hermeneutics.

With *A Lover's Complaint*, Shakespeare participates in the tradition of including a female complaint after a sonnet sequence. Samuel Daniel's *Complaint of Rosamond*, following his sonnet sequence *Delia* (1592), has long been recognized as a model for Shakespeare's own complaint.[1] Considering Shakespeare's demonstrated interest in Spenser's work, it is reasonable to assume that he would have studied the poem that follows Spenser's sonnet sequence, *Amoretti*, just as he studied Daniel's when writing his own version of the form.[2] Of course, he would have found that Spenser's poem does not constitute a female complaint that admonishes illicit sexual desire, but rather a wedding poem that depicts desire's consummation within the framework of Christian matrimony. For this reason, scholars tend to remark on the thematic differences between *Epithalamion* and *A Lover's Complaint* rather than the similarities.

A Lover's Complaint, however, has long been recognized as the most Spenserian of Shakespeare's works. Edmond Malone first observed that "in this beautiful poem, in every part of which the hand of Shakespeare is visible, he perhaps meant to break a lance with Spenser."[3] Colin Burrow confirms Shakespeare's indebtedness to the "elder poet."[4] Michael Schoenfeldt further acknowledges, "*A Lover's Complaint* is Shakespeare sounding like Edmund Spenser on a good day."[5] Other critics, such as John Kerrigan and Patrick Cheney, have explored Spenser's influence on the poem more fully.[6] Brian Vickers even looks to what he calls a "slavish imitation" of Spenser as a basis for eliminating the poem from the Shakespeare canon.[7] Shakespeare, however, does not simply imitate Spenser in *A Lover's Complaint* as Vickers suggests. Instead, Shakespeare joins Spenser in providing not just "an extra meditation on sexual desire and its consequences" but an "extra meditation" on *marriage* after a sonnet sequence.[8] In this way, Shakespeare does not so much imitate Spenser's *Epithalamion* as he revises it for a different context. In *A Lover's Complaint*, Shakespeare reveals that the problem Spenser had hoped to remedy in book I of *The Faerie Queene* has not been resolved. A Marlovian sense of male agency, which preys on female subjectivity within matters of love, continues even as the reign of the real-life Faery Queen is coming (or has come) to a close.

Most likely written either shortly before or after Queen Elizabeth's death, Shakespeare's *A Lover's Complaint* engages with the public debates about clandestine marriage in a transitional time in English history.[9] If Marlowe's *Hero and Leander* enters the literary fray of the 1590s in direct opposition to the sonnet craze, Shakespeare's formal participation in the trend feels almost outdated (his own unconventional sequence was not published until 1609).[10] His focus on clandestine marriage when writing *A Lover's Complaint*, however, is timely: Parliament members seized the transition between Queen Elizabeth's and King James's reigns as an opportunity to put the issue of irregular unions on the political agenda. In 1603, Puritan members of Parliament presented James I with the Millenary Petition, which included pleas for ending the seasonal restraints on weddings and requested "that licences for marriages without banns asked, be more cautiously granted."[11] In particular, they expressed concern about the growing number of untrustworthy clerics (like Shakespeare's Sir Oliver Mar-Text) who made a trade in performing clandestine marriages. The Parliament members elaborate on "the Hurt that comes by barring of askings in the Church, and granting of licences to marry. These marriages are made in places peculiar, which are desired to be annexed to the bishoprics, by vagrant, unlearned, dissolute, drunken, and idle Stipendiaries, Vicars, and Curates: who are placed in the rooms of the rich men; who have divers livings, and are not resident. And they receive the profits; and instead of thankfulness to God, serve him by deputies."[12] In 1604, James I agreed to clarify the definition of marriage by revising certain canon laws. Canons 62 and 63, for instance, declared that marriage be preceded by the announcement of banns and that the service be performed by a duly licensed cleric in the parish church of one of the couple: "No Minister vpon paine of suspension *per triennium ipso facto*, shall celebrate Matrimonie betweene any persons without a Facultie or Licence granted by some of the persons in these our Constitutions expressed, except the Bannes of Matrimonie haue bene first published three seueral Sundaies or Holy dayes in the time of diuine Seruice, in the Parish Churches and Chappels where the saide parties dwel, according to the booke of Common Prayer."[13] While these guidelines were already familiar, they did officially codify the existing regulations. Like any political compromise, however, these developments did not entirely please anyone. They did not satisfy Parliament members who wanted serious reform, and they disappointed those who viewed the canons as imposing on their traditional right to enter into a marriage without ecclesiastical authority.

The marital issues that occupy Spenser's *Epithalamion* and Shakespeare's *A Lover's Complaint*, therefore, reflect the public debates about the benefits of the public surveillance of the marriage ritual, which (presumably) kept sexual predators at bay, and the disadvantages of that surveillance, which resulted in a lack of agency within the matchmaking process. These poems are just as concerned with how someone determines the identity of a prospective spouse as with which vows and rituals transform a couple into husband and wife. How does someone know that a potential spouse will make a good mate, or that a person is even eligible to be married in the first place? For Spenser, public rituals grant lovers access to each other's interiorities, giving them assurance of their partner's virtuous identity. The fickle maid's failure to gain access to her lover's interiority in *A Lover's Complaint* means that she does not recognize her own lover's less-than-virtuous identity until it is too late. Shakespeare thus cautions his readers that marriages that do not occur through "sacred ceremonies" (216) cannot result in the "endlesse matrimony" (217) that Spenser describes in *Epithalamion*.[14]

Sacred Ceremonies in Spenser's *Epithalamion*

In *Epithalamion*, Spenser returns to his poetic agenda in book I of *The Faerie Queene* that nuptial celebrations should be public affairs. Elizabeth Mazzolla observes that Spenser "construes public knowledge about intimacy as a form of approval."[15] I would go further: Spenser construes public approval *as necessary* for intimacy, or, at least, for matrimonial intimacy. While Spenser focuses on the creation of a national consciousness through public ritual in his *Legend of Holiness*, he reveals how public rituals fulfill promises of wedded love made in *Epithalamion*. Despite the increased emphasis on love and companionship within the marital bond, Protestant reformers expressed uncertainty concerning the nature of the marriage ritual: "Did the rite firmly unite lovers, or would it only console them now in the face of the isolation Protestantism descried?"[16] In an uncharacteristic deviation from Calvinist theology, Spenser offers the *Book of Common Prayer*'s public rituals as providing a comforting corrective to marriage's mortal limitations in hardline Protestant doctrine.

Unexpectedly, perhaps, Spenser's *Epithalamion* and Marlowe's *Hero and Leander* have origins in similar poetic frustrations. Both authors value the standards of Petrarchan beauty, but neither is satisfied with the outcomes of Petrarchan courtship. Like Marlowe's Leander, Spenser's bride has all of the physical attributes befitting a Petrarchan mistress:

> Her goodly eyes lyke Saphyres shining bright,
> Her forehead yuory white,
> Her cheekes lyke apples which the sun hath rudded,
> Her lips lyke cherryes charming men to byte,
> Her brest like to a bowle of creame vncrudded,
> Her paps lyke lyllies budded,
> Her snowie necke lyke to a marble towre,
> And all her body like a palace fayre,
> Ascending vppe with many a stately stayre.
>
> *(171–179)*

Considering the autobiographical nature of the poem, this unoriginal catalog might disappoint a reader looking for a more personal description of Spenser's actual bride, Elizabeth Boyle.[17] In his epyllion, Marlowe solves the problem of Petrarchism (or at least the sexual disappointments of Petrarchism) by moving quickly from Leander's physical attributes to the sexual desire (and its fulfillment) that these attributes incite. Spenser, however, rejects this move.

He eschews the Marlovian paradigm by moving directly from his bride's stereotypical physical attributes to her personal interiority. He explains his bride's true allure:

> But if ye saw that which no eyes can see,
> The inward beauty of her liuely spright,
> Garnisht with heauenly guifts of high degree,
> Much more then would ye wonder at that sight.
>
> *(185–188)*

His praise of Elizabeth Boyle's "inward beauty" expresses the typical Platonic ideal of admiring a beloved's soul. That "no eyes can see" this beauty, however, hints at its unique qualities that cannot be adequately described. Furthermore, Platonic spiritual transcendence is not Spenser's goal. Holy matrimony is. Spenser's focus on his bride's "inward beauty" also aligns with the intensifying Protestant rhetoric on the superiority and inwardness of the married state that binds a couple together. Heinrich Bullinger, for instance, claims that of "the riches of the mynde, of the bodye, & of temporall substaunce. The best and mooste precious are the ryches of the mynde."[18] William Whately further waxes that "nuptiall loue . . . is a speciall and peculiar loue, farre more deare and inward than all."[19] The marital bond is not simply a bond of contract, exchange of property, or fulfillment of sexual desire (as Marlowe portrays it). For Spenser, the marital bond's defining feature is not an intermingling of bodies to achieve "one flesh" but an achievement of intersubjectivity with the beloved.

By preceding *Epithalamion* with the *Amoretti* and the "Anacreontics," Spenser demonstrates how a couple must move through a proper and recognizable courtship for this intersubjectivity to occur. The successive genres—sonnet sequence, anacreontic, and epithalamium—map out the prescribed stages of an early modern love affair: courtship, betrothal, and marriage.[20] These stages give a couple the time needed to contemplate the worthiness of the match. Poetic declarations of love and courtship, however, were often accompanied by a kind of haziness. "It can . . . be difficult," Ilona Bell admits, "to know whether a suitor is professing love and desire in order to marry wealth and status, or falsely proposing marriage in order to obtain sexual favors. Sometimes the participants themselves may not know whether their aim is social and material advancement, amorous courtship, or extra-marital seduction."[21] By stating early in the *Amoretti* that he hopes "to knit the knot, that euer shall remaine" (6.14), Spenser identifies that holy matrimony is the goal of his poetic courtship. But how can he expect Elizabeth Boyle to know that his intentions are sincere?

By drawing her into the act of common prayer. As demonstrated in chapter 1, publicly acknowledged courtships and betrothals preferably serve as the Spenserian hallmark of legitimate unions. Bypassing these steps can literally result in no union at all, as seen in the dissolution of Redcrosse and Duessa's clandestine contract. Spenser, therefore, encodes the language from the scriptural readings for the *Book of Common Prayer*'s morning and evening prayers throughout the *Amoretti*.[22] In doing so, he promises not only marriage but also a socially sanctioned one that ensures his beloved that he will follow through. This is not the promise of a union that he could back out of later. When reading the sonnets, the couple further participates in the practice of common prayer that the English reformers hoped would result in the interior transformations of their congregants. Ramie Targoff explains: "Behind the introduction of a liturgy emphasizing the worshippers' active participation and consent lies the establishment's overarching desire to shape personal faith through public and standardized forms."[23] In the *Amoretti*, therefore, Spenser attempts to shape his beloved's faith according to the proper rituals, preparing her for Christian matrimony. Public rituals intended to transform the interior self guide his approach to their private courtship.

Undergoing interior transformations through the act of common prayer thus makes the couple more susceptible to their marital roles. As all readers note, Spenser's beloved seems rather reluctant to be fashioned (perhaps because her role as "submissive wife" is not as appealing as that of "loving and authoritative husband"), and the sequence's vacillation between Petrarchan and anti-Petrarchan approaches underscores Spenser's own difficulty in meeting his goal of self-transformation.[24] Indeed, if the marriage bond is an interior state, as the *Epithalamion* reveals, it requires the couple to prepare their interior selves. In Sonnet 8, Spenser describes how his beloved fashions his interior self:

> You frame my thoughts and fashion me within,
>> you stop my toung, and teach my hart to speake,
>> you calme the storme that passion did begin,
>> strong thrugh your cause, but by your vertue weak.
>
>> *(9–12)*

Rather than inciting the sexual desire that could lead to a clandestine marriage, Elizabeth Boyle "calme[s]" his "passion" as they wait patiently for a proper ceremony. Their courtship does not fashion his public persona as a gentleman (part of *The Faerie Queene*'s promised outcome) but rather his interior one. He further focuses on the need for lovers to gain access to each other's interiorities in Sonnet 45:

> Leaue lady in your glasse of christall clene,
> Your goodly selfe for euermore to vew:
> and in my selfe, my inward selfe I meane,
> most liuely lyke behold your semblant trew.
>
> *(1–4)*

In this first quatrain, Spenser does not blame his beloved for being narcissistic and gluttonous as Shakespeare blames the mirror-gazing young man in his pro-creation sonnets (*Sonnets* 1–17). Instead, Spenser claims that his beloved will find a better, more "trew" mirror within his "inward self." This language forgoes the language of the body for the language of interiority. He frames this idea as a possibility: "*if* your selfe in me ye playne will see" (13). But this suggestion is rhetorical—he knows that his beloved will find herself in his interiority, causing her to love him. Seeing herself thus reflected will enable Elizabeth Boyle to realize that Spenser's love (and his matrimonial promises) is genuine. Without granting his beloved this access through a poetic courtship guided by public ritual, he could not expect her to accept his sincere promises of matrimony.

The rarely mentioned "Anacreontics" reflect the proper brevity of a betrothal. The overtly sexual nature of these poems may appear to undermine the "chaste desires" that Spenser has attempted to cultivate in the preceding sonnets (and that he celebrates in *Epithalamion*). As discussed in relation to the Redcrosse Knight's betrothal with Una, however, participating in a formal betrothal constituted an important step in the courtship process, allowing couples to finalize their nuptial preparations in terms of both material goods and emotional readiness. Although, not waiting too long between the betrothal and the ceremony meant that couples would not be tempted to make their betrothal a "very marriage" before the official solemnization. Spenser admits his impatience for the wedding day, but his inclusion of the "Anacreontics" demonstrates that he and his beloved have undergone a proper waiting period before the ceremony takes place. The brevity of the poems that symbolize the betrothal calls attention to the distressing length of the Redcrosse Knight's betrothal with Una in *The Faerie Queene*. If the "Anacreontics" feel anticlimactic to some readers, the length of Redcrosse's betrothal makes the ending to book I all the less satisfying—and the Faery Queen's insistence that he continue to serve her for six years appears even more inappropriate.

After fostering a courtship based on public ritual in the *Amoretti*, Spenser focuses on the public nature of the solemnization in *Epithalamion*. The natural world—the woods—initiates the communal involvement through the varied refrain: "The woods shall to me answer and my Eccho ring" (18). The woods echo Spenser when he sings "vnto my selfe alone" in the first stanza, emphasizing how even the groom's private early-morning hours have a witness (17). The echoing refrain then becomes increasingly communal until the day is finally over in stanza 17. As James S. Lambert observes, "The ritualized and public utterances that make up *Epithalamion*," including the "call and response" of the echoing refrain, "mimic common prayer."[25] The refrain signals not only the natural world's participation in the day's events but also its consent. By reiterating how the woods "echo," Spenser emphasizes that their response is both immediate and automatic, underscoring the lack of impediments to the marriage. The careful preparations in the preceding marriage poetry ensure that there is no need to hesitate on the wedding day. There are no previous contracts to consider, no unfortunate secrets (such as Redcrosse's relationship with Duessa) to be brought to light. Furthermore, in the final stanzas, the woods cease to echo simply due to the lack of sound, signaling their silent observance rather than their retreat. In addition to the woods, birds constitute another one of the natural world's major participants:[26]

> The merry Larke hir mattins sings aloft,
> The thrush replyes, the Mauis descant playes,
> The Ouzell shrills, the Ruddock warbles soft,
> *So goodly all agree with sweet consent,*
> To this dayes merriment.
>
> *(80–84; emphasis mine)*

Here Spenser openly uses the legal language of consent that Andrew Zurcher finds in *The Faerie Queene*, but not as a private contract between two people.[27] In *Epithalamion*, the contract occurs between the couple and their community, since the community (here represented by the birds) must offer their "sweet consent." If the birds do not consent to the marriage, the nuptials will not go forward. Within the epithalamium tradition, the lack of consent by the birds signals a deficiency in the match, turning a nuptial celebration into an anti-epithalamium.[28]

Having the participation and consent of the natural world, Spenser calls on the community's human inhabitants, including "all the virgins" (111) and "fresh boyes" (112), to participate as well. These participants prepare both the bride and the groom for the ceremony (the bride is surrounded by her entourage as soon as she opens her eyes), provide music, and accompany the couple to the church. Additionally, spectators simply show up to watch: "people [are] standing all about" (143). The inclusion of such casual observers reflects how public a wedding ceremony should be—one does not have to know the couple personally or receive an invitation as a modern reader might expect. A proper wedding, Spenser urges, should be public knowledge, an event that anyone can attend. The participation and approval of witnesses are not just components of the poem's festive tone; they literally facilitate the consecration of the marriage. All participants—bride, groom, and community members—must be of one heart and mind. By using the language of consent within a communal context, Spenser advances the goal of the English reformers to eliminate the confusion surrounding the marriage ritual. To do so, he conflates marriage's legal requirements (the mutual consent of the couple through *de praesenti* spousal vows) with the public solemnization.

By claiming that even classical religion had "sacred rites," Spenser suggests that the public solemnization of the marriage trumps the actual nature of the rituals. Standing on classical precedent, Spenser participates in a marital bacchanalia on which many Protestant reformers would frown, commanding the guests to "poure out the wine without restraint or stay . . . / And sprinkle all the postes and wals with wine, / That they may sweat, and drunken be withall" (250–254). In contrast, Bullinger cautions couples against an "excesse of eatinge [and] drinkynge" after the ceremony, complaining that such wastefulness constitutes an inappropriate use of funds.[29] Within the fictional world of Spenser's poem, however, such practical concerns are not relevant. Though, he does indicate that the bride herself does not necessarily participate in the day's frivolities. In recognition of the seriousness of the occasion, her "sad eyes" remain "fastened on the ground" throughout the wedding ceremony (234). The public celebratory displays, Spenser insists, do not detract from the ceremony's (or the bride's) virtue. Spenser also legitimates the classical elements by emphasizing their religious aspects. He calls on the goddess Juno: "The lawes of wedlock still dost patronize, / And the religion of the faith first plight / With sacred rites hast taught to solemnize" (391–393). In this way, he claims that the public solemnization has precedent even in classical religion. Not adhering to the public rituals, therefore, violates the classical and Christian traditions, both of which are at play in the Christianized epithalamium. Here the public solemnization is what "eternally bind[s]" the "louely band" (396) of marriage. Public knowledge makes the rituals "sacred."

Spenser also infuses the generic elements from classical epithalamia with rituals reminiscent of those in the *Book of Common Prayer* specifically. Melissa E. Sanchez claims that Spenser is "more interested in consummation than ceremony," but Spenser draws attention to the importance of the ceremony by placing it in the poem's central stanza.[30] The rituals take on a decidedly Anglican undertone as the bride proceeds down the aisle of the church:

> Bring her vp to th'high altar that she may
> The sacred ceremonies there partake,
> The which do endlesse matrimony make,
> And let the roring Organs loudly play
> The praises of the Lord in liuely notes,
> The whiles with hollow throates
> The Choristers the ioyous Antheme sing,
> That al the woods may answere and their eccho ring.
>
> *(215–222)*

King observes that "the organ music and choral singing of 'the joyous Antheme' . . . indicate that Spenser sympathized with the ritualism retained by the Church of England."[31] The focus on the "sacred ceremonies" again suggests Spenser's belief that there is more to making a marriage than a contract. Importantly, the priest plays a central role, providing both advice and blessings. The bride, Spenser relates, "before the altar stands / Hearing the holy priest that to her speakes / And blesseth her with his two happy hands" (223–225). By alluding to the language and "sacred ceremonies" of the common prayer book, Spenser uses his marriage poem as a vehicle to express the importance of the Elizabethan rituals.

Some scholars claim that Spenser's emphasis on ritual in *Epithalamion* gives the marriage ceremony the aura of a sacrament.[32] Spenser overgoes Catholic tradition, however, by claiming that the marriage ritual does not grant grace but rather allows the union to last into the afterlife. To do so, he asserts that the "sacred ceremonies" of the wedding service do "endlesse matrimony make" (217). The poem itself, in contrast, is a mere physical "moniment" (433) that will be "endlesse" only for a "short time." Spenser places no such temporal restraints on matrimony itself. The spiritual nature of the marital bond will survive the Day of Judgment. In a wedding sermon, John Donne looks to the verse Hosea 2:19, "And I will mary thee unto me forever," to make a similar claim. Donne first insists that marriage's sacramental status cannot fulfill this decree, observing, "They are somewhat hard driven in the Roman Church, when making marriage a Sacrament" since Roman canon law allows a couple to perform the sacramental act privately between themselves.[33] By insisting that the actual contracting of the marriage occurs during the ceremony itself, Spenser puts full focus on the religious ceremony, making no room for the vestiges of Roman canon law that he dismisses in his *Legend of Holiness*. A simple contract would not make a marriage, much less the "endlesse matrimony" that he celebrates.

Most Protestant reformers, however, insisted that matrimonial bonds did not last into the afterlife. Calvin was particularly firm on this subject, proclaiming that "husband and wife will . . . be separated" in death.[34] William Gouge confirms, "Death is an absolute diremption, and maketh an utter dissolution of the marriage bond."[35] In her work on posthumous love in Renaissance sonnet sequences, Ramie Targoff observes that Spenser moves from the idea of his poetry commemorating his beloved in a classical sense to suggesting it as "the agent of their mutual resurrection."[36] Targoff's reading, however, is hesitant. She notes that Spenser's sonnet sequence is primarily secular, stopping short of making any definite promises about the Christian afterlife. This reading can only be hesitant because it does not take the *Amoretti*'s conclusion—the *Epithalamion*—into account. As Roland Greene observes, "Nearly all editors acknowledge the inseparability of these works by keeping them together."[37] While the love that drives courtship in the *Amoretti* might not make posthumous promises, the love that drives the public solemnization of Christian matrimony in the *Epithalamion* undoubtedly does.

In granting the reader unique access to the marital chamber, Spenser confirms the importance of the sexual consummation to the marriage ceremony, and assuages any doubts or fears concerning the nature of the action. In accordance with generic tradition, the public does accompany the couple to the bedroom. George Puttenham explains the purpose of a noisy celebratory procession: so that "there might no noise be h[e]ard out of the bed cha[m]ber by the shreeking & outcry of the young damosell feeling the first forces of her stiffe & rigorous young man, she being as all virgins tender & weake, and vnexpert in those maner of affaires."[38] Spenser's description of returning home for the consummation, however, is quite different from Puttenham's. Spenser does refer to a noisy procession when saying:

> Harke how the Minstrels gin to shrill aloud
> Their merry Musick that resounds from far,
> The pipe, the tabor, and the trembling Croud,
> That well agree withouten breach or iar.
>
> *(129–132)*

This loud music, however, does not accompany the couple to the bedchamber but rather to the church. When night comes, Spenser declares that the time for noisy celebration is over and begs everyone to quiet down. "Now cease ye damsels," he commands, "your delights forepast" (296). He then asks the bride's fellow virgins to help her to bed in a display of female camaraderie:

> Now night is come, now soone her disaray,
> And in her bed her lay;
> Lay her in lillies and in violets,
> And silken courteins ouer her display,
> And odourd sheetes, and Arras couerlets.
>
> *(300–304)*

Surrounded by her female attendants, the bride is comfortably settled before her friends disperse. Then Spenser and his bride are left completely alone with no noisy celebration outside designed to drown out any female trauma occurring within. In describing the "sacred peace" (354) of the chamber at the time of consummation, Spenser reveals that his own bride will not experience a traumatic sexual experience on her wedding night. Quite unlike Marlowe's Hero. Instead, contradicting Puttenham's description of a typical wedding night, Spenser proclaims, "Let no lamenting cryes, nor dolefull teares, / Be heard all night within nor yet without" (334–335). Spenser affirms that no noises need to occur without the bedchamber because no traumatic noises will occur within. According to Spenser, the marriage ritual reforms the woman's experience of the wedding night from one of painful distress to one of calm assurance. The female community's accompaniment of the couple to the bedchamber also means that everyone knows that their desires are indeed "chaste," and that the bride's "chast wombe" (386) will bring forth legitimate issue. No one will be able to question the legitimacy of their offspring—the exact fear that grips Chapman's Hero after her own clandestine marriage. The public celebration, therefore, provides an important foundation for the couple's private intimacy.

Strangely, however, Spenser does admit that the consummation has one witness: the goddess Cinthia, who "at [the] window peepes" (372). This odd voyeuristic detail, symbolizing Spenser's desire to elicit Queen Elizabeth's approval of the match, illustrates that no aspect of the marriage ceremony is completely private. Spenser's plea that the "fayrest goddesse, do thou not enuy / My loue with me to spy" (376–377) also hints at the queen's control over her courtiers' love lives, which we saw in *The Faerie Queene*'s Belphoebe-Timias episode in chapter 1. Spenser thus gives his wedding a national and even cosmic significance that belies what was probably a relatively small and private event. By portraying his wedding in this way, he suggests that all public ceremonies that take place according to the reformed rituals receive the sanction of the Virgin Queen (no matter how small or insignificant those ceremonies might actually be).

Spenser addresses the problems associated with not following these rituals in his pastoral elegy, *Daphnaïda* (1591). In the elegy, a shepherd, Alcyon, mourns the death of his lover, Daphne, the poem's name for the recently deceased Douglas Howard. Alcyon stands in for her bereaved husband, Arthur Gorges. The elegy is unconventional in that Alcyon's grief remains excessive to the end—the pastoral landscape does not bring him any kind of solace or respite. Not wanting to view Spenser as writing a failed elegy, most scholars read the poem as a warning against extravagant grief.[39] Jonathan Gibson has suggested that Spenser's poem inserts itself into legal disputes over the inheritance of Gorges and Howard's only child, Ambrosia, on Gorges's behalf.[40] After her death, Douglas Howard's father, Henry Howard, second Viscount Bindon, claimed that Ambrosia was a changeling and thus ineligible to inherit his daughter's wealth. He probably would not have attempted to undermine Ambrosia's legitimacy if she were not the product of a clandestine marriage. Indeed, Gorges and Howard married without his consent. The viscount initially contested the marriage by arguing that Gorges had "illicitly enticed Douglas away."[41] His suit was unsuccessful. His daughter's death, however, gave him another opportunity to undermine the marriage.

The clandestine nature of Gorges's marriage with Douglas Howard thus contributed to his woes. Upon learning that Alcyon intends to die alone from grief, *Daphnaïda*'s distressed poet-narrator urges Alcyon to let him "tell the cause" (81) of Alcyon's despair. Otherwise, he reasons, the world may think that "thou for secret crime thy blood hast spilt" (84). As we have learned throughout this book, events shrouded in secrecy can be misinterpreted by the outside world. Whether or not we believe Spenser sympathized with Gorges, it is indisputable that Gorges's irregular union with Douglas Howard created controversies concerning its legitimacy. In this way, the poem becomes a cautionary tale not just about excessive grief but also about clandestinity. Gorges's grief may not have been so excessive if the clandestine nature of his marriage had not heaped legal difficulties on top of his personal tragedy.

In *Epithalamion*, Spenser does admit some discomfort with the public surveillance of the marriage ritual that might have mitigated Gorges's woe. His desire to "let this day let this one day be myne" (125) reads like a plea for privacy amid the celebrating birds, nymphs, and virgins. His fear derives from the possibility that the day's sovereign, Phoebus, might not allow the nuptial events to go forward, pleading, "Doe not thy seruants simple boone refuse" (124). The possibility that Phoebus could refuse the request adds to the troubling tone of uncertainty that many readers discern in the poem. In a strange moment,

Spenser resorts to bargaining. If Phoebus grants the wedding day, then he will sing the god's "prayses loud" (127)—the implication being that if Phoebus does not consent, Spenser might not be such a willing subject. Just as he does in *The Faerie Queene*, Spenser hints at the problems associated with charging the marriage ceremony with political meaning—people, he seems to be acknowledging, do not really like to feel as though they are being watched all the time.

In his epithalamium, however, Spenser informs us that men do not have to reject Petrarchan courtship in favor of a more violent Ovidian framework that allows for clandestine marriage (as Marlowe suggests). Instead, the prayer book's rituals can provide an everlasting bond that rids the wedding night of physical or psychological distress. The key to a mutually fulfilling relationship is to release oneself from the mastery that Petrarchism encourages by fashioning one's interior self through public ritual. In *Hero and Leander*, Marlowe presents Leander's eventual sexual mastery of Hero as a triumph of masculine sexual violence. In *Epithalamion*, Spenser reduces the threat of Ovidian desire to the Echo myth in the varied refrain.[42] Through public nuptials that take place firmly within the approval of the community and nation, Spenser exorcises and dispels the social problems associated with clandestine marriage.

Private Contracts in Shakespeare's *A Lover's Complaint*

Despite Spenser's best efforts, his poetic reformation does not turn all complaints into epithalamia, just as the English Reformation did not put a stop to the deceptive practice of clandestine marriage. A pastoral landscape serves as the site of the maid's solitary confinement in *A Lover's Complaint* rather than a site of matrimonial celebration. In his wedding poem, Spenser's repeated reference to the Echo myth calls attention to how easily a song of love can turn back into a song of lament. In the first lines of his complaint, Shakespeare invokes Spenser's haunting refrain as it reverberates through the distinctly Spenserian landscape. The eavesdropping narrator states that he becomes aware of the maid through her echoing voice:

> From off a hill whose concave womb reworded
> A plaintful story from a sist'ring vale,
> My spirits t'attend this double voice accorded,
> And down I laid to list the sad-tun'd tale.
>
> *(1–4)*

The landscape does not celebrate the maid's match (nor can it since the maid's lover has abandoned her). Instead, it simply "reword[s] / [her] plaintful story." The threat inside the Echo myth from Spenser's *Epithalamion* has not been dispelled but rather unleashed.

A Lover's Complaint also engages in a marital discourse with Spenser's other beautiful marriage poem, *Prothalamion*. Spenser sets his poem, written to commemorate the betrothal of the Earl of Worcester's two daughters, Elizabeth and Katherine Somerset, in an idyllic pastoral landscape on the bank of the Thames. His creation of a new genre marking a betrothal coincides with his insistence that marriage should progress through prescribed stages to be legitimate. As in book I, canto xii, of *The Faerie Queene*, the betrothal takes on the significance of the actual wedding. MacDonald P. Jackson masterfully demonstrates how Shakespeare borrows words and phrases from Spenser's "Spousall Verse" in *A Lover's Complaint*.[43] In particular, Shakespeare appropriates Spenser's marital imagery for his own maid, who also wears her hair loose as she tosses love tokens from her own "maund" (36), or wicker basket, rather than gathering up flowers in celebration of a wedding (as do the nymphs). Jackson mainly uses these connections to date Shakespeare's poem as being written after *Prothalamion*'s 1596 publication date. Brian Vickers further compares the fickle maid with the disappointed narrator of the betrothal poem.[44] Neither considers how the theme of marriage connects the two poems. *Prothalamion*'s subjects, the two swans swimming majestically down the river to London and the brides' nuptials, provide the closest analogue to Shakespeare's maid, especially since both she and the swans are the unconscious subjects of a voyeuristic narrator. In this way, Shakespeare pointedly contrasts the differences between women who participate in clandestine marriages and those who participate in public solemnizations. In *Prothalamion*, the public nature of the nuptials brings order to the landscape, fostering the idea that public ritual orders the realm, and providing solace to the disconsolate narrator who had lost faith in the court. In *A Lover's Complaint*, the maid's lack of proper attention to marital ritual disrupts pastoral tranquility and isolates her from the court where she used to reside. The reason the maid finds herself in such a state is that she has failed to undergo a proper courtship and betrothal leading up to a public ceremony validating her marriage.

Unlike Spenser, Shakespeare does not use his own sonnet sequence to demonstrate the proper uses of courtship and marriage. Instead, his sequence is riddled with the tension between public matrimony and secret contracts. As Heather Dubrow observes, "The sonnets portray a world dominated by legal, social, and verbal bonds."[45] Previous chapters have demonstrated that legal language often points to literary portrayals of clandestine marriage. The language of clandestine marriage infuses the dark lady sonnets in particular.[46] In Sonnet 152, for instance, Shakespeare laments that his mistress has been unfaithful to him and to a third party:

> In loving thee thou know'st I am forsworn,
> But thou art twice forsworn, to me love swearing;
> In act thy bed-vow broke, and new faith torn
> In vowing new hate after new love bearing.
>
> *(1–4)*

By stating that his mistress has broken a "bed-vow," Shakespeare suggests that she has broken a clandestine marital contract sealed by a consummation. Indeed, the *Oxford English Dictionary* confirms this reading by looking to Sonnet 152 to define "bed-vow" as "a promise of fidelity to the marriage bed."[47] Furthermore, since the act of consummation solidified a *de futuro* contract, a "bed-vow" could literally be the vow that constituted the dark lady's clandestine marriage with another lover. The dark lady's seeming participation in a previous clandestine marriage foreshadows the fickle maid's own marital state in *A Lover's Complaint*. Unlike in the *Amoretti*, which Spenser uses to transform his beloved into a loving wife, the maid does not glean any words of wisdom about the proper making of a match from the sonnets that most parallel her own biography.

Even the seemingly wholesome theme of the procreation sonnets does not steer the maid in the right direction. When Shakespeare chastises the young man in Sonnet 1 for being *"contracted* to thine own bright eyes" (5; emphasis mine), he uses marital language: the young man's contractual commitment to his own image means that he believes himself unable to enter into a relationship with anyone else. The fickle maid admits that one reason she participated in a clandestine marriage is that she did not want to succumb to narcissism. She laments: "I might as yet have been a spreading flower, / Fresh to myself, if I had self-applied / Love to myself, and to no love beside" (75–77). If the maid had contracted herself to her "own bright eyes," she suggests, she might still be a "spreading flower." Instead, she observes that her focus on loving her own young man has aged her beyond her years: her beauty is now "spent and done" (11) even if it does "peep . . . through lettice of sear'd age" (14). By participating in an ill-advised clandestine contract, the maid overly compensates for possible narcissistic behavior. She apparently misses Shakespeare's insistence that the young man's child must be the product of legitimate wedlock:

For having traffic with thyself alone,
Thou of thyself thy sweet self dost deceive,
Then how when Nature calls thee to be gone,
What acceptable audit canst thou leave?

(4.9–12)

The legal language of this sonnet, comparing the young man's future child to an "acceptable audit," makes clear that the child must be legitimate. Of course, a clandestine marriage could call a child's legitimacy into question. By claiming that the child must have the legal rights of an heir, Shakespeare insists that the young man must enter into marriage properly in order for his issue to inherit his looks (along with his property), placing an enormous amount of pressure on the transformative effects of the public solemnization.

If we consider the young man of the *Sonnets* to be a model for (or even the same as) the young man in *A Lover's Complaint*, however, we find that he has chosen to interpret the procreation sonnets' decree to marry and have children as loosely as possible. He agrees to marry, but only in a way that allows him to move quickly from one woman (or one wife) to another. A lack of witnesses to their unions means that the jilted women have no real case against him. Catherine Bates emphasizes that the fickle maid is not the only victim of the young man's deception—she is simply one of many that the young man has left in the lurch.[48] The young man of *A Lover's Complaint* fully understands the consequences of his actions, causing him to resemble the purposely deceptive Duessa more than the hopelessly naive Leander. Indeed, the young man seduces his victims by taking advantage of the confusion surrounding the differences between the pre- and post-Reformation marriage ritual.

The young man capitalizes on the Reformation discourse on marriage in his seduction of a nun. He brags to the fickle maid that he "had pow'r to charm a sacred [nun], / Who disciplin'd, ay, dieted, in grace" (260–261), persuading her to leave her cloister. Like Marlowe's Hero, the nun in the young man's tale appears to follow the advice of the Protestant reformers by leaving her celibate life and taking (presumably) a husband. The nun's willingness to leave behind her vows of celibacy certainly confirms the theologians' belief that women cannot be expected to withstand the direct assault of sexual desire, especially after being cooped up in a convent. She falls victim, however, to a matrimonial loophole that the English reformers never bothered to resolve completely. After the young man leaves the nun in disgrace, one can only assume that she was probably better off in the convent.

The maid's willingness to seek solace from a solitary priestly figure hints at the lingering sympathies for Catholic rituals that continued to permeate early modern England, and that may have made her more susceptible to a clandestine marriage. In accordance with the underlying Reformation themes of the poem, critics associate the "reverend man" with the figure of a priest, who encourages the maid to participate in the sacrament of auricular confession.[49] Drawn by the sounds of her lamentations, the old man approaches the maid to determine the "motives of her woe" (63), suggesting his desire to help her achieve spiritual reconciliation. The maid describes how the young man clothed himself "with the garment of a Grace" (316). Just as she participates in a confession reminiscent of a Catholic sacrament, she also apparently believed that her contract with the young man achieved sacramental status. As we have seen, any marriage, even a clandestine one, fulfilled the requirements of the marital sacrament. As Spenser explains in *Epithalamion*, however, only public solemnizations meet the proper requirements of marriage in Protestant England. The "maimed rites" (*Hamlet* 5.1.219) that Shakespeare depicts in *A Lover's Complaint* do not refer to the degradation of Catholic ritual but rather to the maid's failure to participate in the reformed rites of the *Book of Common Prayer*.

When explaining how the young man managed to seduce her, she confirms her confusion concerning the proper rituals. The young man's insistence that his "vows" (179) are "holy" indicates that the maid believed she was participating in the "sacred rites" that Spenser describes in *Epithalamion*. Eschewing a Spenserian emphasis on publicity, the young man scorns the practice of declaring banns, claiming "How coldly those impediments stand forth / Of wealth, of filial fear, law, kindred, fame" (269–270). He declares a need for privacy for true love to come to fruition—giving people the chance to look for impediments corresponds to the equivalent of throwing cold water on the flames of marital desire. The young man's proclamations anticipate the growing popularity of clandestine marriage by license in the Stuart era. Daniel Rogers laments the growing number of couples who marry by license, claiming that "people . . . itch . . . after private marryings" that allow them to "oppose publication."[50] The custom has become so common, he observes, that a person considers himself "but a peasent who declines not this lawful provision of the Church."[51] Rogers does not express this outrage until 1642, but licensed clandestinity was already on the rise during the Jacobean period.[52] In a sense, licensed clandestinity was becoming fashionable, particularly among the wealthy who could better afford it, and the ease with which couples could obtain licenses facilitated the hiding of impediments. Of course, the young man does not seem to have concerned himself even with obtaining a license. The sentiment, however, remains the same—clandestine marriage in any of its forms, whether licensed or not, allowed couples to bypass some (or even all) of the typical impediments to a marriage contract. Doing so gave the marriage an aura of romance to which young women in particular might be susceptible.

Without religious solemnization, however, the maid's intimacy with the young man does not extend beyond the physical. She finds herself in an abandoned state because she allows herself to be fooled by the young man's "tragic shows" (308). Instead of correcting Petrarchism, as Spenser suggests, by focusing on her beloved's "inward beauty," she succumbs to his false Petrarchan rhetoric.[53] The young man deceives her through a disconnect between his interiority and his outward appearance. After describing how the young man's "wat'ry eyes" (281) produced a "brinish current" (284) running down each cheek, the maid laments how she allowed her suitor's histrionics to affect her:

> O father, what a hell of witchcraft lies
> In the small orb of one particular tear!
> But with the inundation of the eyes
> What rocky heart to water will not wear?
>
> *(288–291)*

The young man seduces the maid by convincing her that his tears are an indicator of his love, causing her to believe that she has access to his interiority. Believing that they have achieved the intersubjectivity of the marital bond that Spenser describes with his own bride, the maid consents to the clandestine contract. Clearly, she believed that she was marrying for love, as the domestic manuals suggest, but, as she now realizes, "consents" (131) can be "bewitch'd." A seducer is less likely to bewitch if he must persuade a whole community— not just one woman—that he has honorable intentions. Bypassing the proper rituals, including the public ceremony, therefore, becomes the source of the maid's tragedy—just as Chapman identifies it as being the source of Hero's tragedy in his continuation of Marlowe's epyllion.

The young man's ability to disguise his true identity, allowing him to contract himself to a series of women, also connects the theme of clandestine marriage to the concern over bigamous marriages early in James I's reign. Tobias B. Hug observes that the "definition of marriage and the various ways it could be contracted present[ed] several problems" when determining whether couples had contracted a bigamous marriage.[54] Hug elaborates on how the problem of bigamy is one of identity. A bigamist is a form of imposture, he informs, who often "changed important aspects of their identity, i.e. their marital status and personal circumstances such as wealth."[55] To combat these impostures, Parliament made bigamy a felony, punishable by the death penalty except in instances where a spouse had been absent for seven years (before 1604 bigamy was merely a spiritual offense). One reason Parliament put the act into place was to "stop the practice of 'evil disposed' people going into other counties and contracting new, clandestine marriages."[56] The preamble to the Bigamy Act states: "For asmuch as divers evil disposed persons being married, run out of one county into another, or into places where they are not known, and there become to be married, having another husband or wife living, to the great dishonour of God, and utter undoing of divers honest mens children, and others."[57] In 1563, for instance, Anne Yate accused George Johnson of marrying another woman after having lived with her as man and wife.[58] Deponents testified that George and Anne contracted themselves to one another at Anne's house in front of witnesses. After exchanging spousal vows, the couple may or may not have kissed (according to one witness who could not quite remember) and then ate a "cowple of wodcokes" together in front of the fireplace.[59] George then lived with Anne for several years. As a way of underscoring the relationship's commitment, another witness emphasized that George even brought his "dogges, his horse, and his hawkes" to live with Anne.[60] According to several eyewitness accounts, the couple had clearly entered into a legal marriage, but George was still able to sneak off and marry again clandestinely.

Understanding *A Lover's Complaint* as about clandestine marriage further explains why the maid recounts her lover's speech in such detail: she wishes to prove that she believed she was entering into a marriage. Upon first noticing the maid, the narrator describes her as though she is presenting evidence at a trial, making the old man her judge as much as her confessor. Her "plaintfull story" suggests that the narrator views her as a plaintiff in a legal trial.[61] We can thus read the maid's complaint not simply as a futile exercise in emotional expression but as a serious attempt to blame her husband for abandoning her—just as many women did in the early modern courts.[62] She claims that, unlike his previous lovers, she initially withstood the young man's pleas to doff her "white stole of chastity" (297). Instead, she waits until his promises become matrimonial ones. He laces his seduction with marital language when asking her to "lend . . . soft audience to my sweet design, / And credent soul to that *strong-bonded oath* / That shall prefer and undertake my *troth*" (278–280; emphases mine). The language of oaths and troths is the language of spousal vows. By consenting to his "soft audience," the maid must have understood herself to be entering into a *de futuro* spousal vow. As we learned in Marlowe's *Hero and Leander*, women may be more willing to give up their chastity if they do not actually believe that they are doing so. By claiming that the young man made solemn vows before sleeping with her, the maid insists that she believed they were entering into a marriage.

The maid's superfluity of love tokens further exemplifies the kind of evidence that could be used in an ecclesiastical court trial. Houlbrooke explains that love tokens could carry so much significance during the early modern period that "the most prudent course . . . was to return immediately the gifts of unwelcome suitors" to avoid confusion concerning the seriousness of a relationship.[63] The giving of a love token could express a willingness to marry in the mind of the recipient, or the giver could interpret the acceptance of a token as a sign of consent to a match. As Loreen Giese has shown, the London Consistory Court records from 1586 to 1611 are filled with such debates concerning the meaning of love tokens. In one case, *Alexander Hollinworth v. Ann Hyde*, Ann explains how a go-between, John Griffith, gave her love tokens from his friend Hollinworth. Her acceptance of the tokens caused Hollinworth to presume that they had entered into a contract: "She receyved . . . at severall times bothe the ringes mentioned in this article that with the stone by Griffins wife and thother by Griffin himself, the one ring being . . . not worth . . . iiii shillings . . . and thother is a Counterfitt stone as she hath byn synce towld and . . . it cannot be worth . . . above a noble . . . all which . . . she receyved at the great importunite of Griffin and his wife synce the time of the pretended Contract."[64] Ann's unimpressed assessment of the tokens' worth (not worth four shillings, or not worth "above a noble") indicates that she believed marital tokens should be more costly. However, confusing matters, she sent Hollinworth tokens in return, which, in his mind, confirmed her consent to his marital overtures. The deposition records that "she did not send any of theis tokens uppon Confirmacion of any Contract of marriage . . . butt with what intencion he receyved them she sayethe she cannot tell."[65] Due to the ambiguities surrounding love tokens, it becomes very difficult to tell when—if ever—a couple achieves the intersubjectivity indicative of mutual consent.

Like the hapless Hollinworth, Shakespeare's maid clearly has misinterpreted the significance of the love tokens that she has received from the young man.[66] After she pulls "a thousand favours from a maund" (36), the eavesdropper describes the nature of the tokens:

> Of folded schedules had she many a one,
> Which she perus'd, sigh'd, tore, and gave the flood,
> Crack'd many a ring of posied gold and bone,
> Bidding them find their sepulchres in mud,
> Found yet moe letters sadly penn'd in blood,
> With sleided silk feat and affectedly
> Enswath'd and seal'd to curious secrecy.
>
> (43–49)

Especially since the ring plays a prominent role during the Solemnization of Matrimony in the *Book of Common Prayer*, rings appear most often in the London Consistory Court records as evidence that a wedding contract had taken place. Of course, the meaning of rings, and other love tokens, depended on the context in which they were given, which, naturally, is open to interpretation (as the Hollinworth vs. Hyde case reveals). The maid describes the tokens as bearing "unapproved witness" (53). She believed that the tokens served as "witness" to their contract, but, in the end, these tokens could not offer unequivocal proof of a match. The fact that the young man has merely recycled tokens from previous lovers when giving them to her further demonstrates how difficult it can be to determine intent behind a love token. The unknowable contents of the maid's letters gesture toward these interpretative difficulties. By not allowing us access to the contents, Shakespeare demonstrates how difficult it could be to determine whether love objects, literary or otherwise, were imbued with marital import. Without witnesses to confirm that a spousal contract or ceremony had taken place, tokens rarely carried any weight in the courts, even though they were often used as evidence. The "ocular proof" of a courtship or marriage is meaningless if no one can attest to its meaning.

This suspicion of clandestine marriage aligns itself thematically with plays that Shakespeare was writing around the same time, such as *Hamlet*, *Troilus and Cressida*, and *Measure for Measure* (as well as *Othello*, which will be explored in chapter 5), signaling a shift in the Shakespeare canon that tends to view clandestine marriage sympathetically.[67] In *Hamlet*, Ophelia's father and brother warn her against a relationship with the melancholy prince. While scholars lament that these warnings indicate a disappointing lack of faith in the young woman's own judgment, poems like *A Lover's Complaint* suggest that their fears do have a basis. Alan Stewart demonstrates that the love letters Ophelia returns to Hamlet indicate that they already considered themselves to be contracted with one another.[68] When Ophelia returns the letters, she breaks the contract, but since their contract had no witnesses, Hamlet has no option but to accept. During her mad scenes, Ophelia also refers to the hazy relationship between sex and marriage. "Before you tumbled me," she sings, "You promis'd me to wed" (4.5.62–63). She thus refers to the way in which men pressured women into sleeping with them by suggesting that a marriage would result. In *Troilus and Cressida*, Pandarus invokes the language of the marriage ceremony from the *Book of Common Prayer* immediately before the consummation of the titular lovers:

> Here she is now, swear the oaths now to her that you have sworn to me. . . . Here's 'In witness whereof the parties interchangeably'—Come

in, come in. . . . Go to, a bargain made, seal it, seal it, I'll be the witness.
Here I hold your hand, here my cousin's. If ever you prove false one to
another, since I have taken such pain to bring you together, let all pitiful
goers-between be call'd to the world's end after my name; call them all
Pandars. Let all constant men be Troiluses, all false women Cressids, and
all brokers-between Pandars! Say amen.

(3.2.41–42, 57–59, 197–204)

His language, which focuses on oaths and witnesses and is accompanied by
the holding of hands, lends their consummation the weight of a marital contract. Troilus, however, decides to value his relationship with his fellow men
above his marital bond when allowing Cressida to be traded to the Greek camp.
Cressida and the fickle maid have much in common: each believes she is entering into a marriage when sleeping with an aristocratic young man who later
abandons her.

In *Measure for Measure*, the ultimate treatment of marital contracts speaks
to the ability of the sexual consummation to solidify a marriage no matter how
long ago or ambiguously the original contract took place. Mistress Overdone,
for instance, informs that Lucio "promis'd [Kate Keepdown] marriage" (3.2.200)
but that Kate has been unable to hold him to the promise despite their child
being almost "a year and a quarter old" (201). The play thus makes clear how
young men could use the importance of the consummation to persuade
women to sleep with them, thinking they would be married afterward. In the
end, the duke holds Lucio to the promise by making him officially solemnize
the marriage with Kate. Angelo's unintentional consummation of his betrothal
with Mariana also results in a legally binding marriage. Even though Mariana
and Angelo made *de futuro* vows five years before, the lapse in time and lack
of additional confirmation of the union does not prevent the marriage from
becoming legally binding the moment the consummation takes place. The uncomfortable nature of these unions, since neither Lucio nor Angelo is happy
to be a married man, also underscores how the practice of clandestine marriage could result in unhappy marriages if the schemes of the predatory men
do not work out in their favor.

Both Shakespeare's plays and poems are haunted by the fact that Spenser's
literary agenda—an increased emphasis on public ritual as necessary to the success of marriages and the nation—has failed to come to fruition. When the
maid admits at the end of *A Lover's Complaint* that the young man would (if
given the chance) "yet again betray the fore-betray'd, / And new pervert a reconciled maid" (328–329), she indicates that the failure of the Catholic sacrament of auricular confession goes hand in hand with the misguided perception

that marriage continues to be a sacrament as well. *A Lover's Complaint* reveals that, even after the Elizabethan regime's concerted efforts to institute widespread use of the *Book of Common Prayer*, confusion still existed concerning the proper formation of the marital bond. It emerges as a complaint not just about love and marriage but about the mismatch between the contemporary legal constitution and the social fabric.

As Spenser's *Epithalamion* indicates, however, defusing the confusion over this mismatch comes with a price. The public surveillance of the marital bond to ensure that women do not endure the maid's fate means that even the consummation has a witness. Spenser's recalcitrant bride may be quite lovely, but scholars have puzzled over whether she seems truly "companionable." She glides through the day's events in a state of passive aloofness, remarked upon but never remarking herself. Her sexual encounter on her wedding night may not be traumatic or distressing, but it is also unclear whether she finds the experience enjoyable (as Spenser presumably does). Shakespeare leaves his own maid in a state of tortured subjectivity after allowing her to be fooled by a seducer. Indeed, in a moment of self-awareness, the maid admits that she "knew vows were ever brokers to defiling" (173). The maid, however, has made her own choices rather than allowing herself to be shaped by outside forces. She has not achieved intersubjectivity (or marriage) with her lover, but she has her own voice.

CHAPTER 4

"Lorenzo and His Infidel"

Elopement and the Cross-Cultural Household in Shakespeare's *Merchant of Venice*

In this chapter on *The Merchant of Venice* and the next on *Othello*, I am interested in how Shakespeare uses elopement to explore the possible integration of racial and religious outsiders into white Christian society. In *The Merchant of Venice*, Shakespeare takes the popular stage plotline of clandestine marriage and gives it a cross-cultural twist when a Jew's daughter, Jessica, elopes with a Christian, Lorenzo. Of course, Shakespeare portrays clandestine marriages with a noticeable regularity throughout his canon. Due to their versatility as plot devices, irregular unions occur in every dramatic genre, making for great comedy and great tragedy alike. In comedies, clandestine marriages are the natural by-product of a genre that foregrounds female agency within matters of love and courtship. Some clandestine marriages, however, such as the secret consummation between the eponymous lovers in *Troilus and Cressida* or the unsolemnized union between Claudio and Juliet in *Measure for Measure*, trouble the festive tone typically associated with comedy, contributing to the categorization of these works as "problem comedies."[1] The possibility of a clandestine marriage may give way to a public wedding at the play's end according to comedic convention (Lysander and Hermia's attempted elopement in *A Midsummer Night's Dream*, for instance). Otherwise, clandestine marriages undermine the hallmark of comic closure: the incorporation of a couple back into normative society through Christian matrimony.[2]

Representations of cross-cultural marriage on the Renaissance stage are inevitably clandestine. As New World exploration expanded along with international trade, however, the possibility must have captivated the early modern imagination. Queen Elizabeth's "open letter to the Lord Maiour of London" (1596) complaining of the presence of "blackmoores" reveals a concern about the growing number of racialized others in England, even if the numbers remained relatively small.[3] When looking to Shylock's account of the Jacob and Laban story, Elizabeth A. Spiller observes that "miscegenation is . . . a key theme" in The Merchant of Venice.[4] Launcelot Gobbo's assertion that the marriage of Jews to Christians will "raise the price of hogs" (3.5.24) suggests the belief that romantic alliances with outsiders were economically destabilizing.[5] The range of ways in which a couple could enter into marriage in early modern England meant that cross-cultural unions, whether with racial and/or religious outsiders, through clandestine means could become a real, even if remote, possibility.

If clandestine marriage troubles comic closure, then it seems cross-cultural clandestine marriage would be more the stuff of tragedy than comedy. The fact that Shakespeare adds the elopement of Jessica and Lorenzo to the familiar tale about a wealthy Jew and a flesh bond, and that it is the only instance of cross-cultural marriage in his comedies, should draw our attention to its significance.[6] In Christopher Marlowe's Jew of Malta, the relationship between the Jew's daughter Abigail and her Christian suitor—Shakespeare's inspiration for the Jessica-Lorenzo plotline—does not allow for a happy conclusion, indicating the near impossibility of a successful cross-cultural marriage on the early modern stage. The closest analogue to the Jessica-Lorenzo plotline in Shakespeare's other plays, the elopement between Othello and Desdemona (which will be explored in the next chapter), ends disastrously. In The Merchant of Venice, Shakespeare finds a way to enfold a plot line seemingly better suited to tragedy into a comedic framework.

Most of the scholarship on Jessica and Lorenzo's marriage deploys early modern theories on racial and religious difference to determine whether Jessica successfully effaces her Jewish identity to become a full-fledged member of the Christian community. The scholarly focus stems from the belief that Jewishness signified not only a theological difference during the early modern period but a racial difference as well.[7] A person could not convert from Judaism to Christianity without undergoing a literal bodily change. According to Kim F. Hall, Jessica appears to get around this problem as the other characters deny Shylock's claims of consanguinity with his daughter.[8] M. Lindsay Kaplan further argues that Jessica's female body does not pose a threat to bloodlines since popular Aristotelian theory claimed that women did not contribute any of their own biological makeup to their children.[9] However, scholars have stressed that Jessica's integration into the Christian community at Belmont is not as comfortable as Kaplan suggests. Janet Adelman, for instance, points out that Gratiano's reference to Jessica as an "infidel" (3.2.218) after her marriage, and the fact that Portia and Bassanio "barely register" her presence, indicates that the Christian characters are not ready to accept Jessica as one of their own.[10] Carole Levin agrees that Jessica appears uncomfortable and isolated after her marriage and conversion.[11] This scholarship, however, does not take the clandestine nature of Jessica's wedding vows into account.

By refocusing the scholarly conversation on Jessica and Lorenzo's elopement away from the ambiguities of the female Jewish body and onto the issues at stake in Shakespearean comedy—female agency within courtship and marriage—we can better understand how the couple fits into the play's comedic framework. *The Merchant of Venice* does not end with a grand wedding according to convention, because the couples all exchange their wedding vows offstage in the previous acts, making it one of the few comedies in which Shakespeare explores the marriages that come after the courtships.[12] Up to this point in the critical conversation, scholars have not fully attended to the clandestine (as well as the cross-cultural) nature of Lorenzo and Jessica's marriage and the implications of this for Jessica's integration into Belmont society.[13] The break from generic tradition allows us to compare the complications surrounding Jessica and Lorenzo's secret union with Portia and Bassanio's public one. Shakespeare illustrates that those who elope automatically put themselves into the position of outsider by violating social norms.

Shakespeare does not solve the problem of cross-cultural clandestine marriage in *The Merchant of Venice* by neutralizing or even erasing Jessica's Jewish identity (an impossible feat as the contradictory scholarship on the subject has shown). Instead, he recuperates Jessica's domestic identity as a responsible householder. Since establishing a household was one of the primary goals of early modern marriage, her initial inability to establish a domestic identity after her elopement becomes at least as devastating as her converted Jewish one. To make this argument, I first explore how elopement undermined the ideal of the early modern household, and then how Shakespeare portrays Portia's running of her Belmont estate as representing this ideal. Portia's domestic acumen contrasts with Shylock's own poor household management, which precipitates Jessica's elopement. In light of the emphasis on the proper rule of the domestic space in the play, I further demonstrate how Jessica's elopement

hinders her ability to enter into the Belmont community. The other characters' efforts to establish a domestic identity for the cross-cultural couple prevent them from falling into the tragedy of *Othello*.

Domestic Identity and the Problem of Elopement

Establishing a domestic identity was one of the main purposes of early modern marriage. As William Gouge observes of the marriage ceremony, "by it
men and women are made *Husbands* and *Wives*. It is the onely lawfull means to
make them *Fathers* and *Mothers*. It is the ordinary meanes to make them *Masters*
and *Mistresses*."[14] Such new identities as masters and mistresses of households
came with a new list of responsibilities. David Cressy describes the nature of
the transformation: "Through marriage . . . [a couple's] relationship to domestic authority became transformed. As single and dependent persons they had
followed orders, but as married householders they issued instructions. . . .
Their authority proceeded from their condition."[15] Husband and wife ruled the
household together, but within a hierarchical relationship that defined the husband as the head of household.[16] Domestic handbooks present the woman's
recognition of her husband's superiority as a choice: "The *Voluntary* subjection
is that dutifull respect which inferiours carry towards those whom God hath set
over them."[17] The wife thus ruled the rest of the household through an *"extension* of patriarchal power."[18] Despite this limitation of female authority, however, women did perform significant tasks, including the management of the
household's complex day-to-day affairs and financial matters.

To help husbands and wives better understand their new responsibilities,
the early modern handbooks explain household obligations in elaborate detail. Even though William Perkins claims that "the Holie Ghost in the booke
of the Scriptures, hath in great wisedome commended both Rules for direction, and examples for imitation, to Husbands and Wiues, to Parents and
Children, to Masters and Seruants," the number of early modern handbooks
that provide guidelines for domestic order betrays an anxiety concerning the
subject.[19] Gouge's *Of Domesticall Duties*, for instance, is almost 700 pages long,
providing explicit information concerning the duties of different household
members—husband, wife, parents, children, servants—and their responsibilities to each other, all within the context of Paul's *Letter to the Ephesians*. The
ordering of the household was not something that even Puritan preachers
wanted to leave to personal exegesis.

This interest in the household takes on increased significance when one remembers the early modern commonplace that the domestic space was supposed to be a "seminary for the church and commonwealth." In his own domestic handbook, Robert Cleaver observes that the household "is as it were a little common wealth, by the good gouernment wherof, Gods glorie may be aduaunced, the common wealth which standeth of seuerall families, benefited, and al that liue in that familie may receiue much comfort and commoditie."[20] The domestic space thus became responsible for the grooming of public citizenship.[21] Husbands and wives had to prove themselves worthy of governing their little commonwealths by conducting themselves with propriety and sobriety. They were expected to keep a public profile by attending church regularly, where they sat in positions of privilege, and gave back to the community by paying new taxes. Wives also entered a new community of married women by attending births and the churchings of new mothers. Maintaining a proper household that mirrored the kingdom at large, and participating in all of the duties that went along with that kingdom, allowed all English citizens to participate in the Protestant national project.

This emphasis on establishing a domestic identity after marriage affected when and whom one married. The typical age for marriage was the mid to late twenties.[22] Eric Josef Carlson confirms that "couples married late because they were expected to have the economic resources to maintain a family before marrying, and needed time to accumulate those resources."[23] Members of the upper classes (who were already financially secure) tended to marry at younger ages, but their marriages included extensive negotiations concerning the interchange of property before a ceremony could take place. Marriage bargaining could take months or even years. Naturally, some couples felt impatient with such proceedings. In a 1589 letter to Richard Bagot, the Baron John Lumley writes perplexedly that even though marriage negotiations were under way, his nephew eloped with the bride-to-be before the business had been finalized. Lumley laments that the young couple "haue with more speede then was meete coupled themselves togeather in marriage without the consent and pryvitie of their parents, to [their] vtter subuersion and undooing."[24] To save the couple from domestic and social suicide, he urges his friend "to conferre with their fathers to the end that those speaches and promysses that have bene deluded and made by them both may be performed accordingly, both in the assurance of their lands and otherwayes for Joycnture, for their maintenantes."[25] Before the business was happily resolved, the couple caused their families and friends much distress and anxiety and endangered their own ability to establish an independent household.

Indeed, parents could, and did, withhold dowries and inheritances from children who eloped without their consent. After his elopement with Anne More, John Donne unsuccessfully attempted to persuade his infuriated father-in-law to give the couple her dowry. Expecting to move Sir George More with feelings of paternal sympathy, Donne writes in his first letter to the patriarch after the elopement: "I humbly beg of yow, that she may not, to her danger, feele the terror of your sodaine anger. I know this letter shall find yow full of passion: but I know no passion can alter your reason and wisdome; to which I adventure to commend these perticulers; That yt ys irremediably donne; That if yow incense my lord, yow Destroy her and me; That yt is easye to give us happines; And that my Endevors and industrie, if it please yow to prosper them, may soone make me somewhat worthyer of her."[26] Donne here conflates Anne's marital happiness with their economic well-being, which can only stem from More's generosity. The cheekiness of the statement (in which Donne puns on his own name) reveals that he did not yet understand the enormity of his fault or the depth of his father-in-law's wrath. Sir George remained unmoved, refusing to pay the dowry until years after the couple had been married. Since the couple had not fulfilled their obligations to him—obtaining his consent of the match—he felt no sense of obligation to them.

Even though parental consent was not necessary for a legal marriage (unless the couple was underage), domestic handbooks portray parental approval as important, even a requirement. In *The Christen State of Matrymonye*, Bullinger condemns "prevye contracts" since "in asmuch as the children are not yet come to perfite discretion, they can not contract mariage which requireth vnderstanding: yea, they can nether counsell nor helpe themselves. So that in this behalf the consent of their parents is not only necessary, but also good and profytable for them."[27] This need for consent extended to other members of the household as well, such as servants or apprentices, who were considered extended members of the householder's family.[28] By violating their own household responsibilities, which included respecting the wishes of the household's master (whether a parent or otherwise), an eloping couple seriously jeopardized their ability to establish their own domestic identity after marriage.

Communities did not want destitute or otherwise irresponsible couples setting up households in their midst, and thus they discouraged or prevented clandestine marriages as much as possible. Carlson informs us that hasty marriages followed by the cursory establishment of households "were often identified as principal causes of poverty in England and legal steps were taken to restrict . . . marriage . . . for this reason."[29] Outhwaite further emphasizes the community investment in marriage matches by observing that "although the parish authorities had no legal right to meddle, they could oppose the mar- riages of the poor" by various "informal means such as withholding rights of settlement, housing or employment."[30] These kinds of steps were not re- stricted to the impoverished. Sir George More influenced his friends to have Donne thrown in jail and removed from his employment, thus sabotaging the young man's aspirations to a career at court.[31] More's ability to influence his friends reveals the investment of the wider community in the sanctity of pa- triarchal norms within the household. While some of More's friends may have believed his treatment of the couple to be harsh, they probably did not want their own daughters eloping with brazen young poets either.

The fear of seduction was rampant among the upper classes in the early modern period, and the ease of clandestine marriage made a seducer's suc- cess potentially irrevocable. The seduction of wealthy young people was one of the main reasons for the institution of Lord Hardwicke's Marriage Act, which made clandestine marriages illegal, in 1753. In a debate in the Commons concerning the subject, the attorney general, Dudley Ryder, argued that the act would put "an end to an evil which has been long and grievously com- plained of, an evil by which many of our best families have often suffered."[32] He asks, "How often have we known the heir of a good family seduced, and engaged in a clandestine marriage, perhaps with a common strumpet?"[33] While Ryder makes these comments over a hundred years after Shakespeare wrote his plays, his reasons for the enactment are timeless, reflecting a centuries-long buildup of wealthy parents' fears and frustrations concerning clandestine mar- riage and seduction. Indeed, wealthy families have always wanted their children to make socially advantageous matches. Furthermore, the idea that people should marry within their class rank was a prevailing notion throughout the early modern period.[34] Clandestine marriages by means of seduction not only threatened the wealth and status of elite families but also undermined the very fabric of the hierarchical English society.

Before the passing of the Marriage Act, rape and ravishment laws discour- aged seduction. While modern laws view rape as a crime against a woman's person, early modern laws on rape and ravishment, deriving from the Middle Ages, conflated a daughter with her father's property, viewing the crime as one against her family. Carolyn Sale explains that "ravishment, which may or may not have included forcible sexual intercourse, differed from rape only inasmuch as the seized property included, in addition to the property of the woman, any real property that she stood to inherit."[35] In addition to functioning more as a piece of property under these laws than as a person, a woman could even be held guilty of her own rape. This possibility derives from the 1382 legisla- tion, 6 Richard II, which stated that women could be found guilty of their own ravishment if they consented to the rape later. Emma Hawkes observes that "the fact that some crimes were reconciled by marriages between the rapists and their victims . . . made it possible for women to elope in the guise of ravishment with partners their parents did not approve of and for men to abduct women and arrange advantageous marriages."[36] In this way, the law was put into place not only to discourage fortune hunters but also to limit women's agency within the matchmaking process. Under 6 Richard II, a woman who consented to her ravishment was cut off from all inheritance, dower, or jointure. For all essential purposes, the complicit abduction for marriage rendered the guilty couple dead (at least in terms of matters of inheritance) in the eyes of the law. During the debate concerning Lord Hardwicke's Marriage Act, Rudley observed that even the severity of these laws did not do enough to discourage clandestine marriages of this kind.

Instead, the best course for an early modern household was to prevent elopements from happening in the first place. One of the most important duties of parents was to provide their children with acceptable marriage matches. As Lord Burghley advises his son, Robert Cecil: "Marry thy daughters in time, lest they marry themselves."[37] Of course, this kind of patriarchal surveillance does not have to result in loveless arranged marriages, as Lawrence Stone's scholarship suggested.[38] Many parents genuinely took their children's desires to heart, simply wanting to ensure that suitors had their children's own best interests in mind as well. Indeed, during the public arguments surrounding the Marriage Act, one supporter argued that adultery was more likely in marriages that came out of "fortune-hunting, mercenary unions that clandestinity encouraged" than out of marriages forced on young people by their parents.[39] As Burghley's advice suggests, parents who neglected to perform their duties for their children were at least partially to blame if their children eloped without their consent.

Elopements seriously undermined both the domestic space and, by extension, the Elizabethan commonwealth for which it served as the foundation. By violating their duties to their households, eloping couples thus called their commitment to the entire commonwealth into question. Furthermore, the act of elopement suggested that the heads of household to which the couple belonged did not have control over their subjects. Cut off from the support of their family and friends, elopers compromised their ability to enter into a new community and establish a household of their own. By keeping these issues in mind, we can better understand how Jessica and Lorenzo's elopement threatens the domestic peace of the Belmont community.

The Belmont Estate as the Archetypal Household

In *The Merchant of Venice*, Shakespeare illustrates the ideal that the household should represent a mini-commonwealth through Portia's Belmont estate. By making Belmont the place to which characters retreat from the corrupt life of the city, he establishes the estate as a domestic archetype. Just as the domestic handbooks urge, power within this commonwealth is distributed through a system of checks and balances—Portia presides as the mistress over her household while also closely attending to responsibilities that may or may not align with her personal desires. Shakespeare thus reveals the complexity of patriarchal authority within the early modern household, which could bolster or limit male and female agency alike in order to keep the domestic space running smoothly.

The Belmont estate mirrors Elizabethan England by serving as a place of order over which Portia rules as a virgin queen. Within her court/household, she entertains foreign guests, oversees the management of her property and servants, and takes advice from her courtiers. As a single woman, Portia does not have a husband to mitigate her authority, putting her in an unusual position of power. She calls attention to her own place as an acting female head of household when she gives herself over to Bassanio: "I was the lord / Of this fair mansion, master of my servants, / Queen o'er myself" (3.2.167–169). By giving herself the title of a queen, she places herself in the position of Queen Elizabeth, suggesting that a court is a kind of domestic space and vice versa (of course, quite unlike Queen Elizabeth, Portia has no subjects outside of her household, being queen only "o'er myself"). Adelman compares Portia's statement that she is "Queen o'er myself" to the Ditchley portrait "in which Queen Elizabeth's body takes up virtually the entire space of her kingdom; and the name of her realm slyly figures her female anatomy, as though her kingdom and her body were one."[40] On the one hand, the position of nobility is not incongruous to Portia's aristocratic estate, but, on the other, she emphasizes the singularity of her position: a woman with so much domestic power must surely be a queen.

Shakespeare, however, supplies Portia with another source of patriarchal authority: her father's will. Her father leaves her the Belmont estate with the stipulation that she abide by the courtship ritual outlined by the casket test. In this way, she initially seems to have less agency than other heroines in Shakespeare's comedies. While Rosalind's and Viola's agency within their courtships drive the courtship plots of *As You Like It* and *Twelfth Night*, respectively, Portia laments: "I may neither choose who I would, nor refuse who I dislike; so is the will of a living daughter curb'd by the will of a dead father" (1.2.23–25).

Portia may not exert her own will when choosing her marriage match—an agency that most comic heroines take for granted. Neither Rosalind nor Viola, though, has a household over which to rule. Since Portia has become the master-mistress of her own household through unusual means (inheritance rather than marriage), her adherence to the casket test allows her to demonstrate the patriarchal source of her authority, and the virtues of a responsible householder, outside of the marital bond.

As a single young woman, Portia is dangerously vulnerable to the fortune-hunting schemes that Elizabethan parents of wealthy children feared. The overbearing nature of the casket test, which derives from the *Gesta Romanorum*, thus serves to protect Portia.[41] The will gives her the authority to send away unwelcome suitors once they have hazarded the test. She appears dissatisfied with her lack of agency in the courtship, but also confirms:

> If I live to be as old as Sibylla, I will die as chaste as Diana, unless I be obtain'd by the manner of my father's will. I am glad this parcel of wooers are so reasonable, for there is not one among them but I dote on his very absence, and I pray God grant them a fair departure.
>
> *(1.2.106–111)*

Without her obligation to uphold her dead father's wishes to reject suitors who fail the test, she may not be able to rid herself of unwelcome, or unreasonable, wooers, who may not respect the wishes of a young woman in the same way they respect those of a dead patriarch. By performing his paternal duty to Portia from beyond the grave, her father makes certain that no one can question her marriage's legitimacy or marry her without his approval. She cannot turn into an early modern Penelope with hoards of suitors lusting after her wealth and chastity, and with no good reason to turn them away.

Portia's father polices the domestic identities of the suitors outside of the Belmont estate as well. As the Prince of Arragon reveals, failed suitors must promise *"never* in my life / To woo a maid in way of marriage" (2.9.12–13; emphasis mine). This harsh stipulation does not appear in the *Gesta Romanorum* where the Roman emperor simply dictates that the King of Ampluy's daughter will not marry his son if she chooses incorrectly. By raising the stakes of the casket test, Portia's father ensures that the suitors must truly want to marry Portia. Otherwise, they would not be willing to take the risk. The raised stakes also underscore how the proper establishment of households lies at the foundation of the test: Portia's father denies the unsuccessful suitors the ability to have families of their own. In a play that places such a strong emphasis on domestic responsibilities, the inability to become the head of a family household (not simply the inability to marry Portia) is the ultimate punishment.

The casket test also allows Portia to demonstrate the self-control necessary for responsible householdership. In addition to needing time to gain the necessary resources, couples delayed getting married because young people were considered "incapable of stability."[42] When responding to Nerissa's observation that she has no good reason for her melancholy, Portia acknowledges:

> If to do were as easy as to know what were good to do, chapels had been churches, and poor men's cottages princes' palaces. It is a good divine that follows his own instructions; I can easier teach twenty what were good to be done than to be one of the twenty to follow mine own teaching. The brain may devise laws for the blood, but a hot temper leaps o'er a cold decree.
>
> *(1.2.12–19)*

Even though she cannot pinpoint the source of her sadness, she cannot help feeling so. Douglas Trevor points out that Hamlet, when ruminating on his own famous melancholy, "roots these forces inside of himself, where fluctuations he cannot control make and remake him as a tortured Galenic subject."[43] Portia's speech confirms that similar feelings, although fueled by blood and a "hot temper," could control her actions. The casket test provides a tempering influence to her courtship so that she does not fall prey to the irrational passions of youth that could jeopardize her decision making.

Nerissa helps maintain household order by insisting that her mistress participate in a marriage that will garner public consent. She assures her mistress that her father has devised the casket test so that Portia will love the person who chooses correctly: "The lott'ry that he hath devis'd in these three chests of gold, silver, and lead, whereof who chooses his meaning chooses you, will no doubt never be chosen by any rightly but one who you shall rightly love" (1.2.29–33). Whether this is actually the case is up for debate—and beside the point. Nerissa's main duty is to ensure that Portia's marriage occurs at least within the trappings of patriarchy so that her mistress does not lose her position of authority. Indeed, many theatrical productions emphasize Portia's ability to manipulate the casket test (such as through musical cues or even overt eye rolling) so that her preferred suitor makes the correct choice. Portia's need to prompt Bassanio in these performances suggests a fear that the casket test's purpose to provide a love match is not foolproof (i.e., Portia believes Bassanio could fail to puzzle through the clues and choose incorrectly) while also allowing Portia to retain agency over the matchmaking. Even if Portia does manipulate the casket test, however, the fact that she follows through with it rather than discarding it is what is most important. As the Redcrosse Knight learns when Archimago shows up to forbid the banns at the end of *The Faerie Queene*, book I, appearances matter. Considering Portia's initial dissatisfaction with the casket test, one can only wonder if she would have adhered to its rules without Nerissa's encouragement (as well as knowing that the rest of the members of her household were watching). However, since Portia ends up marrying the suitor of her choice (whether through her father's foresight or her own manipulation of the dictated test), Shakespeare indicates that domestic duties need not result in loveless matches. In the realm of comedy, domestic duties contribute to the fostering of the household.

Portia's father fulfills another paternal duty by making sure that she does not lack for suitors in number or variety. Indeed, the casket test does not screen for race—despite Portia's relief at his failure, the Prince of Morocco has a one-in-three chance of success. Perhaps just as alarming to an early modern audience as the possibility of miscegenation, though, is fortune hunting, which the casket test also does not screen for. Bassanio is just the kind of fortune hunter that Lord Hardwicke's Marriage Act hoped to ward against. After explaining to Antonio the destitution of his estate due to his own profligacy, he launches into his plans to seduce "a lady richly left" in order to fill his beleaguered coffers (1.1.161). Scholars who wish to idealize the Portia-Bassanio match as a happy, successful one usually gloss over the reasons for Bassanio's pilgrimage to Belmont while emphasizing his ability to choose (unprompted) the correct casket.[44] For these scholars, the end justifies the means since Portia and Bassanio do seem to love each other. However, we cannot overlook the significance of Bassanio's seemingly ungentlemanly behavior concerning his desire to woo Portia, and the fact that their marriage also easily could have devolved into a case of seduction and elopement.

Obviously, the casket test cannot prevent fortune hunters from taking their chances, but it does mean that the courtship and marriage take place publicly and within patriarchal trappings. Bassanio cannot seduce Portia and then take her money and run. Of course, when Bassanio learns that Antonio's ships have miscarried, he does hurry off to save his friend. He is able to do so, however, only after Portia, as the head of her household and knowledgeable in its financial matters, dismisses the bond of three thousand ducats as a paltry sum. She gives the money to Bassanio willingly, proclaiming "You shall have gold / To pay the petty debt twenty times over" (3.2.305–306). Bassanio thus departs to save his friend only after obtaining Portia's permission, acknowledging that he has "her good leave" (3.2.324), and only after agreeing to solemnize their marriage in a church. After such a public display of marital commitment in terms of vows and the transference of money, Bassanio could not expect to simply slip away into the night even if he wanted to. In this way, the casket test does not necessarily guarantee that someone does not court Portia for the sake of her money. Instead, it seeks to ensure that the successful suitor must fulfill his marital obligations to Portia and settle down at her Belmont estate. The suitor cannot undermine patriarchal authority any more than Portia. The stable creation of households, and the clear and legitimate transfer of property and inheritance, is what is truly at stake in the casket test.

Nerissa's choice of a marriage partner is also conditioned by her sense of domestic propriety. As Gratiano reveals, Nerissa agrees to marry him "provided that [Bassanio's] fortune / Achiev'd her mistress" (3.2.207–208). Nerissa is not going to leave her employment just to get married. In a similar fashion, domestic handbooks stressed that servants should ask their master's permission when pursuing marriage partners. Servants "ought not to mary while the time of their couenant for seruice lasteth," Gouge explains, "vnlesse their master giue consent thereto."[45] While Nerissa does not ask Portia's permission to marry outright, she agrees to go forward with the marriage only if it will not trouble the Belmont estate by displeasing her mistress. She places her household duty to her mistress above her own personal happiness.

Even though *The Merchant of Venice* may seem a comedy that appears to stifle female agency within matters of love, Shakespeare takes the opportunity to show that comic heroines need not become silent after marriage (as often seems the case when the marriage occurs at the end of the play). By adhering to their proper responsibilities within the household, women can wield a considerable amount of agency within the home. Many scholars take issue with Portia's lack of agency in her courtship (just as Portia initially does) and hail Portia's cross-dressing during the courtroom scene, and her orchestration of the ring trick, as an indication of her ability to undermine the patriarchal framework that confines her otherwise.[46] Jean E. Howard, for instance, lauds Portia for her agency in the courtroom scene and points out that Portia's cross-dressing allows her "to gain control over her sexuality" within marriage by delaying the consummation to a time of her choosing. However, Howard does not consider Portia's marriage as necessary to granting that agency.[47] Portia follows Bassanio to the courtroom to keep an eye on the well-earned husband that her father has chosen for her. Indeed, her marriage differentiates her from Shakespeare's other cross-dressed heroines, Rosalind and Viola, who don men's clothing to court their future husbands. Portia cross-dresses as a means to make sure that her match, arranged with the sanction of her father, household, and community, is a successful one, and she does not trouble patriarchy as much as she benefits from it during the courtroom scene and ring trick.

Through the ring trick, Portia reveals that a husband's domestic identity should take precedence over his community of male friends. Bassanio infamously hesitates to give Portia's ring away until Antonio claims that his friend's love should "be valued 'gainst your wive's commandment" (4.1.451). Bassanio's and Gratiano's commitments to male friendship result in a few tense moments when they believe that they have been cuckolded. Portia capitalizes on this by teaching the men that privileging male friendship over their ties in Christian matrimony could be disastrous, particularly considering that Bassanio now has the Belmont estate to offer as an inheritance. Portia thus overturns the popular discourse on male friendship, which championed the primacy of homosocial networks, by emphasizing Bassanio's inclusion into patriarchal hierarchy through marriage.[48] Bassanio even subconsciously anticipates his possible cuckoldry when he claims that he will die if he ever takes off the ring, further implying that his lineage will die out with him. Portia reminds the men of the importance of marriage when she chides Gratiano for parting with "A thing stuck on with oaths upon your finger / And so riveted with faith unto your flesh" (5.1.168–169). While many of Shakespeare's heroines seem to have agency only during their courtship, and then become silent after marriage, the staging of Portia and Bassanio's marriage in the middle of *The Merchant of Venice* reveals that a married woman could wield considerable agency within her marriage. Counterintuitively, this agency derives from her wifely authority within patriarchal structures. Shakespeare illustrates that Portia's marital agency can derive only from an ideal household where parents, children, and servants all follow their domestic responsibilities.

Jessica and Lorenzo's Elopement

While Jessica and Lorenzo's elopement may seem to follow a comedic paradigm (the cross-dressing heroine marries the suitor of her choice), their marriage violates the domestic ideal associated with Belmont. As a result, their participation in the play's comic ending appears ambiguous. Portia welcomes Lorenzo as Bassanio's friend, but Jessica apparently hangs back since Gratiano must urge Nerissa, "cheer yond stranger, bid her welcome" (3.2.237). Referring to Jessica as a "stranger" confirms her outsider status (even as the wife of Bassanio's friend), and Jessica's discomfort must be obvious indeed if Gratiano notices that she needs cheering up. The new wives may not be eager to welcome Jessica into their community of married women because they do not know her, and because she enters the Belmont estate with no one to commend her as Lorenzo does. No public announcement preceded her wedding to give them a chance to approve of her marriage as they would expect, especially considering that even Nerissa was willing to forgo marriage if it did not suit her mistress. In this way, clandestinity poses a threat to Jessica's marriage just as male friendship threatens Portia's normative one. Jessica, however, has no source of domestic authority from which to defuse the threat.

Jessica's Jewish blood could undermine Belmont's Christian commonwealth. When considering whether Jessica could successfully convert to Christianity, Janet Adelman suggests that marrying across races was understood to taint the bloodlines, and thus national identities, of the fledgling European nation-states.[49] Shylock appeals to the importance of blood to nationhood when describing the Jewish race as a landless religious nation held together by blood ties, referring to his fellow Jews as belonging to a "tribe" (1.3.51, 57, 110), "nation" (3.1.56, 85), or, more specifically, "sacred nation" (1.3.48). Although he claims that Jews have the same "hands, organs, dimensions, senses, affections, passions" (3.1.59–60) as Christians, Shylock insists that they have a different national identity even while living among the other Venetians. Salerio attempts to distance Jessica from Shylock by claiming that her blood differs from his as red wine differs from white (3.1.41–42). This claim, however, made more in mockery of Shylock than in defense of Jessica, does not hold up. Just four scenes later, Launcelot privately informs Jessica that she cannot escape her blood relationship with her father. According to Launcelot, Jessica's physical attributes of fairness, observed by the other characters, do not necessarily guarantee her a Christian identity. He laments: "The sins of the father [Shylock's Jewishness] are to be laid upon the children" (3.5.1–2). Even Jessica does not try to soften or undermine her blood relationship with her father when admitting, "I am a daughter to his blood" (2.3.18). Both Jessica and Shylock express that she is of his "own flesh and blood" even if she exhibits bodily Christian characteristics. Jessica does not—and cannot—deny consanguinity with Shylock. She must find another means, therefore, to distance herself from her Jewish identity if she wishes to integrate into the Christian community.

Thankfully for Jessica, blood ties were not the only way to form religious or national identity in the early modern world. As Richard Helgerson observes, early modern cartographers reveal a transition from "universal Christendom, to dynastic state, to land-centered nation."[50] The boundaries of commonwealths, according to Helgerson, were drawn on maps—not by blood. James Shapiro further observes that countries that emphasized bloodlines as part of their national identities were unsuccessful. Spain's efforts to institute *"limpieza de sangre*, blood laws that distinguished between those of Jewish lineage and Old Christians . . . signaled . . . failure, since adopting them meant abandoning the fundamental tenet of Christianity as a religion based on brotherhood."[51] As we saw in the first chapter, participating in a nation's religious rituals could also constitute an important means of expressing one's commitment to a national identity. Jessica, therefore, does not make her claim to Christianity in bodily or racial terms.

Sidestepping the idea of race altogether, Jessica insists that her wedding vows—not her bodily attributes—will constitute her conversion. When anticipating her marriage, she proclaims that even though she is Shylock's daughter:

> I am not to his manners. O Lorenzo,
> If thou keep promise, I shall end this strife,
> Become a Christian and thy loving wife.
>
> *(2.3.19–21)*

In conflating becoming a Christian with becoming a wife, Jessica indicates that her marriage vows will have a sacramental effect. She later explains to the doubting Launcelot that "I shall be sav'd by my husband, he hath made me a Christian" (3.5.19–20). The term "sav'd" again underscores the sacramental nature of her marriage vows. John Foxe, in *A Sermon Preached at the Christening of a Certaine Jew*, states that Jews could become Christians by "embracing the faith, and Sacramentes of Christ Iesu."[52] Even though marriage no longer constituted a sacrament under the Protestant faith, the marriage ritual, and all other rituals in the *Book of Common Prayer*, constituted the means by which a person could openly express her devotion to both the state and its religion. Jessica (or anyone else in the play) never indicates that she has participated in any other sacramental actions, such as baptism. She puts her entire faith in the marriage ritual as the means through which she will prove her Christianity. When arriving in Belmont, she refers to Shylock and his "countrymen" (3.2.285), as though she now considers herself to be an outsider to the Jews' landless nation. Jessica's focus on her "manners" as being different from Shylock's, therefore, implies that her actions—her participation in the Christian marriage ritual—will differentiate her most emphatically from her father and his Jewishness.

Manners play an important role in distinguishing the Christians from the Jews throughout the play. When she enters the courtroom, Portia fails to see a difference between her husband's cherished friend Antonio and his enemy Shylock, famously remarking, "Which is the merchant here? and which the

Jew?" (4.1.174). Bodily differences between the races, at least in this particular case, are not immediately obvious. Shylock distinguishes himself in the courtroom scene through his adherence to the law, expressing a value system that aligns itself more with Old Testament justice than with the Christian spirit of mercy. In other words, he performs his Jewishness by means of adherence to this value system. The fact that people could participate in "Judaizing," or turn into a Jew, similarly confirms that behavior was crucial to establishing an ethnic identity.[53] Of course, whether Portia and her fellow Christian characters act mercifully in the courtroom scene is up for debate. Instead, as we saw in the previous section, attention to one's domestic responsibilities, even at the potential expense of one's own personal happiness, serves as the foundation for the Christian community at Belmont.

Jessica may claim that she will integrate into the Christian community through matrimony, but a community cannot know if an outsider has participated in a ritual if it has not seen the ceremony take place. When Gratiano calls Jessica an "infidel" as she appears on stage for the first time after the elopement, we should remember that the other characters have not served as witnesses to the marriage. At first glance, Jessica's conversion to Christianity seems far more convincing than her father's. Since Shylock does not wish to convert to Christianity, his conversion will constitute a textbook example of an infelicitous speech act.[54] The other characters, however, do not have the opportunity to witness Jessica's own sincere vows. For all they know, her vows are infelicitous, or even misfire entirely. How can they be sure, for instance, that Jessica and Lorenzo's marriage was even a Christian one? As we have seen, clandestine marriages were the hallmark of Catholic recusants who did not wish to participate in the rituals of the *Book of Common Prayer*. A clandestine marriage suggested that the participants could be religious deviants or, at the very least, had something to hide. We might remember that Gouge condemns clandestine marriages for this reason: "As such seeking of secrecie taketh much from the honour and dignitie of mariage, so it implieth some euill cleauing thereto. . . . For where such meanes as are sanctified for obtaining a blessing on mariage are neglected, what blessing can thereupon be expected?"[55] Unfortunately for Jessica, the impossibility of a public courtship between a Jew and a Christian means that the ritual that leads to community approval of a marriage cannot take place. While living in her father's house, Jessica remained a "pagan" (2.3.11), perhaps waiting for the time when her father solidifies her fate by stipulating that she marry another Jew. Her only option of conversion (at least within the context of the play), however, a clandestine marriage with a Christian, means that the other characters call her marriage vows into question.

Creating a domestic space as a "seminary for the church and common-wealth" could serve as an important avenue for Jessica to demonstrate her commitment to Christian matrimony. Her inability to do so, therefore, further sabotages her conversion narrative. In Jessica and Lorenzo's elopement, reli-gious deviance, or the related issue of miscegenation, is not at stake as much as is the potential disruption of the general commonwealth through the couple's inability to provide for themselves. After discovering that Launcelot has been heckling Jessica about her conversion, Lorenzo chides him for impregnating a woman of another race: "I shall answer that better to the commonwealth than you can the getting up of the Negro's belly; the Moor is with child by you, Launcelot" (3.5.37–39). With these words, Lorenzo conflates the identity of the Jew with that of the Moor. He does not identify race as the problem, though, but rather that Launcelot has not married the woman he has impreg-nated. He has failed to establish a mini-commonwealth, even though he has participated in the marital privilege of sex and reproduction. Extramarital sex and its ability to destabilize the commonwealth at large through bastardy prove more problematic than miscegenation alone.[56]

Despite Lorenzo's recognition of the importance of the domestic space, Jessica and Lorenzo's failure to gain her father's permission for their marriage, and their consequent inability to seek community approval of the marriage, violates the rules of the Belmont household that keep it running smoothly. Making matters worse, since Lorenzo steals Jessica away with the money that supposedly would contribute to her inheritance, they commit a textbook ex-ample of the crime of ravishment under 6 Richard II, placing themselves out-side of the law's protection. Shylock's reported conflation of his daughter with his ducats after her elopement—"My daughter! O my ducats" (2.8.15)—seems devoid of paternal sympathy, but his desire for "Justice! the law!" (2.8.17) is not unreasonable, since she has indeed "stol'n" (2.8.19) his possessions and since Lorenzo has stolen his daughter. Shylock's view of the elopement as a kind of thievery does not simply illustrate the early modern stereotype of Jew-ish greediness but rather establishes his victimhood under the law. He is the victim of Jessica's ravishment. The law is on his side: the Venetian duke helps Shylock search the ships for the eloping couple. Camille Slights observes that Jessica's renouncement of parental protection "makes herself dangerously vul-nerable. The report that the Duke accompanied Shylock to search Bassanio's ship for the runaways (2.8) tells us how much protection Jessica could expect from the state."[57] Indeed, Portia's father implements the casket test in order to avoid the exact situation in which Shylock finds himself. Even if the Chris-tian characters sympathize with Jessica and Lorenzo, or delight at Shylock's misfortune, they cannot afford to undermine the norms that govern their households by ignoring Shylock's grievance completely.

Of course, if Portia's household is exemplary, then Shylock's household serves as its perverse analogue. He finds himself bereft of both fortune and daughter through his own poor household management. Unlike Portia's father, who takes his patriarchal duties seriously even in death, Shylock fails to find his daughter an appropriate husband in order to maintain his fortune's legacy. Jessica complains to Launcelot, "I am sorry thou wilt leave my father so. / Our house is hell, and thou, a merry devil, / Didst rob it of some taste of tedious-ness" (2.3.1–3). The "hell" that Jessica describes does not derive from ill treat-ment at the hands of her father but from boredom. This image starkly contrasts with Portia's own lively household, which features a steady stream of care-fully supervised eligible bachelors—eliminating (or at least mitigating) the possibility of a seducer. Shylock's household, by comparison, is noticeably vacant. As he exits the house, he leaves Jessica with paranoid instructions to "lock up my doors" (2.5.29) and "stop my house's ears" (2.5.34) so that "the sound of shallow fopp'ry" (2.5.35) cannot "enter" (2.5.35). Kathy Lavezzo ex-plores how closed-off households in early modern literature embody Jewish stereotypes, literally demonstrating the Jews' willingness to shut themselves off from religious truth.[58] The specificity of Shylock's instructions, warning Jessica not to "clamber . . . up to the casements then, / Nor thrust your head into the public street / To gaze on Christian fools" (2.5.31–33), suggests that Jessica has done so in the past—curious about the outside world from which she has been isolated. In addition to this inability to participate in youthful pursuits, Jessica has no close household companion as does Portia, and, de-spite Shylock's reference to his former wife, Shakespeare portrays no other female members of the Jewish community. Jessica appears just as cut off from the Jewish community as the Christian one. Her isolation thus serves as a catalyst for her elopement. Shylock's neglect of Jessica's needs and desires as a young woman brings this aspect of his own tragedy on himself. While Portia's father carefully arranges for his own wealth to be passed down to the future generations, Shylock's main concern is to hoard his riches with no thought of his own daughter's welfare.

According to the play's emphasis on domestic responsibilities, Shylock's fail-ure to provide his daughter with a match makes clandestine marriage neces-sary for Jessica and Lorenzo. Their inability to operate within social norms, however, jeopardizes their marriage from the start. When compared with Por-tia's highly public and ritualized courtship, Jessica and Lorenzo appear to have no courtship at all, or at least no meaningful courtship takes place.

Gratiano and Salerio reveal that they think Jessica and Lorenzo elope for the exact reasons that Portia's father implements the casket courtship ritual, and for the reasons that early modern readers would have been suspicious of any clandestine marriage: fortune hunting and/or sexual desire. When Jessica tosses Lorenzo a heavy casket and then returns to the house to "gild [herself] / With some moe ducats" (2.6.49–50), her behavior suggests that Lorenzo's intentions may be more akin to Bassanio's than initially realized. Jessica assumes that Lorenzo may not consider their elopement worth the risk if there is not a substantial financial reward. While waiting for the tardy Lorenzo to show up to whisk Jessica away from her father's house, Gratiano banters with Salerio about Lorenzo's motives. In doing so, he reveals that he also questions Lorenzo's intentions, claiming "Who riseth from a feast / With that keen appetite that he sits down?" (2.6.8–9). His following ten lines ensure that no one misses the point: Gratiano believes that Lorenzo will tire of Jessica after the excitement of the elopement has worn off. The clandestine nature of the marriage, which places the lovers outside of patriarchal authority, also means that Jessica may have less ability to hold Lorenzo to his marriage vows than Portia does. After Lorenzo's entrance, Salerio's comment desiring further conversation on the subject, "Here comes Lorenzo, more of this hereafter" (2.6.20), further implies that there is substance to the banter. That Lorenzo arrives late because he has been busy conscientiously preparing does not occur to either of his friends: the association between clandestine marriage and desire is too powerful to overcome.[59] Since Lorenzo and Jessica have had to hide their courtship from Shylock, they have had little opportunity to test their affections in the public sphere to prove the worthiness of their match, and their marriage encourages gossip, and doubts concerning its sincerity, before it even takes place.

If marriage was intended to provide stability to a household and community, Jessica and Lorenzo flout the responsibilities of married life when reportedly spending her father's fortune on trifles.[60] One lesson that the ring trick teaches Bassanio is that he will have to become more mature in his financial dealings after his prodigal lifestyle as a bachelor. After all, hazarding is for courtship, not marriage. Jessica and Lorenzo's marriage, which takes place outside of the public eye and with no father figure to watch over the spending of his inheritance, means that they feel no obligation to restrict the spending that appears to have bankrupted Venetian citizens already. Instead, they reportedly spend in "one night fourscore ducats" (3.1.109), paralleling Bassanio's sad state at the beginning of the play where he admits that he has squandered his fortune. Joan Ozark Holmer claims that Jessica's "freewheeling caper is not mean-spirited" and that Jessica also may dispose of her father's beloved turquoise ring due to its association with talismanic powers, and thereby "rids herself of such superstition by selling it for a monkey."[61] Portia's ring exchange with Bassanio, though, proves that the symbolic nature of betrothal rings was not limited to Christian or Jewish cultures, and Jessica in fact sells the one object that most connects her with marital values. After expressing his disappointment that Jessica has sold the ring that his wife, Leah, gave him by claiming, "I would not have given it for a wilderness of monkeys" (3.1.122–123), Shylock reveals that the Jewish traditions do include respect and concern for the sanctity of marriage. When Bassanio and Gratiano exclaim that they would rather see their wives dead than Antonio, Shylock exclaims: "I have a daughter— / Would any of the stock of Barrabas / Had been her husband rather than a Christian!" (4.1.295–297). Despite his previous remarks about disowning his daughter, Shylock feels he has reason for concern for her welfare, although the realization that he should have suggested a Jewish husband comes too late. As a result, Jessica's sale of the ring, perhaps sold in an attempt to disassociate herself from her father, only reflects a disregard for the marital values that have currency in both the Christian and Jewish faiths, and the couples' extravagance confirms Gratiano's belief that they marry for passion rather than reason. On the one hand, Jessica may act hastily by eloping with Lorenzo and spending her father's fortune; on the other, the Christian community's racism disallows her from learning the proper purpose of marriage.

As Jessica and Lorenzo walk the moonlit streets of Belmont, they appear to have internalized these doubts concerning their marriage as they compare their relationship with other clandestine marriages and love affairs that ended in tragedy. Any couple that participates in a clandestine marriage cannot but be reminded of their classical literary predecessors. Lorenzo first mentions Troilus and Cressida, musing that "in such a night / Troilus methinks mounted the Troyan walls, / And sigh'd his soul toward the Grecian tents, / Where Cressid lay that night" (5.1.3–6). The fact that Cressida gets traded to the Greek camp because no one knows about her union with Troilus exemplifies the complications surrounding the ease of clandestine marriages. The practice allowed a member of a couple to extricate himself from a marriage almost as easily as he entered it. Jessica alludes to this possibility: "In such a night / Did young Lorenzo swear he lov'd her well, / Stealing her soul with many vows of faith, / And ne'er a true one" (5.1.17–20). While the lovers obviously tease each other in this scene, the "vows of faith" quite literally refer to their wedding vows and her lines speak to early modern fears concerning the ease of conducting (and disavowing) clandestine marriages via spousal vows. Their teasing hints at the possible tragedy that their union could have befallen.

What, then, saves Jessica and Lorenzo from this fate? The Christian characters help secure their domestic identities within a patriarchal framework. Proving the importance of Jessica's need for a domestic identity in order to be incorporated into the Belmont community, Portia's first direct acknowledgment of Jessica occurs just after she gives Lorenzo and his wife command over her estate: "I commit into your hands / The husbandry and manage of my house / Until my lord's return" (3.4.24–26). She thus gives Lorenzo the opportunity to accept a household duty and participate in the proper art of "husbandry." Portia acknowledges that the task may be an "imposition" (3.4.33), but, as a guest that has accepted her "love" (3.4.34), Lorenzo is obliged to accept. Portia also does not neglect Jessica; she suggests her servants "will acknowledge you *and Jessica* / In place of Lord Bassanio and myself" (3.4.38–39; emphasis mine). Jessica's role may not be completely comfortable, but at least she has one.[62] Tellingly, Michael Radford's film version of *The Merchant of Venice* (2004) leaves out this line. Portia commits the rule of her house to only Lorenzo while Jessica remains standing awkwardly in the corridor. The film's desire to portray Jessica as an outsider necessitates that Portia neglect to include Jessica in household responsibilities. Portia's willingness to impose on Jessica in Shakespeare's play thus becomes an important instance of inclusion, and the fact that the imposition takes the form of a domestic duty indicates that the proper oversight of the household is the way in which Jessica and Lorenzo will integrate their cross-cultural marriage into the Belmont community.

In the courtroom scene, Shakespeare gives Shylock the opportunity to contest the legitimacy of his daughter's marriage as though before an early modern church court. Lorna Hutson suggests that Shylock's failure to mention his daughter's elopement contributes to the other characters' pitiless reaction to him, as they would have viewed the elopement as a legitimate grievance.[63] Shylock does not capitalize on the opportunity due to his obsession with taking revenge. The Christian characters, however, reveal their anxiety concerning the elopement by bringing it up themselves. Antonio's reference to Lorenzo as "the gentleman / That lately stole [Shylock's] daughter" (4.1.384–385) confirms the belief that Lorenzo did "play the knave" (2.3.12) when marrying Jessica. Antonio feels it necessary to bring Jessica and Lorenzo within patriarchal norms in order to come to terms with the elopement. The use of the term "stole" within the courtroom—not just as part of the idle banter of Launcelot or Gratiano—confirms that Lorenzo has indeed committed a crime by abducting Jessica from her house, even if she was complicit in the act. By acknowledging that Shylock is a victim, Antonio must defuse the threat that the couple presents to the law since they are indeed guilty. To do so, he forces

Shylock to accept his daughter's marriage by granting the couple an inheritance. In addition to becoming a Christian, Shylock must "record a gift, / Here in the court, of all he dies possess'd / Unto his son Lorenzo and his daughter" (4.1.388–390). Antonio's reference to Lorenzo as Shylock's "son" may come as a surprise since one imagines the Christian characters would prefer to disassociate their friend from his father-in-law as much as possible. To the contrary, Antonio's language makes clear that Shylock must view Lorenzo as his son and must offer his blessing by leaving the couple with an inheritance, in order for the Christian characters to become fully comfortable with the elopement.[64] Shakespeare thus underscores that even though parental consent was not necessary to make a legal match, it was considered necessary if the match was to be viewed as socially acceptable.

The Christian characters thus can feel comfortable that patriarchal norms have been restored, and that Jessica and Lorenzo will come into an inheritance that will secure their financial future. In light of the early modern fears concerning elopement, Lorenzo's statement that Antonio's stipulation "drop[s] manna in the way / Of starved people" (5.1.294–295) reflects the concern that those who elope literally will have no means to provide for themselves and will contribute to the poverty of the community, destabilizing the economic well-being of the state as a whole. His words may seem like an exaggeration since Jessica and Lorenzo are clearly in no danger of starving just yet, but only because they are taking advantage of Portia and Bassanio's generosity. The public acknowledgment and acceptance of Lorenzo and Jessica's marriage that takes place within a courtroom ensures that the marriage takes on the trappings of legitimacy within the eyes of the law, and gives them the ability to move out of their friends' house and into a home of their own. Shakespeare thus defuses the threat of the eloping cross-cultural couple not by proving that Jessica is not a Jew but by proving that she will be able to enter into the Christian community as a responsible householder.

CHAPTER 5

"Are You Fast Married?"

Elopement and Turning Turk in
Shakespeare's *Othello*

Jessica and Lorenzo's cross-cultural clandestine marriage in *The Merchant of Venice* is comedy saved; Othello and Desdemona's is comedy gone horribly awry. *Othello*, with its multicultural Venetian setting and interracial marriage, has long been recognized as Shakespeare's tragic revision of *The Merchant of Venice*. Julia Reinhard Lupton observes, "Both are set in the mercantile city-state of Venice, both employ clearly marked 'others' as central characters, and both use the theme of conspicuous exogamy to heighten the conventional comedic situation of young lovers blocked by an old father."[1] Lupton, however, views Othello more as Shakespeare's rewriting of Shylock than Jessica, and does not consider how his clandestine marriage to Desdemona impacts his identity as a Venetian citizen. In the tragedy, Shakespeare does not make the interracial clandestine marriage between Othello and Desdemona a side plot as he does Jessica and Lorenzo's. Instead, by bringing the clandestine marriage front and center, he places more pressure on it, making it central to the play's tragedy. As the play's protagonist, Othello has no well-meaning Portia who can swoop in and save the day. While Shakespeare makes no attempt to incorporate the couple into a comedic plotline, the play has many characteristics of comedy. As Stephen Rogers attests, "*Othello* achieves much of its tragic power through the adaptation, often the rearrangement or inversion, of techniques, devices, and other materials traditionally belonging to comedy."[2] Indeed, the inversion of the elopement plot that succeeds in Shakespearean comedy should call our attention to why it fails in *Othello*.

Like the figure of the Jew, the figure of the Moor constituted both a religious and racial outsider in early modern literature and society. Much scholarship has focused on Othello's racial otherness, and on how Shakespeare and early modern theatergoers would have defined his racial difference.[3] Michael Neill demonstrates that the term "Moor" could refer to a range of racial identities, describing someone from a specific region of North Africa or from anywhere on the African continent or simply anyone with dark skin.[4] Emily C. Bartels's argument that Othello is simultaneously a racialized outsider *and* Venetian insider (the two subject positions are not mutually exclusive) has become a critical commonplace.[5] Unlike Jessica's Jewish identity, however, Othello's racial identity is literally marked on his skin, suggesting that he could never escape a certain amount of outsider status even if welcomed into Venetian society. No one would ever wonder, "Which is the merchant here? And which the Moor?"

Other criticism focuses less on Othello's fixed racial alterity and more on his fluid religious identity as a Christian convert. The play presents few details of Othello's specific origins, but we know they are pagan or, at the least, non-Christian. Both Lupton and Daniel J. Vitkus have argued for Othello's Muslim origins, claiming that the Moor was almost indistinguishable from the Turk on the early modern stage.[6] Neill informs that the term "'Moor' often came to be used as a blanket term for Muslims of any nationality."[7] Lupton further argues that "for the modern reader or viewer, a black Othello is more subversive, 'other,' or dangerous, in the Renaissance, an Othello more closely resembling the Turks whom he fights might actually challenge more deeply the integrity of the Christian paradigms set up in the play as the measure of humanity."[8] According to Lupton, Othello only truly becomes a member of Christian society when he identifies himself as the Turkish other by committing suicide. Dennis Austin Britton admirably takes a more positive approach to the issue of religious identity.[9] Rather than focusing on the play's fearmongering over conversion and religious otherness, Britton emphasizes how Othello's Christianity allows him to enter into Venetian society, insisting that religious identity trumps racial identity. Despite Othello's racial otherness, the white Venetian society has obviously embraced him. He is a popular general whom Desdemona's father, Brabantio, has allowed to be a house guest, enabling the couple to fall in love in the first place. Despite the differences in their arguments, Vitkus, Lupton, and Britton all suggest that Othello begins to "turn Turk" (or *re-turn* to a Muslim identity) only once he has left the safety of Venice and becomes vulnerable to Iago's machinations in Cyprus. As yet, no one has considered how Othello's clandestine marriage could potentially play a role in his religious turning.

Nevertheless, the clandestine marriage is perhaps *the* most significant revision that Shakespeare makes to his source: Cinthio's *Hecatommithi*. Just as Shakespeare fabricates a story of cross-cultural clandestine marriage to include in his revision of Fiorentino's *Il Pecorone* in *The Merchant of Venice*, he revises his source for *Othello* to include an elopement narrative. As we have seen in *The Merchant of Venice*, entering a Christian community through elopement can be a difficult, tricky business, and remains difficult if the character's religious identity is already slippery or elusive. Othello's willful religious transgression through his clandestine marriage to Desdemona undermines his conversion to Christianity from the outset, indicating that he begins to "turn" even before he leaves Venetian soil. Not only does the clandestine marriage cement Othello's otherness, but it also others Desdemona in Othello's eyes. In *Othello*, clandestine marriage thus creates the skepticism at the heart of Shakespearean tragedy.[10] That the elopement calls the legitimacy of their marriage into question, contributing to Othello's misguided belief in Desdemona's adulterous behavior, ultimately guarantees the play's tragic trajectory.

Elopement and Conversion in Venice

Unlike Jessica, Othello is already a Christian convert at the beginning of the play. When Iago claims that the Moor would be willing to "renounce his baptism" (2.3.343) for the sake of Desdemona, he implies that Othello has converted through the sacrament. The baptism of Muslims was an accepted—and not entirely unheard of—practice in early modern England. Meredith Hanmer's *The Baptizing of a Turke, A sermon preached at the Hospitall of Saint Katherin* recounts the baptizing of a Muslim Turk named Chinano. Britton explains: Hanmer "links . . . race, black skin, geography, and religion by proclaiming that adherence to Islam, like blackness, is the consequence of Noah's curse on Cham and his descendants; like constructions of blackness as a genealogically inherited marker of spiritual cursedness, Muslim faith becomes a racial marker that is inherited by the descendants of Cham because of their progenitor's spiritual depravity."[11] Hanmer thus conflates the identity of the Moor with the identity of the Turk because of their shared predisposition to Islam. To be baptized, Chinano must make a "publike confession of his true faith in Iesus Christ."[12] Hanmer describes how the baptism takes place in a public forum, requiring the convert to speak openly about his faith, specifically outlining his beliefs rather than simply confirming them.[13] Most pertinent to my analysis is the public nature of the examination. The Church of England required conversions of Muslims / Turks through baptism to take place publicly rather than privately—congregations were not expected to accept converts into their midst without witnessing an interrogation of the convert's faith first. Only in that way could a congregation feel satisfied that the conversion was sincere.

The suggestion that Othello could "renounce" the conversion confirms the early modern fear that the sacramental promises of converts were not necessarily absolute. If no one saw the conversion through baptism to begin with, how does anyone even know that it took place? These fears reached a fever pitch in early modern Spain where Moors forced to convert to Catholicism—"Moriscos"—became "subject to increased suspicion and regulation. Conversion did not guarantee belief."[14] As we have seen, it seems very unlikely that the Christian community will embrace Shylock after he presumably undergoes a forced conversion through baptism. Vitkus further argues that the theme of "turning Turk" in *Othello* reflects the early modern audience's "collective anxiety" about religious conversion, particularly in the face of an expanding Islamic empire.[15] He observes that "according to Protestant ideology, the Devil, the pope, and the Turk all desired to 'convert' good Protestant souls to a state of damnation."[16] Entering into a marriage with a Christian woman, therefore, could reinforce Othello's Christianity for the Venetian community, serving as another means through which he demonstrates the "seals and symbols of [his] redeemed sin" (2.3.344). Lupton agrees, claiming that Othello "enters into Christian fellowship and the Venetian polity through *intermarriage* and public service."[17] According to Britton, "Othello's black skin proves to be an insufficient reason for exclusion from either civic or *married* life in Venice."[18]

Othello *is* excluded from married life in Venice, however. He and Desdemona do not get married in a public ceremony with other Venetians acting as sanctifying and affirming witnesses, evincing that the Venetian community has denied their ability to marry. This departs sharply from the *Hecatommithi*. In the original romance, the Moorish captain falls in love with a "virtuous Lady of wondrous beauty called Disdemona."[19] Cinthio is eager to point out that their love is mutual and sincere: "Disdemona, impelled not by female appetite but by the Moor's good qualities, fell in love with him, and he, vanquished by the Lady's beauty and noble mind, likewise was enamoured of her. So propitious was their mutual love that, although the Lady's relatives did all they could to make her take another husband, they were united in marriage and lived together in such concord and tranquility while they remained in Venice, that never a word passed between them that was not loving."[20] At first glance, Shakespeare appears to have followed this plotline closely. To emphasize this, E. A. J.

Honigmann usefully provides footnotes to the corresponding lines in the Arden Shakespeare so that the reader can easily see how Shakespeare is drawing on his source; Neill further observes that Shakespeare "seems to have worked with a version of this text beside him."[21] Shakespeare departs significantly from the way in which the marriage occurs, however—a difference that no critic has emphasized despite Neill's assertion that Shakespeare "seldom departs from his sources without good reason."[22] Following Neill's lead, I would like to consider how paying close attention to the nature of Othello and Desdemona's marriage can influence our understanding of the tragedy. While Disdemona's relatives attempt to persuade her from marrying the Moor, they also appear to reconcile themselves to the match. There is no indication that the couple has to elope after failing to obtain approval for a public ceremony. Since they do not elope, they also have a happily married life residing in Venice. In contrast, Othello and Desdemona leave Venice almost immediately after the elopement. They never reside in Venice as a married couple, so we never have the chance to determine whether the Venetian community would have truly accepted them. If anything, their marriage results in their immediate expulsion from Venetian society—not their inclusion. The elopement is what prevents them from being able to stay in Venice—not Othello's blackness. Shakespeare's revision of his source to include the elopement plot, and the way in which he makes the contestation surrounding the marriage central to the play's entire first act, underscores the significance of the specifically *clandestine* marriage to the tragedy.

Even though Othello is a well-respected citizen of Venice, as both Britton and Bartels demonstrate, Othello and Desdemona know that Brabantio would never consent to their marriage. Otherwise, they would not elope. We do not know the exact nature of the marriage, but Roderigo provides some insight. "At this odd-even and dull watch o'th'night," he explains, Desdemona was "transported with no worse nor better guard / But with a knave of common hire, a gundolier" (1.1.123–125). His description emphasizes the irregularity of the marriage's timing. In his editorial footnote, E. A. J. Honigmann hesitantly suggests that Roderigo's phrase "odd-even" means "neither one thing nor the other, neither night nor day."[23] "Odd-even" may also be Roderigo's way of saying "uneven," since we do know that the elopement occurs in the dead of night when all things should typically be "dull" or sleeping. We also learn from Roderigo that Othello did not help Desdemona get away—quite the opposite of the conscientious Lorenzo, who ensures that he has the help of several friends to assist Jessica in her escape. Desdemona, presumably, is too old to have someone like a nurse help her climb out a window.[24] Instead, Desdemona traverses the watery streets of Venice alone and friendless. Strangely, we find out in act 3 that Cassio served as a go-between for Othello and Desdemona during their courtship. Iago asks Othello: "Did Michael Cassio, when [you] woo'd my lady, / Know of your love?" (3.3.94–95). "He did, from first to last," Othello replies, clarifying that Cassio "went between us very oft" (3.3.96, 100). Desdemona even reminds her husband that Cassio "came a-wooing with you" (3.3.71) when trying to restore Cassio to Othello's good graces. Cassio does know about their love affair, but Othello does not employ his help with the actual elopement. Indeed, when Iago tells him Othello is married, Cassio appears surprised, asking, "To who?" (1.2.52). Apparently, Othello has not confided in him.[25] Othello's decision not to include Cassio in the elopement plans, unlike Lorenzo's employing his own friends, suggests that his trust in Cassio may not be as absolute as it seems. Othello's lack of a close friend or confidant to aid in the elopement speaks to his isolation in Venetian society rather than his inclusion—he does not expect anyone to help him in his plan to elope with Desdemona. On his wedding night, Othello presents himself as an isolated figure rather than one who has the support of a community (or even his trusted lieutenant).

Making matters worse, the couple replaces—or at least appears to replace—the church ceremony with a sexual consummation. Both Roderigo and Iago hint that Desdemona and Othello rely on the sexual consummation to validate the marriage. Roderigo warns Brabantio that Desdemona is in "the gross clasps of a lascivious Moor" (1.1.126), while Iago confirms that "an old black ram / Is tupping your white ewe" (1.1.88–89). Their tasteless references imply that the eloping couple has not rushed to a church to perform the necessary rites (as do, for instance, Romeo and Juliet) but to the bedroom. Of course, it is not entirely clear that this is the case. Some critics have questioned whether the marriage is actually consummated. T. G. A. Nelson and Charles Haines, for instance, have argued that the lack of a sexual consummation is why Othello becomes prey to Iago—he is so overcome by sexual frustration.[26] If the marriage is not consummated, then one could argue that there is no marriage at all. Brabantio does not make this part of his case against the couple, however, suggesting that he believes Iago's account of Desdemona and Othello's sexual activity. When Desdemona begs to go with Othello to Cyprus, she insinuates the role of sexual appetite in the elopement, stating that if he goes to war without her, "the rites for why I love him are bereft me" (1.3.257). Here she intimates that the "rites" are sexual ones that could not be performed if they are apart. Othello realizes that Desdemona's expression of sexuality might be problematic—he assures the Venetian senators that he does not feel similarly:

Let her have your voice.
Vouch with me, heaven, I therefore beg it not
To please the palate of my appetite,
Nor to comply with heat (the young affects
In [me] defunct), and proper satisfaction;
But to be free and bounteous to her mind.
And heaven defend your good souls, that you think
I will your serious and great business scant
[For] she is with me. No, when light-wing'd toys
Of feather'd Cupid seel with wanton dullness
My speculative and offic'd [instruments],
That my disports corrupt and taint my business,
Let housewives make a skillet of my helm,
And all indign and base adversities
Make head against my estimation!

(1.3.260–274)

While Desdemona's language could be taken to have a sexual connotation, Othello insists that this language does not apply to him: his age exempts him from lust since his "young affects" are "defunct." Marital sex, Othello claims, will not distract him from his handling of military affairs or dull his ability to be a warrior. He will not "great business scant." He would not have to make such a speech, however, if it were not a concern—he is eager to assuage the Venetian Senate's fears concerning the oft-assumed role of sexuality in clandestine marriage. Even if sexual desire is not the actual reason for their marriage, Desdemona and Othello cannot escape the perception that this was potentially the case, particularly since the elopement appears unplanned and happens in the middle of the night.

Iago relies on the presumed role of sexual appetite in the elopement, absent from the original plot, to set his plan against the Moor in motion. Iago explains to the hopeful Roderigo:

It cannot be long that Desdemona should long continue her love to
the Moor . . . nor he his to her. It was a violent commencement in her,
and thou shalt see an answerable sequestration. . . . The food that to
him now is as luscious as locusts, shall be to him shortly as [acerb] as
[the] coloquintida. She must change for youth; when she is sated with
his body, she will find the [error] of her choice. [She must have
change, she must].

(1.3.341–352)

The sudden, "violent" nature of the love resulting in a precipitous clandestine marriage cannot last long—both Desdemona and Othello will soon tire of one another. He further claims that Desdemona and Othello are not well suited:

> When the blood is made dull with the act of sport, there should be, [again] to inflame it and to give satiety a fresh appetite, loveliness in favor, sympathy in years, manners, and beauties—all which the Moor is defective in. Now for want of these requir'd conveniences, her delicate tenderness will find itself abus'd, begin to heave the gorge, disrelish and abhor the Moor; very nature will instruct her in it and compel her to some second choice.
>
> *(2.1.226–235)*

Iago explains how clandestine marriage results in mismatched couples, not just in terms of race but also in years and manners. In his treatise *Matrimoniall Honour*, Daniel Rogers warns that the practice of clandestine marriage encourages such mismatched couples. Without the guidance of family and friends, couples may not even realize they are unsuited until a contract has been made. "When it appears, that the one partie is unqualified for the other," he further admonishes, "then they that made [the union] may break it."[27] Rogers laments that due to the clandestine nature of their contracts, mismatched couples could more easily break their marriage vows. Communal approval is necessary to ensure that such ill-advised marriages do not occur. Iago suggests that Desdemona will soon realize that Othello is "unqualified" for marriage since he is "defective" in looks, age, and manners. According to this theory, Desdemona's love for Othello is not sincere like the love between the Moor and Disdemona in the original romance, but is simply a lust that can be satiated. Iago thus uses the circumstances surrounding the marriage to claim that Desdemona and Othello's marriage will not last. Once Desdemona regains her senses, she will have a "second choice." Iago's implication here is that Desdemona will have the ability to choose not just another sexual partner but another husband, perhaps by refuting the clandestine marriage and marrying again. Iago would not be able to make these claims if Othello and Desdemona had married in a church ceremony, as do Cinthio's lovers.

Othello thus inadvertently aligns himself with the excessive sexual desire that was associated with the Turks and Islam through the very act of his elopement. Edward Kellett associates Muhammad with lechery in a 1627 sermon: "That great seducer *Mahomet*, was a salacious, lustfull *Amoroso*; and his intemperate lasciuiousnesse, was wayted on by infirmities and sicknesses correspondent to his lewdness."[28] Edward Aston, in *The Manners, Lawes, and Cvstomes of all Nations*, claims that Islam's "incredible allurement" was in "giuing to his people free liberty and power to pursue their lustes and all other pleasures."[29] Even Othello's epileptic seizure links him with the early modern connection between epilepsy and excessive sensuality.[30] Othello's religious otherness is marked on his body not only through his racial difference but also through his physical infirmity. He does not enter into Christian matrimony but rather confirms his religious otherness, renouncing his baptism in the process, by marrying clandestinely even before he comes on stage for the first time.

When meeting Othello immediately after the elopement, Iago hints that the clandestine marriage will enable Desdemona to have a "second choice." Feigning concern, he anxiously inquires, "Are you *fast* married?" (1.2.11; emphasis mine). The term "fast" could mean not only "firmly" or "fixed" but also "tightly" or "securely" so "as to not permit . . . detachment."[31] Iago further suggests that Desdemona's unhappy father will detach the couple from one another if their marriage is not "fast" or was not performed in such a way to make it fast. This is a perfectly legitimate worry since we have learned that some marriages could indeed be more "fast" than others depending on the kind of evidence that could be provided demonstrating that a marriage has taken place. Iago further proclaims:

> That the magnifico is much belov'd,
> And hath in his effect a voice potential
> As double as the Duke's. He will divorce you,
> Or put upon you what restraint or grievance
> The law (with all his might to enforce it on)
> Will give him cable.
>
> (1.2.12–17)

According to Iago, Brabantio is a powerful Venetian citizen—one who has the wherewithal to pressure the duke in the matter of his daughter's elopement. Iago warns, therefore, that Brabantio might even have the ability to "divorce" the couple, an otherwise rare occurrence in early modern society.[32] In a modern sense, divorce was simply not available. The church courts, however, could grant two types of divorces: *a vinculo matrimonii* and *a mensa et thoro*.[33] A divorce *a vinculo matrimonii* occurred if a "dirimentary impediment" voided the marriage ab initio. Essentially, the church courts determined that a marriage never existed in the first place, allowing the couple to marry again (in this case, Desdemona might have a "second choice"). A divorce *a mensa et thoro* released a couple from their legal obligation to cohabit (they were not, however, allowed to marry again).[34] If Brabantio is not able to obtain a divorce for his daughter, Iago presumes that Brabantio will use the law to punish the couple another way.

Despite the sense of impropriety surrounding their nocturnal marriage, Othello and Desdemona are not the only ones conducting important business in Venice in the dead of night. The duke is also unexpectedly "in council" (1.2.92). Even though the duke is clearly attending to important matters of state, Brabantio claims that his case is important enough to interrupt:

> Bring him away;
> Mine's not an idle cause. The Duke himself,
> Or any of my brothers of the state,
> Cannot but feel this wrong as 'twere their own;
> For if such actions may have passage free,
> Bond-slaves and pagans shall our statesmen be.
>
> (1.2.94–99)

With this proclamation, Brabantio insists that the issue of clandestine marriage is an issue of national importance, momentous enough to drag the duke away from an emergency meeting in the middle of the night. Furthermore, Brabantio makes the argument that his grievance is not a personal one—the interests of all "brothers of the state" are at stake in the issue of clandestine marriage. By using the word "brothers," he excludes Othello from the population of Venice since the Moor is not a brother or related by blood to anyone in the city. Brabantio's claim that the allowance of middle-of-the-night elopements will make Venetians "pagans" also hints that Othello's elopement with Desdemona has undermined the Moor's Christianity—only a pagan would elope with someone's daughter without her father's consent. According to this rationale, if the Venetians allow the elopement to go unpunished, then they themselves will turn Turk. Accusing Othello of being "damn'd" (1.2.63), Brabantio emphasizes how Othello's religious otherness—not his racial otherness—causes his actions to fall outside of the law. If Brabantio had been willing to accept Othello as a houseguest because of his Christian identity, as Britton argues, the patriarch changes his mind about Othello's Christianity the moment he learns of the elopement. Brabantio questions whether Othello was ever Christian or merely masquerading as Christian so as to seduce his daughter. Similar to Spenser at the end of the *Legend of Holiness*, Brabantio believes that marriages that take place outside of the proper religious frameworks should not be valid, and are even outside the realm of Christianity.

When Brabantio uses the same language as Shylock to express his grievance over his daughter's elopement, he suggests that the conflation of a daughter with one's possessions was not an idea reserved for Jewishness on the early modern stage. Iago first borrows Shylock's language to announce the elopement: "Awake: what ho, Brabantio! thieves, thieves, thieves! / Look to your house, your daughter and your bags! / Thieves, thieves!" (1.1.79–81). With these words, Iago makes it seem as though the theft of a daughter alone is not enough reason to get out of bed. Brabantio's initial statement of disbelief— "What tell'st thou me of robbing? This is Venice; / My house is not a grange" (1.1.105–106)—further underlines how Othello others himself through the act of elopement. According to Brabantio, Venetians do not rob each other, either of household goods or of daughters. Brabantio picks up Iago's language to increase his claim's exigence when gaining entrance to the duke. He repeatedly refers to Othello as a thief, proclaiming, "Down with him, thief!" (1.2.57) and "O thou foul thief, where hast thou stow'd my daughter?" (1.2.62), and complaining that Desdemona has been "stol'n from me" (1.3.60). On the one hand, his conflation of Desdemona with goods that can be stolen seems like callous objectification.[35] On the other, Brabantio carefully uses language that could aid him in obtaining a divorce. If Othello has "stolen" Desdemona, then it means she may not have consented to the elopement, implying that she has been abducted against her will. In this scenario, a divorce *a vinculo matrimonii* could be possible.

Just as Iago predicts, the duke is sympathetic to Brabantio's claims—despite being busy, the duke holds an impromptu ecclesiastical trial to handle the marital dispute. And Brabantio does consider himself to have sufficient grounds to contest the marriage. He demands a trial, proclaiming, "I'll have't disputed on" (1.2.75). Curiously, no one doubts that a marriage or marital contract of some sort has actually taken place. When Brabantio asks, "Are they married, think you?" (1.1.167), Roderigo replies, "Truly, I think they are" (1.1.168). Brabantio, therefore, does not claim that some kind of marriage has not occurred, insisting instead that Desdemona and Othello's marriage is not "fast" because Othello must have "bound" Desdemona (1.2.65) in "chains of magic" (1.2.65). He declares that Desdemona could not have consented in the eyes of the law, since Othello "hast practic'd on her with foul charms, / Abus'd her delicate youth with drugs or minerals / That weakens motion" (1.2.73–75). Diane Purkiss observes that Brabantio's accusation is "the only time we see something like a trial for witchcraft dramatized on the Renaissance stage."[36] When considering that witchcraft could be a capital offense, Brabantio's statement becomes that much more significant.[37] He turns his pursuit of the elopers, quite literally, into a witch hunt: Othello stands not just to lose Desdemona but also, potentially, his life. The duke agrees that trickery or beguilement resulting in clandestine marriage would be sufficient cause for punishment, assuring Brabantio:

> Who e'er he be that in this foul proceeding
> Hath thus beguil'd your daughter of herself,
> And you of her, the bloody book of law
> You shall yourself read in the bitter letter
> After your own sense; yea, though our proper son
> Stood in your action
>
> (1.3.65–70)

He certifies that Desdemona could not have been "herself" if Othello used witchcraft when persuading her to elope, and therefore she would not be married. His language also conforms to the urgency of Brabantio's request. In stating that he would not let his own son go unpunished for such an action, he confirms that irregular unions are indeed a concern of the entire state—a concern that would trump his own duty as a father to protect his son from a potentially capital offense.

Brabantio, however, is not able to offer any "ocular proof" (3.3.360) that Othello used magic outside of his own word and speculation. Othello, of course, does confirm that an elopement has taken place: "That I have ta'en away this old man's daughter, / It is most true; true I have married her" (1.3.78–79). Othello insists, though, that he did not bewitch Desdemona but rather told her stories of his adventurous exploits. In doing so, he makes Brabantio's "belief in literal witchcraft look naïve" since he proves that being able to tell an interesting story is the "only . . . witchcraft I have us'd" (1.3.169).[38] The duke agrees that there is not enough evidence to confirm witchcraft, proclaiming, "To vouch this is no proof, / Without more wider and more [overt] test" (1.3.107–108). After hearing how Othello wooed Desdemona with stories of his foreign adventure, he even admits, "I think this tale would win my daughter too" (1.3.171). The duke rules that the telling of and listening to stories is a perfectly legitimate means of courtship, and perhaps a particularly effective one since he speculates that even his own daughter would have been susceptible to it. Early modern fathers should take heed. The duke and the senators may sympathize with Brabantio's predicament (they profess that they are sorry for it), but the duke's hands are tied: he cannot dissolve the marriage.

Just as Othello does not enlist Cassio's help during the elopement, he does not call Cassio as a witness at the trial, even though go-betweens would have been standard witnesses during ecclesiastical court trials.[39] Instead, Cassio stands by silently as Othello explains his courtship with Desdemona, completely cutting out any role that Cassio played.[40] Perhaps Othello does not want to get his lieutenant in trouble. Or perhaps he is not sure if Cassio's testimony will have much more weight than his own. While Cassio is not a racial or religious outsider, he is not a Venetian—he is Florentine (1.1.20). His own status as an outsider could undermine his testimony. Othello also indicates that he wants to stand on his own merit. He dismisses Iago's initial warning that Brabantio will be angry:

> Let him do his spite;
> My services which I have done the signiory
> Shall out-tongue his complaints. 'Tis yet to know—
> Which, when I know that boasting is an honor,
> I shall [provulgate]—I fetch my life and being
> From men of royal siege, and my demerits
> May speak, unbonneted, to as proud a fortune
> As this that I have reach'd.
>
> (1.2.17–24)

Here Othello does not claim that he will prove his marriage by calling on witnesses or by describing the ceremony or trothplighting that would give legitimacy to the match. Instead, he claims that his military deeds in the service of the signiory should legitimate his marriage. This, however, does not seem quite right. While Othello's military deeds are clearly admirable, they cannot take the place of a marriage ceremony. Othello reveals that he does not understand the importance of having witnesses to validate the marriage—marriages are supposed to have the support of a couple's family and community, not be based solely on the individuals' personal characteristics or merits. In contrast, Jessica and Lorenzo have defenders during the courtroom scene in *The Merchant of Venice* who secure their well-being. When failing to call on his friends by proudly looking to his public service instead, Othello indicates that he does not understand the role of community in making an early modern marriage successful—a fatal error.

The courtroom scene, however, does at least give Desdemona a chance to claim that she consented to the match, confirming that she was "herself" when making the decision to elope. When Brabantio asks her to whom she most owes obedience, he asks her to provide proof of her identity. Is she a daughter? Or a wife? Desdemona answers with the latter. "I do perceive here a divided duty" (1.3.181), she observes:

I am hitherto your daughter. But here's my husband;
And so much duty as my mother show'd
To you, preferring you before her father,
So much I challenge that I may profess
Due to the Moor, my lord.

(1.3.185–189)

Despite the clandestine nature of her vows, Desdemona has undergone the successful transformation from daughter to wife—an early modern woman's identity hinges upon to whom she owes allegiance. Desdemona understands this and responds accordingly. Upon hearing his daughter's testimony, Brabantio admits defeat: "God be with you! I have done" (1.3.189). Desdemona's testimony is enough for her father—he does not try to claim that she is too young or that the marriage has not been consummated. While Brabantio disapproves of her choice, he is willing to honor it. Backed into a corner, he offers his consent: "Come hither, Moor: / I here do give thee that with all my heart" (1.3.192–193). Brabantio makes clear, however, that he does not do so willingly, lamenting, "I had rather to adopt a child than get it" (1.3.191). Again conflating Desdemona with his monetary wealth by calling her a "jewel" (1.3.195), he also acknowledges that Desdemona is not a mere object but a woman who has chosen to give herself away. Early modern marriage law does allow for female agency. He claims, however, that he would turn into a Shylock if he had other children, observing "thy escape would teach me tyranny, / To hang clogs on them" (1.3.197–198). Brabantio suggests that becoming an overcontrolling patriarch would constitute a kind of religious turning that he would prefer to avoid. Referring to daughters as objects crosses the Christian-Jewish divide in Shakespeare's Venetian plays, but disallowing daughters' opportunities to fall in love is a characteristic of overbearing Jewish fathers only.

Brabantio cannot deny that he has given Desdemona the chance to fall in love with Othello by inviting the Moor into his household. Unlike the reclusive Shylock, Brabantio is perfectly happy to entertain foreign guests. Othello testifies that "her father lov'd me, oft invited me" (1.3.128) to his house. While Brabantio's "love" for Othello could simply refer to common social courtesy in this context, he clearly liked and enjoyed Othello's company since he invited the general "oft." Othello reveals the reason for Brabantio's frequent invitations: he "questioned me the story of my life / From year to year—the [battles], sieges, [fortunes] / That I have pass'd" (1.3.129–131). Like his daughter, Brabantio hangs on Othello's stories of daring exploits. As the ruler of his household, Brabantio is responsible for who does and does not gain access to it. In a sense, he has only himself to blame if his daughter runs off with a man that he willingly invited into his own home on numerous occasions.

Brabantio has done his duty as an early modern father, however, by providing Desdemona with what he considers to be acceptable alternatives. He laments: "She shunn'd / The wealthy curled [darlings] of our nation" (1.2.67–68). Here he suggests that Desdemona has had many appropriate (i.e., native Venetian) suitors from which to choose. She has rejected them. Clearly, he has not been paying close attention to her when he says Othello is someone (or something) that she "fear'd to look on" (1.3.98). Othello's description of their courtship indicates that they spent time alone as he expanded on his stories that she did not have a chance to hear in full while attending to her household duties, explaining, "That I would all my pilgrimage dilate, / Whereof by parcels she had something heard / But not [intentively]" (1.3.153–155). Considering the lack of privacy in early modern households, it seems strange that Brabantio has neglected to notice his daughter listening attentively to a man visiting his house. He falls victim to his own inability to exercise his patriarchal authority, failing to see his daughter falling in love in front of his very eyes. Indeed, the idea that Desdemona might fall in love with Othello precisely because she does "fear" him and "for the dangers [he] had passed" (1.3.168) does not even enter his mind despite the fact that he himself seems to enjoy Othello's company for the same reasons.

The duke expresses discomfort with Brabantio's reluctant acceptance of the match. He issues a "sentence" that he hopes will put the eloping couple into Brabantio's favor:

When remedies are past, the griefs are ended
By seeing the worst, which late on hopes depended.
To mourn a mischief that is past and gone
Is the next way to draw new mischief on.

(1.3.202–205)

Here the duke basically tells Brabantio to get over it: what is done is done. Though he does imply that Othello has indeed stolen Desdemona when stating, "The robb'd that smiles steals something from the thief" (1.3.208). The duke's acknowledgment that Othello has stolen Desdemona is significant: he hints that Othello has committed a crime. His willingness to gloss over this detail speaks to Othello's important role in the Venetian community—the duke does not try to do anything else to make amends or smooth over the issue as the Christian characters do when requiring Shylock to leave Jessica an inheritance. The duke also needs his most valuable general in the impending battle against the Turks. Brabantio, however, is not so easily consoled. He classifies the duke's attempt at reconciliation as "Turkish": "So let the Turk of Cyprus us beguile" (1.3.210). Brabantio first asserts that the deception associated with clandestine marriage parallels the acts of deception associated with the Turks. He then asserts here that the duke's acceptance of Othello and Desdemona's clandestine marriage causes his fellow Venetians to turn Turk as well.

Further troubling his religious identity, Othello's clandestine marriage does not perform the proper function of transforming him into a householder. He admits that he never really wanted to settle down when telling Iago:

> But that I love the gentle Desdemona,
> I would not my unhoused free condition
> Put into circumscription and confine
> For the sea's worth.
>
> (1.2.25–28)

His wistful reference to his "unhoused free condition" suggests that Othello prefers being a bachelor. He is willing to confine himself or settle down only for the sake of his love for Desdemona. This sounds romantic. It also sounds, however, like Othello is not necessarily ready to take on the responsibilities of married life. Furthermore, Othello *has not* settled down. During the trial scene, he reveals that he is not a homeowner; he must uncomfortably admit that Desdemona has no place to stay while he is off at war. Britton reads Othello as a character of the romance genre. As Una must learn at the end of book I of *The Faerie Queene*, soldiering is for bachelors—not for husbands— since the Redcrosse Knight must leave her behind to continue fighting for the Faery Queen. Redcrosse cannot officially marry Una until his military duties are over. Othello attempts to remedy his lack of preparation for his married state, telling the duke that he craves:

> Fit disposition for my wife,
> Due reference of place and exhibition,
> With such accommodation and besort
> As levels with her breeding.
>
> (1.3.236–239)

His request may seem like kind regard for his spouse—he wants Desdemona to enjoy the upper-class comforts that she is used to—but setting up a domestic space is really something that he should have done in advance. Not doing so serves only to underline the hastiness of the elopement, intimating that the proper thought and care were not put into the preparations. Jessica and

Lorenzo's own elopement now seems well organized in comparison—at least they had Portia's Belmont household in which to take refuge. They had a plan. Even more importantly, they had help.

The duke's immediate response that Desdemona should stay with her father provides another opportunity for Brabantio to bestow a blessing on the marriage. This is a crucial moment in the play's tragedy—a request that would actually give Desdemona a place to reside in Venice and demonstrate her commitment to Christian matrimony. Underscoring his disapproval of the marriage even in his defeat, however, Brabantio immediately rejects this suggestion: "I will not have it so" (1.3.240). Since Desdemona no longer recognizes herself as having duty to him as her father, he no longer recognizes himself as having a duty to her. He will not provide her with houseroom. Brabantio, unlike Portia, does not give the couple a chance to act out the domestic responsibilities associated with marriage. He thus condemns the marriage to failure—punishing the couple as Iago forewarned—even before they leave for Cyprus.

Sowing Skepticism on Cyprus

On Cyprus, Iago manages to exploit the ambiguity surrounding Othello's marriage vows not by causing his community to question their legitimacy but by causing Othello himself to question their legitimacy. Presumably, as she declares during the courtroom scene, Desdemona's marriage vows have transformed her from loving daughter to faithful wife. Iago, however, suggests that the clandestine marriage should cause Othello to doubt Desdemona's virtuous identity. Brabantio has already warned Othello that the act of elopement has disrupted her selfhood: "Look to her, Moor, if thou hast eyes to see; / She has deceiv'd her father, and may thee" (1.3.292–293). Iago builds on these suspicions when reminding Othello, "She did deceive her father, marrying you" (3.3.206). Brabantio and Iago advise Othello that the clandestine marriage gives him reason to doubt her virtue. Considering how quickly Othello falls for Iago's hints and warnings, he seems to have already been experiencing doubts concerning the nature of the marriage. Even before demanding to see the "ocular proof" (3.3.360), he laments, "She's gone. I am abus'd" (3.3.267). Just as Brabantio claims that the act of elopement causes Othello to turn away from his virtuous Christian identity, Othello claims Desdemona is susceptible to deceptive "turning." After striking his wife in a shocking instance of domestic violence, he tells Lodovico: "Sir, she can turn, and turn; and yet go on / And turn again" (4.1.253–254). Othello believes that Desdemona's potential for deceptive behavior—a belief that would not exist if their marriage had not been clandestine—justifies his behavior. Harry Berger Jr. claims that *Othello* "is about the meaning and effects of fear of adultery."[41] I would go further. *Othello* is about how *clandestine marriage* creates the fear of adultery. Whether that fear is correct is beside the point—clandestine marriage sows seeds of distrust that can cause marriages to fail.

Indeed, Othello admits that his jealous imaginings are far worse than any unknown truth. He tells Iago: "I had been happy, if the general camp, / Pioners and all, had tasted her sweet body, / So I had nothing known" (3.3.345–347). The mere thought that Desdemona could be unfaithful results in his farewell speech to a "tranquill mind" (3.3.348). The issue is not that Desdemona has been unfaithful but that Othello *thinks* that she has been and can never unthink it—not, at least, until he kills her. In *Matrimoniall Honour*, Rogers further explains the dangerous role that imagination plays in conducting clandestine marriages, elucidating that a union without a proper ceremony is simply a "union of imagination."[42] While not denying the legality of private contracts, Rogers recommends a public marriage since it is "an union of state and condition, standing in right, and law, above all private affection."[43] According to Rogers, the public ceremony creates the proper "condition" for marriage—it is as though couples that marry clandestinely do not actually inhabit a proper married "state." A "union of imagination" is a union that may not actually exist. The members of the couple that marry publicly cannot simply change their minds later about their married condition as Othello fears Desdemona has done by committing adultery.

Othello does attempt to correct the fault of his clandestine marriage when ordering his soldiers to celebrate his marriage alongside the military triumph during their first night on Cyprus. A herald announces: "It is Othello's pleasure, our noble and valiant general, that upon certain tidings now arriv'd, importing the mere perdition of the Turkish fleet, every man put himself into triumph; some to dance, some to make bonfires, each man to what sport and revels his [addiction] leads him; for besides these beneficial news, it is the celebration of his nuptial" (2.2.1–7). Again, Othello reveals his lack of planning when organizing his marriage. Rather than arranging for a celebration of his nuptials where both he and Desdemona reside, he must celebrate their marriage when they are abroad. The marriage is not even the main reason for the celebration. It is "besides." The couple does not have the support of family and friends who are married householders themselves, but the highly inadequate support of a cohort of bachelors. In this way, Othello mixes his business—war and soldiering—with his domestic life.

Since Othello does not give up his military exploits before getting married, he also makes himself vulnerable to the outside forces of other men. At the end of *The Merchant of Venice*, the couples pair off, suggesting that heterosexual coupling is more important than same-sex friendship—at least in a play with a happy ending. Othello's continued commitment to his military life means that he must remain attached to fraternal bonds with the men serving under him. Othello's reluctance to give up his relationships with other men allows him to enter into an inappropriately close relationship with Iago—a relationship that begins as a courtship. Iago carefully woos Othello using the language of love during the temptation scene that convinces the Moor of his wife's deceit.[44] Iago proclaims: "My lord, you know I love you" (3.3.117), "now I shall have reason / To show the love and duty that I bear you / with franker spirit" (3.3.193–95), "I humbly do beseech you of your pardon / For too much loving you" (3.3.212–213), "I hope you will consider what is spoke / Comes from [my] love" (3.3.216–217), "I thank you for this profit, and from hence / I'll love no friend, sith love breeds such offense" (3.3.379–380). After wooing Othello in this manner, Iago tells the Moor that he will assist him in his "sacred vow" of revenge:

> Othello: *He kneels.*
>   Now, by yond marble heaven,
>   In the due reverence of a sacred vow
>   I here engage my words.
>
> Iago: Do not rise yet.
>   *Iago kneels.*
>   Witness, you ever-burning lights above,
>   You elements that clip us round about,
>   Witness that here Iago doth give up
>   The execution of his wit, hands, heart,
>   To wrong'd Othello's service! Let him command,
>   And to obey shall be in me remorse,
>   What bloody business ever.
>   *They rise*
> Othello: I greet thy love,
>
> ·   ·   ·   ·   ·   ·   ·   ·   ·
>
>   Now art thou my Lieutenant.
> Iago: I am your own for ever.
>
> *(3.3.460–480)*

The formality of this pact, echoing the language of the marriage ceremony, is astonishing. As Neill observes, "If there is any act of adultery in the play, this surely is it."[45] This is not just an act of adultery, however. This act constitutes the only marriage or trothplight in the play that we actually witness. We never witness any kind of marital vow made between Othello and Desdemona, yet here we witness the making of a formal pact between Othello and Iago. The stars are not the only witnesses; the audience members are as well. This kind of witnessed formality gives Othello reason to trust Iago. He enters into this relationship with his male friend because he doubts the fastness of his own marriage. Here Shakespeare reveals the dangers of clandestine marriage. Since Othello feels uncertain of the legitimacy of his marriage to Desdemona, he creates a second unholy union with Iago. It is he—not Desdemona—who makes a "second choice." Something that would not be possible—or at least not necessary in Othello's mind—if the marriage had been public.

Not only does Othello remain overly committed to his relationships with other men on Cyprus, but Desdemona does as well. Without a household to run like Portia, Desdemona lacks the employment of a wife, involving herself in Othello's employment instead. If Portia teaches Bassanio to privilege his marriage above his friendship with Antonio when settling down at Belmont, Desdemona has no such impulse since there is no domestic space to control and protect. Natasha Korda confirms, "It is Desdemona's concern with affairs of state, rather than those of the household—with political, rather than domestic oeconomy—that both accords her tragic stature and ultimately brings her to a tragic end."[46] Desdemona's inability to concern herself with domestic responsibilities directly results from the clandestine nature of her marriage that did not include the establishment of a household. Rather than pushing Othello's male friends away, therefore, Desdemona vows friendship with Cassio:

> If I do vow a friendship, I'll perform it
> To the last article. My lord shall never rest,
> I'll watch him tame and talk him out of patience;
> . . . .
> I'll intermingle every thing he does
> with Cassio's suit.
>
> *(3.3.21–26)*

Like Othello's vow to Iago, this is also the only such intimate oath that we see Desdemona make in the play—to a man who is not her husband. While Desdemona remains faithful to her husband, her willingness to help Cassio overshadows her clandestine marriage vows, at least in the mind of Othello. Iago narrates her "innocently flirtatious palm-paddling with Cassio": "He takes her by the palm; ay, well said, whisper. With as little web as this will I ensnare as great a fly as Cassio" (2.1.167–169).[47] This "paddling of palms" resembles the hand holding between Polonius and Hermione that so enrages Leontes in *The Winter's Tale*. The king concludes: "To mingle friendship far is mingling bloods" (1.2.109). Of course, Leontes infamously refuses to recognize that his wife is acting on his command. In light of Leontes's insane jealousy that does not even require an Iago to stoke its flames, it is no wonder that Othello falls prey to a similar sentiment. Shakespeare warns of the dangers of a wife becoming too intimate with her husband's male friends—an intimacy that never would have happened if Desdemona had not felt compelled to follow Othello to Cyprus, or if Othello himself had been willing and able to set up a household and settle down after his elopement.

The clandestine marriage also legitimates the importance of the handkerchief to the tragedy's plotline. The handkerchief plot derives from Cinthio—something that easily, as Lynda E. Boose observes, could have been left out.[48] Instead, Shakespeare keeps the plot device, so unsatisfactory for some critics, and puts even more pressure on it. It is the only token of the marriage that we see, even if an inadequate one and even though we know Cassio went between Othello and Desdemona with other tokens. The seeming "trifle" has been the subject of much derision and much scrutiny. Thomas Rymer notoriously proclaimed in frustration: "So much ado, so much stress, so much passion and repetition about an Handkerchief! Why was not this call'd the *Tragedy of the Handkerchief*? . . . Had it been *Desdemona's* Garter, the Sagacious Moor might have smelt a Rat: but the Handkerchief is so remote a trifle, no Booby, on this side *Mauritania*, cou'd make any consequence from it."[49] Korda has argued that Othello's focus on the handkerchief is excessive by early modern standards, contending, "Both women and Africans were in varying ways vilified as being attached in the wrong way or to too great an extent to material objects."[50] In this way, Othello's obsession with the handkerchief and its whereabouts becomes a part of the play's racism.[51]

As we have seen, however, tokens, even small, seemingly inconsequential ones, can play big roles in early modern courtship and marriage customs, far disproportionate to their size. The fact that Othello and Desdemona's marriage was clandestine only contributes to the importance of the handkerchief in their relationship. Emilia confirms this when Desdemona accidentally lets it drop: "She so loves the token / (For he conjur'd her she should ever keep it) / That she reserves it evermore about her / To kiss and talk to" (3.3.293–296). We have not seen Desdemona and Othello exchange rings or vows of any kind as symbols of their troth. The handkerchief thus stands in for the wedding ring. As Berger observes, the handkerchief operates in a similar fashion to the ring that Portia gives Bassanio. When giving Desdemona the handkerchief, Othello makes her "responsible for the power she has and potentially guilty for its misuse. . . . The compensatory function of the ring is identical to that of the handkerchief."[52] When Desdemona loses the handkerchief, therefore, Othello registers its loss in the way that Portia registers Bassanio's giving away of the ring. A modern reader might be more sympathetic to Portia: what kind of husband gives away his wedding ring? But the handkerchief carries the same significance for Othello. In her examination of ecclesiastical court depositions, Diana O'Hara confirms that handkerchiefs could be used as evidence in cases concerning matrimonial disputes.[53] While a handkerchief might not seem as weighty an object as, say, a ring, it was "evidently customary for the male suitor to woo with gifts, sometimes referred to in an indiscriminate way as 'divers tokens' or 'small trifles.'"[54] "Trifles," objects with seemingly little monetary value, actually hold great significance when used in matters of courtship and matrimony. It may also be fair to say that these trifles carry greater significance for couples that have married clandestinely. The trifles become more than trifles when presented as evidence in a matrimonial dispute. In early modern courtrooms, trifles became the "ocular proof" that a marriage had taken place.

Furthermore, Othello makes clear that the handkerchief is not a trifle. It is a family heirloom—an object of great worth to him even outside of his relationship with Desdemona. Giving the token magical characteristics contributes to his identity as a religious other. After denying his use of magic when telling Desdemona stories of love and adventure, he mysteriously describes the handkerchief's properties: "There's magic in the web of it." (3.4.69). The Egyptian sibyl who gave it to his mother was a "charmer," he reveals, that "could almost read the thoughts of people" (3.4.57–58). A reader cannot help but be reminded of Othello's pagan background. O'Hara demonstrates, however, how love tokens were often associated with magical properties in early modern England. She explains, "A host of superstitions surrounded such gifts, and their properties, considering the evidence for belief in the efficacy, and mechanistic nature of magic and the role of village wizards and pedlars who distributed love magic, and other popular products. Indeed, the quasi-magical dimension of gift-giving cannot be ignored, since the giving of objects arguably served to symbolise and effect stages in marriage. The potential exists for gifts and tokens to take on the character of charms."[55] The understanding is that such tokens, imbued with a kind of magic that transformed a couple into husband and wife, could not simply be thrown away or tossed aside. While Shakespeare's audience may not have approved of the use of magic in general, Othello's belief in the handkerchief's magical qualities might not have seemed so pagan or outlandish. It is Othello's failure to participate in the marriage ceremony that permanently others him, not necessarily his relationship with the handkerchief.

Othello's uncharacteristic mistreatment of her makes Desdemona realize that he does not believe their marriage to be "fast." To assuage his doubt, she asks Emilia to lay their wedding sheets on their bed (4.2.105). Desdemona wants to re-create their marriage night, either as a way of reliving that night or as a way of legitimating a marriage that remains uncertain. Whether the marriage remains unconsummated increases in exigence here. If Othello and Desdemona truly have not had a chance to consummate the marriage, their marriage really might not be "fast"—couples could renege on a marriage that had not been consummated. Even though her father did not make it an issue during the courtroom scene, Desdemona may be anxious to solidify the marriage once and for all so as to put Othello's mind at ease. During this scene, Emilia also confirms that Desdemona's elopement has isolated her in a way that makes her vulnerable:

> Hath she forsook so many noble matches?
> Her father? and her country? and her friends?
> To be call'd whore? Would it not make one weep?
>
> *(4.2.125–127)*

Here Emilia confirms not only Brabantio's statement that Desdemona rejected many worthy suitors but also that Desdemona married without the approval of "her country, and her friends"—her father's disapproval is not the only one of importance. Emilia speaks to the social network required to make an early modern marriage successful. Due to the clandestine nature of her marriage, Desdemona has no family or friends to turn to when her husband accuses her of infidelity—she is dangerously isolated in a world made up primarily of men, some of whom quite literally mean her harm. No one can vouch for the sincerity of her vows or of her virtue.

Once in Cyprus, Othello and Desdemona's marriage fails not just because Othello is a converted other but because he has difficulty comprehending Desdemona's own otherness. He cannot fathom Desdemona's virtue without being able to see it. Andrew Sisson explains: "Iago compels Othello to become aware that his marriage depends upon his partnership with a virtue that cannot be known, displayed, judged, or valued in a way that would satisfy him of its reality."[56] Stanley Cavell expounds further: "Nothing could be more certain to Othello than that Desdemona exists; is flesh and blood; is separate from him; other. This is precisely the possibility that tortures him. . . . His professions of skepticism over her faithfulness are a cover story for a deeper conviction; a terrible doubt covering a yet more terrible certainty, an unstable certainty"[57] Of course, the whole purpose of the marriage ceremony is to make a couple "one flesh" so that they are not separate, can never be alien to one another. The purpose of the ceremony is to dispel the skepticism that Cavell identifies. Without the ceremony, the conversion to man and wife is incomplete, or at least seems incomplete to the couple's community or even to the couple themselves as the case here. Has a marriage truly occurred or not? On the wedding night, the consummation, which Cavell dwells on, is not the only important event performed offstage—we do not see Othello and Desdemona's vows of faith as they plight their troth. When Othello says that he has married Desdemona, he implies that a brief ceremony or simply a handfasting—something—has taken place. What did the couple say? How did they say it? The inability to know these things calls the fastness of the clandestine marriage into question. If Othello had been able to hold a proper church ceremony surrounded by friends, family, and neighbors, he would have witnessed a public affirmation of Desdemona's virtue—the "ocular proof" of her faithfulness would not depend so much on a handkerchief, an object so easily stolen or misplaced. Othello would thus be less willing to consider any claims to the contrary—a heartbroken father or a manipulative friend could not suggest that Desdemona's vows were insincere.

The inability to differentiate between true speech acts and false ones without the ceremony of matrimony thus lies at the heart of *Othello*. Without a proper ceremony, Othello cannot determine the sincerity of Desdemona's love and instead falls prey to Iago's own false oaths that have a distinct ceremonial sheen. The purpose behind the growing emphasis on the public marriage ceremony in the late Elizabethan period as the only way to enter into a marriage was to disambiguate the meaning behind speech acts that allowed seducers (like Iago) to deceive their lovers and allowed religious outsiders to continue practicing in Protestant England. Of course, unfortunately for Othello, the impossibility of a public courtship and marriage between a Moor and a white woman means that he has no choice but to participate in a clandestine marriage and embrace the identity of the "malignant and . . . turban'd Turk" that he abhors (5.2.353). Othello scolds his men for excessive drinking when proclaiming "Are we turn'd Turks" (2.3.170) on his first night in Cyprus. In doing so, he suggests that becoming inebriated and participating in brawls results in the excesses associated with Islam rather than with Christian soldiers. Thankfully for his men, this conversion need be only a temporary one—one that they can shake off as they sober up and return to their senses. Since Othello turns Turk through his legal marriage vows, however, the process is permanent. He cannot escape the conversion until it is complete and ultimately damns him.

Conclusion

Incestuous Clandestine Marriage in John Ford's
'Tis Pity She's a Whore

As the previous chapters have demonstrated, fictions of clandestine marriage allowed early modern authors to engage with the social, religious, and political discourses on the practice and with each other. The pervasive nature of these fictions confirms that clandestine marriage was a defining issue of the late Elizabethan and Jacobean eras. Up to this point, I have focused on uncovering fictions of clandestine marriage that are not immediately obvious to a modern reader or have not garnered sustained critical consideration as such. One popular fiction of clandestine marriage from the Elizabethan era, however, demands more of our attention: Shakespeare's *Romeo and Juliet*. Required reading for almost every high school student in the United States, *Romeo and Juliet* has become one of the most celebrated love stories of all time. The tragedy's countless theatrical and film adaptations attest to its enduring popularity. *Romeo and Juliet* also captivated early modern audiences and authors, who appropriated its story, language, and lessons just as modern filmmakers do today.[1] In this conclusion, I explore *Romeo and Juliet's* legacy in John Ford's *'Tis Pity She's a Whore*. In doing so, I suggest that we do not need to see Ford's revision of Shakespeare's play as being "derivative" but rather as revealing how the practice of clandestine marriage continued to play a central role in early modern culture and literature into the Caroline period.[2]

Scholars have long recognized *Romeo and Juliet* as providing a backdrop for Ford's play.[3] Both plays focus on the meteoric rise and precipitous fall of forbidden love. In addition to the young lovers, Ford retains the characters of Shakespeare's friar, the comic nurse, and the matchmaking patriarch; the very language of these characters often echoes that of their Shakespearean counterparts. Clearly, Ford expected to conjure Shakespeare's popular play in the minds of his audience members as they watched his tragedy of incest unfold. But to what end? Bruce Thomas Boehrer links the theme of incest in *'Tis Pity* to a royalist agenda, arguing that the play "explores what might happen if the individual nuclear family were to be assigned independent value as a political unit—if it were to be dissociated from the language of royal absolutism and viewed as a perfectly self-contained political entity."[4] According to this argument, Ford's portrayal of incest suggests the degradation of moral values in the absence of monarchy. Emily C. Bartels observes that the theme of incest constitutes the most crucial plot difference between the two plays. While Shakespeare's lovers "marry before they satisfy their desires," she observes, "marriage is absolutely out of the question" for Annabella and Giovanni.[5] I will demonstrate, however, that Ford's appropriation of the clandestine marriage plotline is what forces us to take Annabella and Giovanni's incestuous relationship seriously. In particular, I argue that Ford associates his play not with a royalist agenda, as Boehrer suggests, but with a political agenda that condemns the role of Catholicism in the Caroline court. In this way, *'Tis Pity* is just as much about the controversy surrounding clandestine marriage in the latter stages of the English Renaissance as it is about the controversy surrounding incest.

By the 1620s, when *'Tis Pity* was written, the growing strain between Puritanism and Arminianism contributed to escalating debates about marriage.[6] More radical members of Parliament had always expressed dissatisfaction with the precepts of the Elizabethan Religious Settlement, particularly with the ceremonial aspects of the *Book of Common Prayer*'s marriage service and with the seemingly arbitrary seasonal restrictions on when marriages could take place. Charles I's refusal to take these grievances seriously and work with Parliament to resolve them contributed to the increasing political tension. The Long Parliament's clamor for marriage reform demonstrates that frustration over the nature of the marriage ritual played a role in the general movement toward the regicide. Indeed, if some members of Parliament viewed the Caroline regime as exhibiting an undesirable favoritism toward Catholicism, this perception was wrapped up with a perceived leniency toward the practice of clandestine marriage. The "Root and Branch" petition blamed "the government of archbishops and lord bishops, deans and archdeacons" for a number of social evils, including "the growth of popery," "the licensing of marriages without banns asking," and "the great increase and frequency of whoredoms and adulteries, occasioned by the prelates' corrupt administration of justice."[7] As we have seen throughout this book, the practice of clandestine marriage, including "the licensing of marriages without banns asking," often went hand in hand with fears concerning the "growth of popery." In 1641, the dismantling of the established Church of England began, abolishing the authority and regulating forces of the church courts along with it. The Commons appointed an assembly to create a new church government and liturgy to replace the *Book of Common Prayer*. One of the Commons' requests to the assembly was to "consider of some Course to prevent the Mischiefs that happen by clandestine Marriages, and by the marrying of People by Laymen."[8] By looking forward to this history, we can see that the practice of clandestine marriage not only was at the heart of the Reformation but also played a role in the events leading to the English Revolution.

Like clandestine marriage, the general topic of incest permeated early modern culture. Church officials argued over the definition of incest and how to interpret the prohibited degrees of kinship laid out in Leviticus.[9] The Church of England regularly issued pamphlets to clarify the dizzying array of incestuous possibilities.[10] Incest's association with transgressive desire further links the act with the transgressive desire often associated with clandestine marriage.

Romeo and Juliet's own passionate love certainly contradicts the careful delineation between sexual desire and the kind of marital companionship that most Protestant moralists espoused. Dympna Callaghan links this disapproval with the couple's Catholicism. She consents that the association of clandestine marriage with Catholic nuptial rites may "have made them decidedly less sympathetic to an Elizabethan audience than they seem to contemporary theatergoers."[11] Lawrence Stone has even gone so far to claim that an early modern audience would have been entirely disapproving of the lovers since they bring "destruction upon themselves by violating the norms of the society in which they lived."[12] An early modern audience, therefore, may have been ready to condemn Romeo and Juliet for similar reasons that they would condemn Annabella and Giovanni.

Shakespeare's tragedy, however, easily affords a sympathetic reading of the young lovers. In *Romeo and Juliet*, clandestine marriage does not serve as a site of deception for the purpose of sexual fulfillment that so often marks the negative literary portrayals of clandestine marriage that we have seen. Instead, Juliet rejects the hastiness sometimes associated with irregular unions when proclaiming during the balcony scene, "I have no joy of this contract to-night" (2.2.117). Even though she agrees to exchange "love's faithful vow" (2.2.127) with Romeo, which could serve as a *de praesenti* contract, she also insists that they properly solemnize their nuptials so that the vows are not "too rash, too unadvis'd, too sudden" (2.2.118) (or at least are less so). She dictates her terms to Romeo. By insisting that they participate in the religious "rite," she refuses to acknowledge a mere "contract" as a marriage, even though such a contract would have been legally binding under canon law. In doing so, Juliet ensures that Romeo cannot renege on his marital vows, and that the basis of his vows does not derive from desire alone—he must profess a love for her that will last over time in the presence of at least one other witness (i.e., Friar Laurence). Romeo's willingness to participate in an actual solemnization confirms the sincerity of his matrimonial promises in the eyes of both Juliet and the audience.

Since Annabella and Giovanni are siblings, they cannot gain the consent of even an unscrupulous friar to marry them via a religious solemnization. The horrified Bonaventura associates Giovanni's incestuous lust with a "devilish atheism" (1.1.8) that "fill[s] the world."[13] Richard A. McCabe observes that Giovanni's rejection of religious precepts "reflects that of a new and more rationalistic age."[14] When justifying his love for his sister, however, Giovanni's language echoes that of the Protestant marital discourses that championed the virtues of wedded love, and that might have made an early modern audience more open to Shakespeare's young lovers. He proclaims:

> Say that we had one father, say one womb
> (Curse to my joys) gave both us life and birth:
> Are we not therefore each to other bound
> So much the more by nature, by the links
> Of blood, of reason, nay, if you will have't,
> Even of religion, to be ever one—
> One soul, one flesh, one love, one heart, one all?
>
> *(1.1.28–34)*

Giovanni's obsession with disputation hinges on his attempt to situate his desire within a widely accepted religious framework. Here he conjures the popular biblical definition of marriage that a man and woman become "one flesh" (Genesis 2:24). According to Giovanni's perverse logic, the fact that he and Annabella already make up "one flesh" since they shared "one womb" means that, in a sense, they are married already. Shockingly, the kind of discourse that allows Protestant Reformers to exalt the marital bond in similar terms serves Giovanni's attempt to justify entering into a sexual relationship with his sister. The discourse of wedded love that many scholars now view as one of the period's defining legacies, a discourse that contributed to the rise of companionate marriage, thus fuels the first portrayal of sibling incest on the early modern stage.

Annabella and Giovanni cannot solemnize their marriage as do Romeo and Juliet, but the practice of clandestine marriage enables them to imbue their vows of faith with marital meaning. After realizing that they love one another, they enter into a marital contract:

> *Annabella*:   On my knees,
> Brother, even by our mother's dust, I charge you,
> Do not betray me to your mirth or hate.
> Love me or kill me, brother.
> *Giovanni*:   On my knees,
> Sister, even by my mother's dust, I charge you,
> Do not betray me to your mirth or hate.
> Love me or kill me, sister.
>
> *(1.2.261–267)*

This scene resembles the clandestine contract between the Duchess and Antonio in *The Duchess of Malfi*, discussed in the introduction.[15] Quite unlike the Duchess and Antonio's expressions of love and fidelity, Annabella and Giovanni's vows constitute a negative injunction: "love me or kill me." Their contract is perverse, but it also carries weight and solemnity. The siblings seal their "troth" with a kiss before consummating the match. While an early modern audience would not have believed that Annabella and Giovanni could enter into a legal union, neither could Romeo and Juliet, at least not without parental consent. By lowering the age of his heroine from his source's sixteen to having "not seen the change of fourteen years" (1.2.9), Shakespeare distances his fiction of clandestine marriage from actual marital law in early modern England. That does not keep us—or their fellow characters—from taking their union seriously, however. In a conversation with her father, Annabella further reveals that she and Giovanni have exchanged tokens symbolizing their union:

> *Florio*: Where's the ring,
>   That which your mother in her will bequeathed
>   And charged you on her blessing not to give't
>   To any but your husband? Send back that.
> *Annabella*: I have it not.
> *Florio*: Ha! have it not? Where is't?
> *Annabella*: My brother in the morning took it from me,
>   Said he would wear't today
>
> *(2.6.39–45)*

The disappointed Florio has no choice but to accept Annabella's willingness to part from the ring as a sign of youthful caprice. The reader knows, however, that Annabella believes Giovanni to be the "husband" to whom her mother "charg'd" her to give the ring. The fact that Annabella makes this statement so openly, even though her father cannot possibly understand its meaning, demonstrates the extent to which she believes her relationship with her brother constitutes a veritable marriage. The brother and sister do not consider themselves to be merely fulfilling their sexual desire. They have entered into a bond of love that carries marital significance.

Both the Elizabethan and Caroline plays demonstrate that clandestine marriage creates another important marital problem (explored in chapter 3): bigamy. Juliet's nurse experiences no qualms when suggesting that Juliet enter into a second marriage with Paris (who makes Romeo look like a "dishclout" [3.5.219] anyway). Indeed, once Juliet finds herself betrothed to Paris against her will, her nurse suggests that her young charge simply move forward with the marriage:

> I think it best you married with the County.
> .   .   .   .
> Beshrow my very heart,
> I think you are happy in this second match,
> For it excels your first; or if it did not,
> Your first is dead, or 'twere as good he were
> As living here and you no use of him.
>
> (3.5.217–225)

The nurse implies that Juliet's father has made a better match for Juliet than Juliet has made for herself—a statement with which an early modern audience would probably agree. Furthermore, since Romeo's exile means that he and Juliet cannot cohabitate, the nurse reasons that they do not have a proper marriage. Romeo and Juliet's inability to fulfill their domestic duties associated with marriage, to be "of use," means that, in the nurse's mind, the marriage does not exist. For all essential purposes, Romeo "is dead, or 'twere as good as he were," since they cannot establish a household together. The nurse thus makes a valiant (though shaky) effort to invalidate Juliet's first marriage within a legal framework (Romeo's dead anyway) so as to make room for a new one. Since Juliet makes her marital vows clandestinely, the nurse argues, they have no social currency.

The idea that private and public contracts can exist simultaneously also makes room for bigamy in 'Tis Pity She's a Whore. The friar forwards a public solemnization of a marriage as a solution to Annabella's pregnancy. He announces, "'Tis thus agreed: / First, for your honour's safety, that you marry / The Lord Soranzo" (3.6.35–37). He further implies that her marriage to Soranzo will go hand in hand with the dissolution of her incestuous relationship when continuing: "next, to save your soul, / Leave off this life and henceforth live to him" (3.6.37–38). The friar oversees a handfasting between Annabella and Soranzo to ensure that she will go through with the match, but he also insists that the handfasting does not constitute a marriage when stating that he will "perform [the ceremony] on the morning sun" (3.6.55). In her private confession, Annabella acknowledges that her ceremonial marriage with Soranzo takes precedence over her incestuous contract with Giovanni. She prays that the "blessed friar" has "joined in ceremonial knot my hand / To him whose wife I now am" (5.1.24–26). Following the lead of Juliet's nurse, Annabella believes that the public ceremony trumps clandestine vows.

Giovanni, however, rejects such claims. Insisting that his union with Annabella constitutes one of "matchless love" (2.5.46), he proclaims that Annabella's marriage with Soranzo will "damn her" (2.5.41) rather than result in her salvation. As McCabe observes, "Scene by scene the distinction between marriage, fornication, and adultery is . . . eroded."[16] In Giovanni's mind, however, his marriage to Annabella remains irrevocable—just as Juliet views her own marriage to Romeo. He will not live in bigamy. In the end, Giovanni kills Annabella rather than releasing her from their marriage vows, which did include the imperative "Love me or kill me" after all. Both his refusal to release Annabella from the bonds of matrimony and his insistence on adhering to their vows' violent undertones point to the dangers of assuming that one could easily get out of an ill-advised irregular union, even an incestuous one.

While Shakespeare's tragedy affords some sympathy for the young lovers, Ford's play reveals that such sympathetic portrayals of clandestine marriage are no longer possible. When Giovanni enters the stage with Annabella's heart on a dagger, any sympathy we had for the young lovers, or at least for Giovanni, is gone.[17] 'Tis Pity does not end with an attempt at reconciliation as does Romeo and Juliet, but with a corrupt cardinal remarking: "Of one so young, so rich in nature's store, / Who could not say ''Tis pity she's a whore?'" (5.6.162–163). Annabella and Giovanni will not be remembered for their love and commitment to one another, as are Romeo and Juliet, but for Annabella's whorish nature. As we have seen again and again, people, particularly women, who marry clandestinely open themselves up to unsavory perceptions, whether those perceptions are fair and warranted or not. Annabella and Giovanni's love may elicit our pity, but not our admiration.

Ford's dark revision of Shakespeare's play thus suggests a fear that the practice of clandestine marriage could result in couples not just eloping in defiance of their family's wishes but marrying clandestinely in defiance of the very laws of nature.[18] In penning his cautionary tale, therefore, Ford points to the dangers of England's continued adherence to Roman canon law long after Spenser's rejection of it in *The Faerie Queene*, book I, and during a time when Catholicism held favor in the English court. In Ford's play, the discourses of wedded love that became so popular during the early modern period become unmoored from any legal apparatus, encouraging couples to define the marital bond, at least within the realm of fiction, entirely for themselves.

Notes

Introduction

1. All Shakespeare quotations are from *The Riverside Shakespeare*, ed. G. Blakemore Evans et al., 2nd ed. (Boston: Houghton Mifflin, 1997) and are cited parenthetically in text.

2. *The Book of Common Prayer: The Texts of 1549, 1559, and 1662*, ed. Brian Cummings (Oxford: Oxford University Press, 2011), 157.

3. *Book of Common Prayer*, 158.

4. David Bevington observes, for instance, that wedding ceremonies rarely occurred on the early modern stage because they were boring and illegal due to the "governmental strictures against derogation or abuse of the *Book of Common Prayer*." David Bevington, *Action Is Eloquence: Shakespeare's Language of Gesture* (Cambridge, MA: Harvard University Press, 1984), 142.

5. For his history of the practice, see R. B. Outhwaite, *Clandestine Marriage in England, 1500–1850* (London: Hambledon Press, 1995). See also Eric Josef Carlson, *Marriage and the English Reformation: Family, Sexuality and Social Relations in Past Times* (Oxford: Blackwell, 1994), 88–102; and Lawrence Stone, *Uncertain Unions: Marriage in England 1660–1753* (Oxford: Oxford University Press, 1992), 22–32.

6. See B. J. Sokol and Mary Sokol, *Shakespeare, Law, and Marriage* (Cambridge: Cambridge University Press, 2003), 93–116; and Ann Jennalie Cook, *Making a Match: Courtship in Shakespeare and His Society* (Princeton, NJ: Princeton University Press, 1991), 185–233. In her *Courtships, Marriage Customs, and Shakespeare's Comedies* (New York: Palgrave Macmillan, 2006), Loreen L. Giese draws on court depositions, which frequently describe clandestine marriages, to contextualize courtship and marriage in *The Two Gentlemen of Verona* and *Twelfth Night*. For her incredible work cataloging consistory court depositions in the London Metropolitan Archives, see Loreen L. Giese, *London Consistory Court Depositions, 1586–1611* (London: London Record Society, 1995). I draw on her invaluable research throughout this book to identify records pertaining to clandestine marriages.

7. *Oxford English Dictionary*, s.v. "clandestine, adj."

8. Medieval church law largely derives from the *Concordance of Discordant Canons* of Gratian of Bologna (ca. 1140) and the *Decretals of Gregory IX* (1234). Together, these volumes make up the *Corpus of Canon Law*, or the law "canonized" by the pope. For the canons on the legality of clandestine marriages, see Gratian 2.30.5–10. The fourth book of the *Decretals* includes a section entitled *De clandestine desponsatione*. For scholarship on medieval canon law, see R. H. Helmholz, *Marriage Litigation in Medieval England* (Cambridge: Cambridge University Press, 1974); and R. H. Helmholz, *Roman*

Canon Law in Reformation England (Cambridge: Cambridge University Press, 1990), 1–27.

9. See Henry Swinburne, *A Treatise of Spousals, or Matrimonial Contracts* (London, 1686). Swinburne wrote this treatise, published posthumously, circa 1600. The treatise's length (240 pages) demonstrates the anxiety concerning spousal vows.

10. For a more detailed explanation of the definition and division of spousal vows, see Swinburne, *Treatise of Spousals*, 5–11.

11. Swinburne, 8.

12. Swinburne, 12.

13. See Martin Ingram, *Church Courts, Sex and Marriage in England, 1570–1640* (Cambridge: Cambridge University Press, 1987); and Ralph Houlbrooke, *Church Courts and the People during the English Reformation, 1520–1570* (Oxford: Oxford University Press, 1979).

14. On the canons relating to marriage, see Helmholz, *Roman Canon Law*, 69–73.

15. Punishments usually included fines or excommunication. On the punishments of the church courts, see Ingram, *Church Courts*, 215–218.

16. Ingram, 213.

17. Outhwaite, *Clandestine Marriage*, 20. Following Outhwaite's lead, I use the terms "irregular union" and "clandestine marriage" interchangeably.

18. I have condensed Outhwaite's categories for the sake of brevity and to include only those categories that pertain to pre-Restoration England. For more detail on these levels of clandestinity, see Outhwaite, *Clandestine Marriage*, 19–50.

19. Peter Holland, "Shakespeare, William (1564–1616)," in *Oxford Dictionary of National Biography*, ed. David Cannadine (Oxford: Oxford University Press, 2004). Holland also informs: "The vicar who officiated at Temple Grafton, if that was indeed where they married, was John Frith, known for his ability to cure hawks but also 'Unsound in religion', according to a survey in 1586 of the Warwickshire clergy, again a possible indication of Shakespeare's Catholicism." See Samuel Schoenbaum, *William Shakespeare: A Documentary Life* (Oxford: Oxford University Press, 1975), 71.

20. On the Fleet marriages, see Roger Lee Brown, "The Rise and Fall of the Fleet Marriages," in *Marriage and Society: Studies in the Social History of Marriage*, ed. R. B. Outhwaite (London: Europa Publications, 1981), 117–136; and John Southerden Burn, *The Fleet Registers: Comprising the History of Fleet Marriages and Some Account of the Parsons and Marriage-House Keepers* (London: Rivingtons, 1833).

21. Burn, *Fleet Registers*, 12.

22. Heinrich Bullinger, *The Christen State of Matrymonye* (London, 1552).

23. See William Gouge, *Of Domesticall Duties* (London, 1622); and Robert Cleaver, *A Godlie Forme of Hovsholde Government* (London, 1598).

24. Gouge, *Of Domesticall Duties*, 205.

25. *Book of Common Prayer*, 157.

26. Lawrence Stone, *The Family, Sex and Marriage in England, 1500–1800* (New York: Harper & Row, 1977); and Steven Ozment, *When Fathers Ruled: Family Life in Reformation Europe* (Cambridge, MA: Harvard University Press, 1983). Ozment corrects Stone's portrait of early modern life as being devoid of affect, although his insistence that patriarchy fostered warm and loving families sometimes borders on the extreme. Literary scholars have since questioned the rise of companionate marriages. On the

incompatibility between companionate marriage and marital hierarchy, see Frances E. Dolan, *Marriage and Violence: The Early Modern Legacy* (Philadelphia: University of Pennsylvania Press, 2008).

27. Carlson, *Marriage and the English Reformation*, 107–108.

28. Bullinger, *Christen State*, fol. 54v.

29. Transcript of the proceedings, with depositions, etc., of a royal commission to enquire into an alleged marriage between Edward Seymour, Earl of Hertford, and the Lady Katherine Grey, 7 Feb 1562–12 May 1562, British Library Add. MS 33749, 45v.

30. British Library Add. MS 33749, 30v.

31. While no evidence indicates Lady Katherine's intent to seize the throne, Queen Elizabeth's fears were not unjustified. Henry VIII's will made Lady Katherine one of his direct heirs, and Lady Katherine's sister, the unfortunate Jane Grey, had already been executed for participating in a plot to take the throne.

32. British Library Add. MS 33749, 43v.

33. British Library Add. MS 33749, 44r.

34. British Library Add. MS 33749, 44r.

35. British Library Add. MS 33749, 31r.

36. On the historical Duchess of Amalfi and Webster's sources, see Leah S. Marcus, introduction to *The Duchess of Malfi*, by John Webster, ed. Leah S. Marcus (London: Arden Early Modern Drama, 2009), 16–23. On how Webster's play references the clandestine marriage of Arbella Stuart, see Sara Jayne Steen, "The Crime of Marriage: Arbella Stuart and *The Duchess of Malfi*," *Sixteenth Century Journal* 22, no. 1 (1991): 61–76.

37. All Webster quotations are from *The Duchess of Malfi*, ed. Leah S. Marcus (London: Arden Early Modern Drama, 2009) and are cited parenthetically in text.

38. David Colclough, "Donne, John (1572–1631)," in *Oxford Dictionary of National Biography*, ed. David Cannadine (Oxford: Oxford University Press, 2004).

39. John Carey, *John Donne: Life, Mind and Art* (London: Faber and Faber, 1981), 58.

40. M. Thomas Hester, Robert Parker Sorlien, and Dennis Flynn, eds., *John Donne's Marriage Letters in the Folger Shakespeare Library* (Washington, DC: Folger Shakespeare Library, 2005), 16.

41. Carey, *John Donne*, 58–59.

42. Henry Ansgar Kelly, *Love and Marriage in the Age of Chaucer* (Ithaca, NY: Cornell University Press, 1975), 165.

43. Kelly, 177. For his full argument on clandestine marriage in the Middle Ages and in medieval literature, see Kelly, 163–244.

44. Brian Cummings, "Notes to Matrimony 1549," in *The Book of Common Prayer: The Texts of 1549, 1559, and 1662*, ed. Brian Cummings (Oxford: Oxford University Press, 2011), 711.

45. For the Elizabethan *Book of Common Prayer*'s marriage service, see *Book of Common Prayer*, 157–164. For the Sarum's marriage service, see *Manuale ad vsum percelebris ecclesie Sarisburiensis* (Rouen, 1543), fol. 47r–56r.

46. Cummings, "Notes to Matrimony," 712.

47. *Book of Common Prayer*, 157.

48. *Book of Common Prayer*, 157.

49. *Book of Common Prayer*, 160.

50. Gouge, *Of Domesticall Duties*, 205.

51. Gouge, 205.

52. John Donne, "Sermon Preached at a Mariage (the marriage of Mistress Margaret Washington at the church of St. Clement Danes, May 30, 1621)," in *The Sermons of John Donne*, vol. 3, no. 11, ed. Evelyn Mary Spearing Simpson and George Reuben Potter (Berkeley: University of California Press, 1957), 3–4.

53. Gouge, *Of Domesticall Duties*, 205.

1. Reforming Clandestine Marriage in Spenser's *Faerie Queene*, Book I

1. See David Quint, "The Boat of Romance and Renaissance Epic," in *Romance: Generic Transformation from Chrétien de Troyes to Cervantes*, ed. Kevin Brownlee and Marina Scordilis Brownlee (Hanover, NH: University Press of New England, 1985), 178–202; David Quint, *Epic and Empire: Politics and Generic Form from Virgil to Milton* (Princeton, NJ: Princeton University Press, 1993); Patricia A. Parker, *Inescapable Romance: Studies in the Poetics of a Mode* (Princeton, NJ: Princeton University Press, 1979); and Barbara Fuchs, *Romance* (New York: Routledge, 2004).

2. On Spenser's theological allegory, see Darryl J. Gless, *Interpretation and Theology in Spenser* (Cambridge: Cambridge University Press, 1994). For an analysis of English Reformation iconography, see John N. King, *Tudor Royal Iconography: Literature and Art in an Age of Religious Crisis* (Princeton, NJ: Princeton University Press, 1989).

3. For his argument on the relationship between the *Book of Common Prayer* and English national identity, see Timothy Rosendale, *Liturgy and Literature in the Making of Protestant England* (Cambridge: Cambridge University Press, 2007), 34–69.

4. Rosendale, 37.

5. Rosendale, 38.

6. C. S. Lewis, *The Allegory of Love: A Study in Medieval Tradition* (Oxford: Oxford University Press, 1936), 338–347. For an extension of Lewis's thesis, see James W. Broaddus, *Spenser's Allegory of Love: Social Vision in Books III, IV, and V of "The Faerie Queene"* (Madison, NJ: Farleigh Dickinson University Press, 1995). See also Thomas P. Roche Jr., *The Kindly Flame: A Study of the Third and Fourth Books of Spenser's "Faerie Queene"* (Princeton, NJ: Princeton University Press, 1964); and Lauren Silberman, *Transforming Desire: Erotic Knowledge in Books III and IV of "The Faerie Queene"* (Berkeley: University of California Press, 1995).

7. See John N. King, *Spenser's Poetry and the Reformation Tradition* (Princeton, NJ: Princeton University Press, 1990), 155; and Richard Mallette, *Spenser and the Discourses of Reformation* (Lincoln: University of Nebraska Press, 1997), 84–142.

8. Andrew Zurcher, *Spenser's Legal Language: Law and Poetry in Early Modern England* (Cambridge: D. S. Brewer, 2007), 89.

9. Andrew Hadfield, "Spenser and Religion—yet Again," *Studies in English Literature, 1500–1900* 51, no. 1 (2011): 35.

10. E. W. Ives, "Henry VIII (1491–1547)," in *Oxford Dictionary of National Biography*, ed. David Cannadine (Oxford: Oxford University Press, 2004). On Henry VIII's separation from Catherine of Aragon and marriage to Anne Boleyn, see also Eric Josef Carlson, *Marriage and the English Reformation: Family, Sexuality and Social Relations in Past Times* (Oxford: Wiley-Blackwell, 1994), 67–73; and Carole Levin, *The Reign of Elizabeth I* (New York: Palgrave, 2002), 5–8.

11. Ives, "Henry VIII."

12. Martin Luther, "An Open Letter to the Christian Nobility," in *Works of Martin Luther*, trans. Charles M. Jacobs (Philadelphia: A.J. Holman Company, 1915), 2:149.

13. Carlson, *Marriage and the English Reformation*, 67.

14. John Calvin, *Institutes of the Christian Religion*, ed. John T. McNeill, trans. Ford Lewis Battles (Philadelphia: Westminster Press, 1960), 2:1484.

15. Calvin, 1:405.

16. Martin Bucer, "De Regno Christi," in *Melanchthon and Bucer*, ed. and trans. Wilhelm Pauck (Philadelphia: Westminster Press, 1969), 320.

17. See Carlson, *Marriage and the English Reformation*, 42. The Ten Articles reduce the number of sacraments from seven (Baptism, Penance, Holy Eucharist, Matrimony, Confirmation, Holy Orders, and Extreme Unction) to three (Baptism, Penance, and Holy Eucharist). The Thirty-Nine Articles (1563), which continue to serve as the basis of Anglican Church doctrine, recognize only two sacraments: Baptism and Holy Eucharist.

18. Carlson, *Marriage and the English Reformation*, 42–43.

19. Helmholz, *Roman Canon Law*, 69. On how the medieval English church had been moving toward this Tridentine reform, see Sue Niebrzydowski, "Encouraging Marriage in facie ecclesiae: The Mary Play 'Betrothal' and the Sarum Ordo ad faciendum Sponsalia," *Medieval English Theatre* 24 (2002): 44–61.

20. On the *Reformatio Legum Ecclesiasticarum*, see Helmholz, *Roman Canon Law*, 35–37.

21. Ingram, *Church Courts*, 192–193. Ingram specifically looks at the spousal contracts in Wiltshire during the years 1565–1640.

22. Outhwaite, *Clandestine Marriage*, 21–26. See also Carlson, *Marriage and the English Reformation*, 124–126.

23. Helmholz, *Roman Canon Law*, 72.

24. Helmholz, 72.

25. *Book of Common Prayer*, 192.

26. For their recounts of their English exploits, see William Weston, *The Autobiography of an Elizabethan*, trans. Philip Caraman (London: Longmans, Green, 1955); and John Gerard, *The Autobiography of an Elizabethan*, trans. Philip Caraman (London: Longmans, Green, 1956).

27. David Cressy, *Birth, Marriage, and Death: Ritual, Religion, and the Life Cycle in Tudor and Stuart England* (Oxford: Oxford University Press, 1997), 322.

28. Cressy, 322.

29. Dom Hugh Aveling, "The Marriages of Catholic Recusants, 1559–1642," *Journal of Ecclesiastical History* 14, no. 1 (1963): 74. Aveling further observes that marrying in the Protestant church appears to have been "tantamount to apostasy" for recusants (71).

30. Eric Josef Carlson, "Marriage Reform and the Elizabethan High Commission," *Sixteenth Century Journal* 21, no. 3 (1990): 449.

31. Carlson, 449.

32. Carlson, 448.

33. In his introduction to *The Book of Common Prayer: The Texts of 1549, 1559, and 1662* (Oxford: Oxford University Press, 2011), Brian Cummings confirms that "Archbishop John Whitgift imposed severe sanctions against those who refused to accept

the Act of Uniformity. . . . Opposition to the bishops became tantamount to sedition against the monarch, so increasingly what now seem arcane questions of church furniture and dress and custom became pointed scenes of dissent" (xxxvi).

34. Carlson, "Marriage Reform," 449.

35. See Susan Doran, "Keys [*née* Grey], Lady Mary: (1545?–1578)," in *Oxford Dictionary of National Biography*, ed. David Cannadine (Oxford: Oxford University Press, 2004). Other courtiers who had clandestine marriages include Henry Wriothesley (Elizabeth Vernon), Mary Shelton (John Scudamore), and Bridget Manners (Robert Tyrwith).

36. Johanna Rickman, *Love, Lust, and License in Early Modern England: Illicit Sex and the Nobility* (Burlington, VT: Ashgate, 2008), 68. The increase in clandestine marriages suggests that while courtiers clearly felt that they could not gain the queen's initial consent for their unions, they were willing to hazard her displeasure. A few months in the Fleet or a temporary exile from court was apparently worth the risk to marry one's beloved.

37. Rickman, 43.

38. Rickman, 68.

39. Rickman, 39.

40. Lord Thomas Howard and Margaret Douglas are the most famous victims of this decree. See David M. Head, "'Beyng Ledde and Seduced by the Devyll': The Attainder of Lord Thomas Howard and the Tudor Law of Treason," *Sixteenth Century Journal* 13, no. 4 (1982): 3–16.

41. John Strype, *The Life and Acts of John Whitgift, D.D.: The Third and Last Lord Archbishop of Canterbury in the Reign of Queen Elizabeth* (Oxford: Clarendon Press, 1822), 2: 400.

42. Hadfield, "Spenser and Religion," 29.

43. All Spenser quotations are from *The Faerie Queene*, ed. A. C. Hamilton, Hiroshi Yamashita, and Toshiyuki Suzuki, 2nd ed. (Harlow: Longman, 2001) and are cited parenthetically in text.

44. *Oxford English Dictionary*, s.v. "assurance, n.," I.1a-b.

45. *Oxford English Dictionary*, s.v. "assurance, n.," I.2.

46. See, for example, Catullus's Carmen 61.

47. On the anti-epithalamion as a genre, see Virgina Tufte, *The Poetry of Marriage: The Epithalamium in Europe and Its Development in England* (Los Angeles: Tinnon-Brown, 1970), 37–56.

48. On Duessa's connection to the Catholic Church, see Gless, *Interpretation and Theology*, 123–125; King, *Tudor Royal Iconography*, 118–119; and D. Douglas Waters, *Duessa as Theological Satire* (Columbia: University of Missouri Press, 1970). On Duessa as a possible figure of Elizabeth, see Andrew Hadfield, "Duessa's Trial and Elizabeth's Error: Judging Elizabeth in Spenser's *Faerie Queene*," in *The Myth of Elizabeth*, ed. Susan Doran and Thomas S. Freeman (London: Palgrave Macmillan, 2003), 56–76.

49. Gouge, *Of Domesticall Duties*, 205.

50. Richard A. McCabe has urged scholars to be more willing to connect Duessa's identity in book I with her identity in book V. See McCabe, "The Masks of Duessa: Spenser, Mary Queen of Scots, and James VI," *English Literary Renaissance* 17, no. 2 (1987): 224–242. On Duessa's role as a figure for Mary, Queen of Scots, see Anthea

Hume, "Duessa," in *The Spenser Encyclopedia*, ed. A. C. Hamilton, Donald Cheney, W. F. Blissett, David A. Richardson, and William W. Barker (Toronto: University of Toronto Press, 1990), 229–230; and Andrew Hadfield, *Edmund Spenser: A Life* (Oxford: Oxford University Press, 2012), 193–194.

51. On Thomas Howard and the Norfolk affair, see Michael A. R. Graves, "Howard, Thomas, Fourth Duke of Norfolk (1538–1572)," in *Oxford Dictionary of National Biography*, ed. David Cannadine (Oxford: Oxford University Press, 2004).

52. On Redcrosse's omission of his relationship with Duessa as representative of *The Faerie Queene*'s general narrative inconsistencies, see Jacqueline T. Miller, "The Omission in Red Cross Knight's Story: Narrative Inconsistencies in *The Faerie Queene*," *ELH* 53, no. 2 (1986): 279–288.

53. For his "survey" of Spenser's legal diction, see Zurcher, *Spenser's Legal Language*, 82–88.

54. On Duessa as a Dido figure, see John Watkins, *The Specter of Dido: Spenser and Virgilian Epic* (New Haven, CT: Yale University Press, 1995), 90–112.

55. Virgil, *Aeneid*, trans. H. Rushton Fairclough, Loeb Classical Library 63 (Cambridge, MA: Harvard University Press, 1967), IV.125–127.

56. Virgil, IV.172.

57. I would like to thank Ryan Crennen for this alternative reading of the Latin.

58. Colin Burrow, *Epic Romance: Homer to Milton* (Oxford: Clarendon Press, 1993), 36–39.

59. On Augustine's Christianized reading of the Dido episode, see Robert R. Edwards, *The Flight from Desire: Augustine and Ovid to Chaucer* (New York: Palgrave Macmillan, 2006), 25–27.

60. Ovid, *Heroides*, 2nd ed. revised by G. P. Goold, trans. and ed. Grant Showerman, Loeb Classical Library 41 (Cambridge, MA: Harvard University Press, 1977), VII.92.

61. Ovid, VII.17.

62. Spenser's opening lines of *The Faerie Queene* specifically imitate the lines prefixed to early modern editions of the *Aeneid*, which reference the Virgilian career path, or the "rota Virgiliana." Spenser then surpasses Virgil's intent by claiming an intent to sing not only of "arma virumque" (arms and the man) (I.1) but of "Knights and Ladies gentle deeds" (I.Proem.1.5). On the "rota Virgiliana," see Katharine Cleland, "Rota Virgiliana," in *The Princeton Encyclopedia of Poetry and Poetics*, ed. Roland Greene and Stephen Cushman, 4th ed. (Princeton, NJ: Princeton University Press, 2012), 1226–1227. On how Spenser's own literary career revises and Christianizes the "rota Virgiliana," see Patrick Cheney, *Spenser's Famous Flight: A Renaissance Idea of a Literary Career* (Toronto: University of Toronto Press, 1993); and David Scott Wilson-Okamura, "Problems in the Virgilian Career," *Spenser Studies* 26 (2011): 1–30.

63. Gouge, *Of Domesticall Duties*, 201.

64. Hadfield, "Spenser and Religion," 34.

65. Hadfield, "Duessa's Trial," 57 (emphasis mine). See also King, *Spenser's Poetry and the Reformation Tradition*, 142; Douglas Brooks-Davies, "Una," in *The Spenser Encyclopedia*, ed. A. C. Hamilton, Donald Cheney, W. F. Blissett, David A Richardson, and William W. Barker (Toronto: University of Toronto Press, 1990), 704–705; Andrew Hadfield, "John Bale and the Time of the Nation," in *Literature, Politics, and National*

Identity: Reformation to Renaissance (Cambridge: Cambridge University Press, 1994), 51–80.

66. *Book of Common Prayer*, 159.

67. *Manuale ad vsum*, fol. 48r.

68. On the relationship between the betrothal scene and the *Sarum Missal*, see Harold L. Weatherby, *Mirrors of Celestial Grace: Patristic Theology in Spenser's Allegory* (Toronto: University of Toronto Press, 1994), 61–75; and Hadfield, "Spenser and Religion," 31.

69. Gouge, *Of Domesticall Duties*, 200.

70. Broaddus, *Spenser's Allegory of Love*, 50. See also Lewis, *Allegory of Love*, 339; A. C. Hamilton, *The Structure of Allegory in "The Faerie Queene"* (Oxford: Clarendon Press, 1961), 168–169; Roche, *Kindly Flame*, 168; Paul J. Alpers, *The Poetry of "The Faerie Queene"* (Princeton, NJ: Princeton University Press, 1967), 120–122.

71. Rachel E. Hile, "The Limitations of Concord in the Thames-Medway Marriage Canto of *The Faerie Queene*," *Studies in Philology* 108, no. 1 (2011): 79.

72. Lisa Celovsky, "Early Modern Masculinities and *The Faerie Queene*," *English Literary Renaissance* 35, no. 2 (2005): 210–247.

73. Gouge, *Of Domesticall Duties*, 203.

74. Heinrich Bullinger, *The Christen State of Matrymonye* (London, 1552), fol. 54r.

75. Letter to Robert Cecil, January 1594/5, quoted in J. R. Brink, "The Masque of the Nine Muses: Sir John Davies's Unpublished 'Epithalamion' and the 'Belphoebe-Ruby' Episode in *The Faerie Queene*," *Review of English Studies* 23, no. 92 (1972): 446. On the Belphoebe/Timias episode and the Ralegh-Throckmorton affair, see also William A. Oram, "Spenser's Raleghs," *Studies in Philology* 87, no. 3 (1990): 341–362, esp. 354–362; William A. Oram, "Elizabethan Fact and Spenserian Fiction," *Spenser Studies* 4 (1983): 33–47; and Cheney, *Spenser's Famous Flight*, 111–148.

76. In Longus's *Daphnis and Chloe*, the titular couple are both exposed at birth and brought up by shepherds, only to have their nobility later revealed.

77. *Oxford English Dictionary*, s.v. "closely, adv.," 3.

78. The *Oxford English Dictionary* defines "wed" as "to become the spouse of (a person) by participating in a *prescribed ceremony*" (emphasis mine). *Oxford English Dictionary*, s.v. "wed, v.," 3a.

79. In "The Uncertainty of Courtesy in Book VI of *The Faerie Queene*," *Spenser Studies* 14 (2000): 215–232, Douglas A. Northrop observes that "Book Six in particular is generally seen as lacking sustained or even significant incidental allusion to historical persons or events," and none of the episodes "increase our general understanding of courtesy" (215). He does not mention Pastorella's parents.

80. See Susan Doran, "Seymour [née Grey], Katherine, Countess of Hertford: (1540?–1568)," in *Oxford Dictionary of National Biography*, ed. David Cannadine (Oxford: Oxford University Press, 2004).

81. M. Lindsay Kaplan, *The Culture of Slander in Early Modern England* (Cambridge: Cambridge University Press, 1997), 16.

82. See James Nohrnberg, *The Analogy of "The Faerie Queene"* (Princeton, NJ: Princeton University Press, 1976), 732–733.

83. The relationship between the 1590 (books I–III) and 1596 (books IV–VI) editions of *The Faerie Queene* has long been elusive. On the unity of *The Faerie Queene*, see

Northrop Frye, "The Structure of Imagery in *The Faerie Queene*," in *Fables of Identity: Studies in Poetic Mythology* (New York: Harcourt, Brace & World, 1963), 69–87. Frye argues that the first three books reflect and enhance the second three books. According to this theory, books I and VI, II and V, and III and IV are "analogous" to each other. On the potential shift in Spenser's political outlook between the 1590 and 1596 editions, typically reading the 1590 edition as celebrating Elizabeth, while reading the 1596 edition as reflecting Spenser's disillusionment with Elizabeth's reign and even with his entire poetic project, see Richard Neuse, "Book VI as Conclusion to *The Faerie Queene*," *ELH* 35, no. 3 (1968): 329–353. For an overview of the scholarly disappointment in the 1596 edition, see Theresa Krier, "*The Faerie Queene* (1596)," in *A Critical Companion to Spenser Studies*, ed. Bart van Es (New York: Palgrave Macmillan, 2006), 191–193.

84. Isabel G. MacCaffrey, *Spenser's Allegory: The Anatomy of Imagination* (Princeton, NJ: Princeton University Press, 1976), 388.

2. "Wanton Loves and Young Desires"

1. Marlowe used Musaeus's *Hero and Leander* as his source text, but he expands on and embellishes the original. With its 409 heroic couplets, Marlowe's "unfinished" poem is three times as long as Musaeus's version. See Gordon Braden, "The Divine Poem of Musaeus," in *The Classics and English Renaissance Poetry: Three Case Studies* (New Haven, CT: Yale University Press, 1978), 55–153. For an analysis of the four English versions of *Hero and Leander* written before 1700, see Stephen Orgel, "Musaeus in English," *George Herbert Journal* 29, nos. 1–2 (2005–2006): 67–75. For Marlowe's elaboration on his source text as a rhetorical exercise, see William P. Weaver, "Marlowe's Fable: *Hero and Leander* and the Rudiments of Eloquence," *Studies in Philology* 105, no. 3 (2008): 388–408. By looking to "the mechanics of rhetorical amplification," Weaver claims that "Marlowe's imitational technique in *Hero and Leander* derives from a grammar school exercise of paraphrasing short narratives" (390).

2. For scholarship that suggests the poem is unfinished, see Louis R. Zocca, "Marlowe and His Imitators," in *Elizabethan Narrative Poetry* (New York: Octagon Books, 1970), 232–247; and Douglas Bush, "Marlowe: *Hero and Leander*," in *Mythology and the Renaissance Tradition in English Poetry*, new rev. ed. (New York: W. W. Norton, 1963), 121–136. For the influential article that has encouraged scholars to view the poem as complete, see Marion Campbell, "'*Desunt Nonnulla*': The Construction of Marlowe's *Hero and Leander* as an Unfinished Poem," *English Literary History* 51, no. 2 (1984): 241–268. Campbell's essay provides extensive information on the poem's history, as well as a summary of the scholarship on the poem's status as a "fragment." See also W. L. Godshalk, "*Hero and Leander*: The Sense of an Ending," in "*A Poet and a Filthy Play-Maker*": *New Essays on Christopher Marlowe*, ed. Kenneth Friedenreich, Roma Gill, and Constance B. Kuriyama (New York: AMS Press, 1988), 293–314.

3. Ilona Bell claims that Elizabethan poets intended their love poetry to be read by a female audience. See Bell, *Elizabethan Women and the Poetry of Courtship* (Cambridge: Cambridge University Press, 1998).

4. Marlowe's rejection of the sonnet in favor of the Ovidian erotic narrative becomes significant when considering that other authors, such as Shakespeare, wrote both. On the lack of subjectivity in Marlowe's poetry, see Joanne Altieri, "*Hero and*

Leander: Sensible Myth and Lyric Subjectivity," *John Donne Journal* 8, nos. 1–2 (1989): 151–166. On Petrarchism's association with effeminacy, see Mark Breitenberg, *Anxious Masculinity in Early Modern England* (Cambridge: Cambridge University Press, 1996), esp. 134–136. For her classic work on Petrarchism and its widespread influence in Renaissance England, see Heather Dubrow, *Echoes of Desire: English Petrarchism and Its Counterdiscourses* (Ithaca, NY: Cornell University Press, 1995).

5. M. C. Bradbrook, *Shakespeare and Elizabethan Poetry: A Study of His Earlier Work in Relation to the Poetry of the Time* (London: Chatto and Windus, 1965), 59.

6. Scholars also use the term "epyllion" (or "minor epic") to refer to the Ovidian erotic narratives that were popular during the 1590s. See William Keach, *"Hero and Leander,"* in *Elizabethan Erotic Narratives: Irony and Pathos in the Ovidian Poetry of Shakespeare, Marlowe, and Their Contemporaries* (New Brunswick, NJ: Rutgers University Press, 1977), 85–116; Clark Hulse, *Metamorphic Verse: The Elizabethan Minor Epic* (Princeton, NJ: Princeton University Press, 1981); Georgia E. Brown, "Breaking the Canon: Marlowe's Challenge to the Literary Status Quo in *Hero and Leander,*" in *Marlowe, History, and Sexuality: New Critical Essays on Christopher Marlowe*, ed. Paul Whitfield White (New York: AMS Press, 1998), 59–76; and Brown, "Gender and Voice in *Hero and Leander,*" in *Constructing Christopher Marlowe*, ed. J. A. Downie and J. T. Parnell (Cambridge: Cambridge University Press, 2000), 148–163.

7. On the poem's homoeroticism, see Gregory W. Bredbeck, *Sodomy and Interpretation: Marlowe to Milton* (Ithaca, NY: Cornell University Press, 1991), 110–134; Bruce R. Smith, *Homosexual Desire in Shakespeare's England: A Cultural Poetics* (Chicago: University of Chicago Press, 1991), 132–136; and Jonathan Goldberg, *Sodometries: Renaissance Texts, Modern Sexualities* (Stanford, CA: Stanford University Press, 1992), 127–128. While Marlowe's inclusion of homoeroticism draws our attention to its presence, Alan Sinfield reminds us that "same-sex passion drew little attention" in Renaissance England. "Marlowe's Erotic Verse," in *Early Modern English Poetry: A Critical Companion*, ed. Patrick Cheney, Andrew Hadfield, and Garrett A. Sullivan Jr. (Oxford: Oxford University Press, 2007), 132.

8. Patrick Cheney explores the implications of Chapman's epic alterations in terms of Marlowe's Ovidian *cursus* in "Marlowe, Chapman, and the Rewriting of Spenser's England in *Hero and Leander,*" in *Marlowe's Counterfeit Profession: Ovid, Spenser, Counter-Nationhood* (Toronto: University of Toronto Press, 1997), 238–258.

9. Chapman's experimentation with the epyllion in *Ovid's Banquet of Sense* (1595) also implies that he did not have a problem with the sexual nature of the genre.

10. All quotations of Marlowe's *Hero and Leander* and Chapman's continuation are from *The Collected Poems of Christopher Marlowe*, ed. Patrick Cheney and Brian J. Striar (New York: Oxford University Press, 2006) and are cited parenthetically in text by sestiad and line number. For a study of Marlowe's fascination with the myth of Tantalus throughout his oeuvre, see Fred B. Tromly, *Playing with Desire: Christopher Marlowe and the Art of Tantalization* (Toronto: University of Toronto Press, 1998).

11. The *Oxford English Dictionary* defines "tender" as "to regard or receive favourably." *Oxford English Dictionary*, s.v. "tender, v.2," 3b.

12. Campbell, *"'Desunt Nonnulla,'"* 241.

13. Scholars have suggested that Marlowe here invites the male reader to participate in the narrator's homoerotic fantasies. In *Hero and Leander*, Keach observes: "The

fact that Leander elicits Marlowe's best erotic writing is not in itself as important as the way in which Marlowe projects a homoerotic fascination with Leander as part of the narrator's persona" (95). And Claude J. Summers argues that "the objectification of Leander is complemented by the poem's blithe assumption of a universal homoerotic impulse." "*Hero and Leander*: The Arbitrariness of Desire," in *Constructing Christopher Marlowe*, ed. J. A. Downie and J. T. Parnell (Cambridge: Cambridge University Press, 2000), 135. For a Freudian analysis of Hero and Leander's positions as desiring subjects and objects throughout the poem, see David Lee Miller, "The Death of the Modern: Gender and Desire in Marlowe's *Hero and Leander*," *South Atlantic Quarterly* 88, nos. 3–4 (1989): 757–787. Miller observes that "any person, male or female, may at a given time act as either the subject or object of desire" (779).

14. Brown, "Breaking the Canon," 64. William P. Walsh, however, disagrees that Marlowe flouts morality when arguing that "Marlowe gives us concrete moral grounds on which to condemn the passion of Hero and Leander." "Sexual Discovery and Renaissance Morality in Marlowe's *Hero and Leander*," *Studies in English Literature, 1500–1900* 12, no. 1 (1972): 34. Walsh makes his argument by claiming that Hero and Leander fail to view procreation as the endpoint of their passions.

15. In *Astrophel and Stella* (1591), Astrophel blames Cupid for making Stella's hair a net that traps her lovers (12.1–2), but the closest Astrophel gets to Stella is when she is sleeping in the Second Song. In his *Amoretti* (1595), Spenser claims that his beloved's hair is indistinguishable from its covering net of gold (37).

16. Burton's *Anatomy of Melancholy*, of course, was not the only such treatise. See also Ian Frederick Moulton, "Jacque Ferrand's *On Lovesickness*: Love and Medicine," in *Love in Print in the Sixteenth Century: The Popularization of Romance* (New York: Palgrave, 2014), 145–182.

17. On the relationship of love melancholy with Petrarchism, see Danila Sokolov, "'Love Gave the Wound, Which While I Breathe Will Bleed': Sidney's *Astrophil and Stella* and the Subject of Melancholy," *Sidney Journal* 30, no. 1 (2012): 27–50.

18. Robert Burton, *The Anatomy of Melancholy*, ed. Thomas C. Faulkner, Nicolas K. Kiessling, and Rhonda L. Blair, 6 vols. (Oxford: Clarendon Press, 1994), 3:149. Breitenberg explores the effeminizing nature of melancholy. in *Anxious Masculinity*, 35–68.

19. All quotations from "The Nymph's Reply" and from "The Passionate Shepherd to His Love" are from *The Collected Poems of Christopher Marlowe*, ed. Cheney and Striar, and are cited parenthetically in text.

20. See Catherine Bates, *The Rhetoric of Courtship in Elizabethan Language and Literature* (Cambridge: Cambridge University Press, 1992).

21. See Arthur Marotti, "'Love Is Not Love': Elizabethan Sonnet Sequences and the Social Order," *ELH* 49, no. 2 (1982): 396–428.

22. Cheney notes that "the 'minor epic' *Hero and Leander* endangers the erotic cult at the centre of Elizabethan nationhood" (*Marlowe's Counterfeit Profession*, 240).

23. Bruce Brandt points out that Marlowe is joking here. Lovers do not actually kill themselves or each other, he insists. The phrase instead refers to Hero's bloody business of sacrificing turtledoves. Whether the human lovers literally kill one another, however, is not necessarily important for my reading. Whether he is joking or not, Marlowe highlights the absurdity and futility of Petrarchan courtship. See Bruce

Brandt, "Marlowe's Amplification of Musaeus in *Hero and Leander*," *Early Modern Literary Studies* 17, no. 23 (2014): 1–15, esp. 7–9.

24. See William A. Oram, "Raleigh, the Queen, and Elizabethan Court Poetry," in *Early Modern English Poetry: A Critical Companion*, ed. Patrick Cheney, Andrew Hadfield, and Garrett A. Sullivan Jr. (Oxford: Oxford University Press, 2007), 113–124.

25. Valerie Traub offers a fascinating analysis of Queen Elizabeth's iconography; see "The Politics of Pleasure: or, Queering Queen Elizabeth," in *The Renaissance of Lesbianism in Early Modern England* (Cambridge: Cambridge University Press, 2002), 125–157.

26. On the conflict between artifice and reality, see Judith Haber, "'True-Loves Blood': Narrative and Desire in *Hero and Leander*," *English Literary Renaissance* 28, no. 3 (1998): 372–386. Haber claims that the blazons of both Hero and Leander reinforce "the suggestion that all truth is artifactual" (376).

27. See Harry Berger Jr., *The Absence of Grace: Sprezzatura and Suspicion in Two Renaissance Courtesy Books* (Stanford, CA: Stanford University Press, 2000).

28. Baldassarre Castiglione, *The Book of the Courtier*, ed. W. E. Henley, trans. Thomas Hoby (London, 1900), 48.

29. See Walter Raleigh, introduction to *The Book of the Courtier*, ed. W. E. Henley, trans. Thomas Hoby (London, 1900), lxxx. On the relationship between Marlowe and this episode in *The Book of the Courtier*, see L. E. Semler, "Marlovian Therapy: The Chastisement of Ovid in *Hero and Leander*," *English Literary Renaissance* 35, no. 2 (2005): 159–186, esp. 162–167. Semler looks to the classical origins of these passages.

30. Musaeus, *Hero and Leander*, ed. Thomas Gelzer, trans. Cedric Whitman, Loeb Classical Library 421 (Cambridge, MA: Harvard University Press, 1975). All translations of Musaeus quotations will be cited parenthetically in text. The original Greek reads:

> Εἰπέ, θεά, κρυφίων ἐπιμάρτυρα λύχνον Ἐρώτων
> καὶ νύχιον πλωτῆρα θαλασσοπόρων ὑμεναίων
> καὶ γάμον ἀχλυόεντα, τὸν οὐκ ἴδεν ἄφθιτος Ἠώς,
> καὶ Σηστὸν καὶ Ἄβυδον, ὅπῃ γάμον ἔννυχον Ἡροῦς
> νηχόμενόν τε Λέανδρον ὁμοῦ καὶ λύχνον ἀκούω,
> λύχνον ἀπαγγέλλοντα διακτορίην Ἀφροδίτης,
> Ἡροῦς νυκτιγάμοιο γαμοστόλον ἀγγελιώτην,
> λύχνον, Ἔρωτος ἄγαλμα.
>
>   (1–8)

31. The original Greek reads: "ἡμετέρην παράκοιτιν ἔχων ἐνὶ δώμασιν Ἡρώ" (81).

32. The original Greek reads: "'Ὡς οἱ μὲν κρυφίοισι γάμοις συνέθεντο μιγῆναι, / καὶ νυχίην φιλότητα καὶ ἀγγελίην ὑμεναίων" (221–222).

33. The original Latin reads: "Interdum metuo, patria ne laedar et inpar / dicar Abydeno Thressa puella toro" (XIX.99–100).

34. Brown, for instance, rejects the social implications of Hero and Leander's relationship when arguing that "Marlowe's *Hero and Leander* is presented as a locus of private recreative activity for both writer and reader, as well as its protagonists" ("Breaking the Canon," 62).

35. Keach, "*Hero and Leander*," in *Elizabethan Erotic Narratives*, 90. On Spenser's portrayals of the Venus-Virgo figure, see Anthony Di Matteo, "Spenser's Venus-Virgo:

The Poetics and Interpretive History of a Dissembling Figure," *Spenser Studies* 10 (1992): 37–70.

36. John Calvin, *Commentaries on the Epistles to Timothy, Titus, and Philemon*, trans. William Pringle (Edinburgh: T. Constable, 1856), 131.

37. Calvin, 132–133.

38. Noricus Philadelphus, *Wie alle Clöster und sonderlich Junckfrawen Clöster in ain Chrstilichs wesen möchten durch gottes gnade gerbracht werden* (1524), quoted in Steven Ozment, *When Fathers Ruled: Family Life in Reformation Europe* (Cambridge, MA: Harvard University Press, 1983), 18.

39. *Oxford English Dictionary*, s.v. "affied, adj."

40. In a discussion of this same scene, William P. Weaver confirms that Marlowe uses marital language that is often ignored. Weaver explains that Hero's sexual awakening occurs in classical terms as she transitions from *parthenos* (virgin) to *numphê* (bride). According to Julius Caesar Scaligar, the beguiling of the nymph by Cupid is part of the wedding rites. In this way, Marlowe "preserves . . . elements of the ancient [marital] ritual" found in the original. William P. Weaver, *Untutored Lines: The Making of the English Epyllion* (Edinburgh: Edinburgh University Press, 2012), 62.

41. Gouge, *Of Domesticall Duties*, 200.

42. Bullinger, *Christen State of Matrymonye*, fol. 54v; Gouge, *Of Domestical Duties*, 198.

43. Roy Strong, *Artists of the Tudor Court* (London: Victoria & Albert Museum, 1983), 75.

44. Giese, *Courtships*, 128.

45. London Metropolitan Archives, DL/C/219/419r, quoted in Giese, *Courtships*, 128.

46. Swinburne, *Treatise of Spousals*, 1.

47. Swinburne, 226.

48. The *Oxford English Dictionary* defines "rite" as "a prescribed act or observance in a religious or other solemn ceremony." *Oxford English Dictionary*, s.v. "rite, n.," 1a.

49. William Whately, *A Bride-Bvsh, or a Wedding Sermon.* (London, 1617), 19.

50. Traub, *Renaissance of Lesbianism*, 82.

51. Summers also emphasizes the violence of the consummation scene (*"Hero and Leander,"* 145). For his positive reading of the consummation scene, see Gordon Braden, "Hero and Leander in Bed (and the Morning After)," *English Literary Renaissance* 45, no. 2 (2015): 205–230.

52. Helga Duncan, "'Headdie Ryots' as Reformations: Marlowe's Libertine Poetics," *Early Modern Literary Studies* 12, no. 2 (2006): 1.

53. Duncan, 2.

54. Bredbeck also reads this digression as an exposure of the Renaissance "market marriage" (*Sodomy and Interpretation*, 122–126).

55. Hero's parents also appear in Musaeus's original. In his rendition, Hero expresses that her parents would never consent to the match. She goes as far to suggest that without her parents' approval, the marriage will not be lawful, stating, "T'is cleere, that Law / by no meanes will approue" (499–500).

56. Summers, *"Hero and Leander,"* 144–145.

57. Phoebe speaks Marlowe's line rather than Rosalind, but Rosalind also falls in love at first sight with Orlando—she knows that love should be tested first, however, rather than acted on.

58. Clifford Leech sympathizes with Hero's plight when pointing out that, while "Chapman's gods are not the overgrown debauched schoolboys of Marlowe," Chapman "recognizes fully that Venus has no right to make such a demand. Her indignation is the result of her own excess." "Venus and Her Nun: Portraits of Women in Love by Shakespeare and Marlowe," *Studies in English Literature, 1500–1900* 5, no. 2 (1965): 266. In this way, Chapman suggests that he must punish Hero and Leander as a result of Marlowe's own interpretation of their myth.

59. Frederick James Furnivall, ed., *Child-Marriages, Divorces, and Ratifications &c. in the Diocese of Chester, A.D. 1561–6* (London: Early English Text Society, 1897), 59–61, 196.

60. Furnivall, 60.

61. Furnivall, 60

62. Furnivall, 59, 61.

63. Furnivall, 61.

64. In his letter "To the Commune Reader" at the beginning of his faithful translation, Chapman praises Marlowe's poem, while also claiming that it differs from his current project. George Chapman, "Musaeus: Of Hero and Leander," in *The Works of George Chapman: Poems and Minor Translations* (London: Chatto and Windus, 1875), 93–94.

3. Sacred Ceremonies and Private Contracts in Spenser's *Epithalamion* and Shakespeare's *A Lover's Complaint*

1. See John Kerrigan, introduction to *The Sonnets and A Lover's Complaint*, by William Shakespeare (New York: Viking, 1986), esp. 18–24; and Bell, *Elizabethan Women*, 145–151.

2. On the relationship between Shakespeare and Spenser, see J. B. Lethbridge, ed., *Shakespeare and Spenser: Attractive Opposites* (New York: Palgrave Macmillan, 2008).

3. Edmond Malone, *The Plays and Poems of William Shakespeare: In Ten Volumes* (London, 1790), 10:371. See especially note 4.

4. Colin Burrow, introduction to *The Complete Sonnets and Poems*, by William Shakespeare (Oxford: Oxford University Press, 2002), 139.

5. Michael Schoenfeldt, *The Cambridge Introduction to Shakespeare's Poetry* (Cambridge: Cambridge University Press, 2010), 112.

6. On the Spenserian echoes in *A Lover's Complaint*, see John Kerrigan, *Motives of Woe: Shakespeare and 'Female Complaint': A Critical Anthology* (Oxford: Clarendon Press, 1991), 21, 30, 39–51. Kerrigan's volume first brought *A Lover's Complaint* the serious critical attention that it deserves. For his argument concerning how Shakespeare confronts his two fellow authors, Spenser and Marlowe, in *A Lover's Complaint*, see Patrick Cheney, *Shakespeare, National Poet-Playwright* (Cambridge: Cambridge University Press, 2004), 239–266.

7. Brian Vickers, *Shakespeare, "A Lover's Complaint," and John Davies of Hereford* (Cambridge: Cambridge University Press, 2007), 69. For another argument calling Shakespeare's authorship of *A Lover's Complaint* into question, see E. Y. Elliott Ward and Robert J. Valenza, "Glass Slippers and Seven-League Boots: C-prompted Doubts about Ascribing *A Funeral Elegy* and *A Lover's Complaint* to Shakespeare," *Shakespeare Quarterly* 48, no. 2 (1997): 177–207. For his exhaustive study refuting the claims (particularly Vickers's) that Shakespeare did not write *A Lover's Complaint*, see MacDonald P.

Jackson, *Determining the Shakespeare Canon: "Arden of Faversham" and "A Lover's Complaint"* (Oxford: Oxford University Press, 2014).

8. Burrow, introduction to *The Complete Sonnets and Poems*, 140.

9. On the dating of *A Lover's Complaint*, see Burrow, 138–140; Kerrigan, *Motives of Woe*, 39–51, 208. Kerrigan dates the writing of *A Lover's Complaint* to the years 1602–1605, though it was published in 1609 (208).

10. On the dating of Shakespeare's *Sonnets*, see A. Kent Hieatt, Charles W. Hieatt, and Anne Lake Prescott, "When Did Shakespeare Write *Sonnets* 1609," *Studies in Philology* 88, no. 1 (1991): 69–109; MacDonald P. Jackson, "Vocabulary and Chronology: The Case of Shakespeare's Sonnets," *Review of English Studies* 52, no. 205 (2001): 59–76; MacDonald P. Jackson, "Rhymes in Shakespeare's *Sonnets*: Evidence of Date of Composition," *Notes and Queries* 46, no. 2 (1999): 213–219; MacDonald P. Jackson, "Dating Shakespeare's Sonnets: Some Old Evidence Revisited," *Notes and Queries* 49, no. 2 (2002): 237–241; and Burrow, introduction to *The Complete Sonnets and Poems*, 103–111. For her influential argument that Shakespeare authorized the *Sonnets*, see Katherine Duncan-Jones, "Was the 1609 Shake-Speares Sonnets Really Unauthorized?," *Review of English Studies* 34, no. 134 (1982): 151–171. For a refutation of this argument, see Arthur F. Marotti, "Shakespeare's Sonnets as Literary Property," in *Soliciting Interpretation: Literary Theory and Seventeenth Century English Poetry*, ed. Elizabeth D. Harvey and Katharine Eisaman Maus (Chicago: University of Chicago Press, 1990), 143–173.

11. Henry Gee and William Hardy, *Documents Illustrative of English Church History* (London: Macmillan, 1896), 510.

12. Strype, *The Life and Acts of John Whitgift*, 2:375.

13. *Constitutions and Canons Ecclesiastical* (London, 1604), L3r-L3v.

14. All quotations from Spenser's shorter poems are from *The Shorter Poems*, ed. Richard A. McCabe (London: Penguin, 1999) and are cited parenthetically in text.

15. Elizabeth Mazzola, "Marrying Medusa: Spenser's *Epithalamion* and Renaissance Reconstructions of Female Privacy," *Genre* 25, nos. 2–3 (1992): 203.

16. Mazzola, 193.

17. Due to the poem's autobiographical nature, I follow the scholarly convention of referring to the poet-narrator as Spenser. On Spenser's actual marriage to Elizabeth Boyle, see Hadfield, *Edmund Spenser: A Life*, 296–322.

18. Bullinger, *Christen State of Matrymonye*, fol. 45v.

19. Whately, *Bride-Bvsh, or a Wedding Sermon*, 8.

20. See Carol V. Kaske, "Spenser's *Amoretti* and *Epithalamion* of 1595: Structure, Genre and Numerology," *English Literary Renaissance* 8, no. 3 (1978): 271–295.

21. Bell, *Elizabethan Women*, 9.

22. See King, *Spenser's Poetry and the Reformation Tradition*, 165. On the *Amoretti*'s correspondence to the liturgical calendar, see Kaske, "Spenser's *Amoretti* and *Epithalamion*"; A. Kent Hieatt, "A Numerical Key for Spenser's *Amoretti* and Guyon in the House of Mammon," *Yearbook of English Studies* 3 (1973): 14–27; Alexander Dunlop, "The Unity of Spenser's *Amoretti*," in *Silent Poetry: Essays in Numerological Analysis*, ed. Alistair Fowler (New York: Barnes and Noble, 1970), 153–169; William C. Johnson, "Spenser's *Amoretti* and the Art of the Liturgy," *Studies in English Literature, 1500–1900* 14, no. 1 (1974): 47–61; G. K. Hunter, "Unity and Numbers in Spenser's *Amoretti*," *Yearbook of English Studies* 5 (1975): 39–45.

23. Ramie Targoff, *Common Prayer: The Language of Public Devotion in Early Modern England* (Chicago: University of Chicago Press, 2001), 18. Targoff asserts that "what is strikingly, and mistakenly, absent from our accounts of the Elizabethan settlement is . . . the belief that external practices might not only reflect but also potentially transform the internal self" (3).

24. On the conflict between Petrarchism and anti-Petrarchism in Spenser's *Amoretti*, see Heather Dubrow, *Echoes of Desire: English Petrarchism and Its Counterdiscourses* (Ithaca, NY: Cornell University Press, 1995), 75–81.

25. James S. Lambert, "Spenser's *Epithalamion* and the Protestant Expression of Joy," *Studies in English Literature, 1500–1900* 54, no. 1 (2014): 87.

26. On the importance of avian imagery to Spenser's career, see Cheney, *Spenser's Famous Flight*.

27. See Zurcher, *Spenser's Legal Language*, 249.

28. On birds cursing—rather than celebrating—a wedding as indicative of an anti-epithalamium, see Virginia Tufte, *The Poetry of Marriage: The Epithalamium in Europe and Its Development in England* (Los Angeles: Tinnon-Brown, 1970), 38–39. Spenser's cataloging of birds that must approve of the marriage recalls a Chaucerian text: the social marriage poem *The Parliament of Fowls*. On *The Parliament of Fowls* as an epithalamion, see Sarah Emsley, "'By Evene Acord': Marriage and Genre in the 'Parliament of Fowls,'" *Chaucer Review* 34, no. 2 (1999): 139–149. Thanks to Elizabeth Fowler for suggesting this connection to me.

29. Bullinger, *Christen State of Matrymonye*, fol. 56v. The wasted funds, Bullinger observes, could go to helping the poor instead.

30. Melissa E. Sanchez, "'Modesty or Comeliness': The Predicament of Reform Theology in Spenser's *Amoretti* and *Epithalamion*," *Renascence* 65, no. 1 (2012): 17. On the ceremony's centrality, see King, *Spenser's Poetry*, 175.

31. King, *Spenser's Poetry*, 175. On Spenser's use of the *Book of Common Prayer* in *Epithalamion*, see also William C. Johnson, "'Sacred Rites' and Prayer-Book Echoes in Spenser's 'Epithalamion,'" *Renaissance and Reformation* 12, no. 1 (1976): 49–54.

32. On the sacramental imagery in *Epithalamion*, see David Chintz, "The Poem as Sacrament: Spenser's *Epithalamion* and the Golden Section," *Journal of Medieval and Renaissance Studies* 21, no. 2 (1991): 251–268.

33. Donne, "Sermon Preached at a Mariage," 3.

34. John Calvin, *Calvin's New Testament Commentaries: A Harmony of the Gospels*, trans. A. W. Morrison, ed. David W. Torrance and Thomas F. Torrance (Grand Rapids, MI: William B. Eerdmans, 1972), 3:102.

35. Gouge, *Of Domesticall Duties*, 228.

36. Ramie Targoff, *Posthumous Love: Eros and the Afterlife in Renaissance England* (Chicago: University of Chicago Press, 2014), 152.

37. Roland Greene, "*Amoretti* and *Epithalamion* (1595)," in *The Oxford Handbook of Edmund Spenser*, ed. Richard A. McCabe (Oxford: Oxford University Press, 2010), 257.

38. George Puttenham, *Arte of English Poesie* (London, 1589), 41.

39. See William A. Oram, "Daphnaida and Spenser's Later Poetry," *Spenser Studies* 2 (1981): 141–158. Rachel E. Hile has gone so far to suggest that Spenser satirizes Gorges's grief. See Rachel E. Hile, *Spenserian Satire: A Tradition of Indirection* (Manchester: Manchester University Press, 2017), 38–63.

40. Jonathan Gibson, "The Legal Context of Spenser's *Daphnaïda*," *Review of English Studies*, n.s., 55, no. 218 (2004): 24–44.

41. Gibson, 27.

42. On the Echo myth in *Epithalamion*, see Joseph Loewenstein, "Echo's Ring: Orpheus and Spenser's Career," *English Literary Renaissance* 16, no. 2 (1986): 287–302; and Judith Deitch, "The Girl He Left Behind: Ovidian *imitatio* and the Body of Echo in Spenser's *Epithalamion*," in *Ovid and the Renaissance Body*, ed. Goran V. Stanivukovic (Toronto: University of Toronto Press, 2001), 224–238.

43. See MacDonald P. Jackson, "Echoes of Spenser's *Prothalamion* as Evidence against an Early Date for Shakespeare's *A Lover's Complaint*," *Notes and Queries* 37, no. 2 (1990): 180–182.

44. Vickers, *Shakespeare, "A Lover's Complaint," and John Davies*, 56–57.

45. Heather Dubrow, *Captive Victors: Shakespeare's Narrative Poems and Sonnets* (Ithaca, NY: Cornell University Press, 1987), 246.

46. On Shakespeare's portrayals of broken trothplights as a link between the *Sonnets* and *A Lover's Complaint*, see Ilona Bell, "Rethinking Shakespeare's Dark Lady," in *A Companion to Shakespeare's Sonnets*, ed. Michael Schoenfeldt (Malden, MA: Blackwell, 2007), 293–313.

47. *Oxford English Dictionary*, s.v. "bed-vow (n.)."

48. Catherine Bates, "The Enigma of *A Lover's Complaint*," in Schoenfeldt, *A Companion to Shakespeare's Sonnets*, 426–440.

49. For a thorough exploration of Shakespeare's engagement with ritualized confession in *A Lover's Complaint*, see Paul Stegner, "A Reconciled Maid: *A Lover's Complaint* and Confessional Practices in Early Modern England," in *Critical Essays on Shakespeare's "A Lover's Complaint": Suffering Ecstasy*, ed. Shirley Sharon-Zisser (Burlington, VT: Ashgate, 2006), 79–90. See also Kerrigan, *Motives of Woe*, 39–42. On the "reverend man" as a Spenserian figure, see Cheney, *Shakespeare, National Poet-Playwright*, 247.

50. Daniel Rogers, *Matrimoniall Honour* (London, 1642), 110.

51. Rogers, 110.

52. See Jeremy Boulton, "Itching after Private Marryings? Marriage Customs in Seventeenth-Century London," *London Journal* 16, no. 1 (1991): 15–34.

53. On the use of rhetoric as a tool of seduction, see Jon Harned, "Rhetoric and Perverse Desire in *A Lover's Complaint*," in Sharon-Zisser, *Critical Essays on Shakespeare's "A Lover's Complaint*," 149–164.

54. Tobias B. Hug, *Impostures in Early Modern England: Representations and Perceptions of Fraudulent Identities* (Manchester: Manchester University Press, 2010), 24.

55. Hug, 24.

56. Bernard Capp, "Bigamous Marriage in Early Modern England," *Historical Journal* 52, no. 3 (2009): 541.

57. I Jac. I, cap. XI, "An Act to restrain all persons from marrying until their former wives and former husbands be dead."

58. Furnivall, *Child-Marriages, Divorces, and Ratifications*, 57–59.

59. Furnivall, 58.

60. Furnivall, 58.

61. On the maid's complaint as a criminal confession, see Katharine A. Craik, "Shakespeare's *A Lover's Complaint* and Early Modern Criminal Confession," *Shakespeare Quarterly* 53, no. 4 (2002): 437–459.

62. For his work on women in the Court of Requests, see Tim Stretton, *Women Waging Law in Elizabethan England* (Cambridge: Cambridge University Press, 1998).

63. Houlbrooke, *Church Courts and the People*, 61. See also Diana O'Hara, *Courtship and Constraint: Rethinking the Making of Marriage in Tudor England* (Manchester: Manchester University Press, 2000), 57–98.

64. London Metropolitan Archives, DL/C/215/114v-115r, quoted in Giese, *Courtships*, 132.

65. London Metropolitan Archives, DL/C/215/115v, quoted in Giese, *Courtships*, 133.

66. On the tokens as connecting Daniel's *The Complaint of Rosamond* and Shakespeare's *A Lover's Complaint*, see Kenji Go, "Samuel Daniel's *The Complaint of Rosamond* and an Emblematic Reconsideration of *A Lover's Complaint*," *Studies in Philology* 104, no. 1 (2007): 82–122.

67. Scholars have long noted the connection between Shakespeare's plays in the early seventeenth century and *A Lover's Complaint*. MacDonald P. Jackson has also looked to words that occur in Shakespeare's late plays, especially *Cymbeline*, to disprove Vickers's thesis that Shakespeare did not write the poem. See MacDonald P. Jackson, "*A Lover's Complaint, Cymbeline,* and the Shakespeare Canon: Interpreting Shared Vocabulary," *Modern Language Review* 103, no. 3 (2008): 621–638.

68. Alan Stewart, *Shakespeare's Letters* (Oxford: Oxford University Press, 2008), 231–260.

4. "Lorenzo and His Infidel"

1. The classic work on festivity in Shakespeare's comedies is C. L. Barber, *Shakespeare's Festive Comedy: A Study of Dramatic Form and Its Relation to Social Custom* (Princeton, NJ: Princeton University Press, 1959). For the work that popularized the category of the problem comedy, see William Witherle Lawrence, *Shakespeare's Problem Comedies* (New York: Frederick Ungar, 1960). Lawrence defines comedies such as *Measure for Measure* and *Troilus and Cressida* as problem comedies because "instead of gay pictures of cheerful scenes, to be accepted with a smile and a jest, we are frequently offered unpleasant and sometimes even repulsive episodes, and characters whose conduct gives rise to sustained questioning of action and motive" (3). On marriage in the problem comedies *All's Well That Ends Well* and *Measure for Measure*, see Richard P. Wheeler, *Shakespeare's Development and the Problem Comedies: Turn and Counter-Turn* (Berkeley: University of California Press, 1981).

2. For marriage as comic closure, see Northrop Frye, *A Natural Perspective: The Development of Shakespearean Comedy and Romance* (New York: Columbia University Press, 1965). See also Lisa Hopkins, *The Shakespearean Marriage: Merry Wives and Heavy Husbands* (New York: St. Martin's Press, 1998), 16–33; and Ejner J. Jensen, *Shakespeare and the Ends of Comedy* (Bloomington: Indiana University Press, 1991).

3. *Acts of the Privy Council Volume 26, 1596–1597*, ed. John Roche Dasent (London: Her Majesty's Stationery Office, 1902), 16. On racialized others in early modern England, see Sujata Iyengar, *Shades of Difference: Mythologies of Skin Color in Early Modern England* (Philadelphia: University of Pennsylvania Press, 2005). On race in early modern drama in particular, see Mary Floyd-Wilson, *English Ethnicity and Race in Early Modern Drama* (Cambridge: Cambridge University Press, 2003).

4. Elizabeth A. Spiller, "From Imagination to Miscegenation: Race and Romance in Shakespeare's *The Merchant of Venice*," *Renaissance Drama* 29 (1998): 144.

5. Lloyd Edward Kermode elaborates that "frustrations about overcrowding and economic strain led to urban unrest, and . . . strangers 'provided a convenient scapegoat' for expressing that frustration in sometimes violent ways." *Aliens and Englishness in Elizabethan Drama* (Cambridge: Cambridge University Press, 2009), 2.

6. For an overview of the play's sources, see John Russell Brown, introduction to *The Merchant of Venice*, by William Shakespeare (London: Arden Shakespeare, 2006), xxvii–xxxi. Shakespeare's most immediate source was Giovanni Fiorentino's *Il Pecorone* (Milan, 1558).

7. For the argument on Jewishness as simply a theological difference, see G. K. Hunter, "The Theology of Marlowe's *The Jew of Malta*," *Journal of the Warburg and Courtauld Institutes* 27 (1964): 211–240. For the seminal work on Jewishness as being shaped by early modern discourses of race, gender, and nationhood, see James Shapiro, *Shakespeare and the Jews* (New York: Columbia University Press, 1996).

8. Kim F. Hall, "Guess Who's Coming to Dinner? Colonization and Miscegenation in *The Merchant of Venice*," *Renaissance Drama* 23 (1992): 87–111, esp. 102–103. For Hall's argument on the racial significance of the terms of fairness and blackness in the early modern period, see *Things of Darkness: Economies of Race and Gender in Early Modern England* (Ithaca, NY: Cornell University Press, 1995). According to Hall, the other characters also appear to view Jessica as a Christian already since they repeatedly label her as "fair."

9. M. Lindsay Kaplan, "Jessica's Mother: Medieval Constructions of Jewish Race and Gender in *The Merchant of Venice*," *Shakespeare Quarterly* 58, no. 1 (2007): 1–30.

10. Janet Adelman, *Blood Relations: Christian and Jew in "The Merchant of Venice"* (Chicago: University of Chicago Press, 2008), 73.

11. Carole Levin and John Watkins, *Shakespeare's Foreign Worlds: National and Transnational Identities in the Elizabethan Age* (Ithaca, NY: Cornell University Press, 2009), 85–87, 96–101. Levin observes that Jessica, even after her conversion, is "still considered to be [a] Jew . . . rather than [a] Christian" (86).

12. See Hall, "Guess Who's Coming to Dinner?"; and Karen Newman, "Portia's Ring: Unruly Women and Structures of Exchange in *The Merchant of Venice*," *Shakespeare Quarterly* 38, no. 1 (1987): 19–33. Hall points out that the play ends with an "evocation of adultery" (104); and Newman claims that, far from idealized statements of love, "the play ends on an obscene pun on *ring* and a commonplace joke about female sexuality and cuckoldry" (32).

13. On the possibilities and limitations of interracial marriage in relation to Jessica's conversion, see Brett D. Hirsch, "'A Gentle and No Jew': The Difference Marriage Makes in *The Merchant of Venice*," *Parergon* 23, no. 1 (2006): 119–129. Hirsch argues that the characters label Jessica as "fair" to legitimate the marriage before it has taken place, but cease to do so afterward—which emphasizes the incompleteness of the conversion. The article does not take the clandestine nature of the marriage into account.

14. Gouge, *Of Domesticall Duties*, 213.

15. Cressy, *Birth, Marriage, and Death*, 287.

16. Frances E. Dolan's study, *Marriage and Violence: The Early Modern Legacy*, explores the paradox of the early modern marriage that stressed both hierarchy and equality between the sexes.

17. Gouge, *Of Domesticall Duties*, 27.

18. Cressy, *Birth, Marriage, and Death*, 287 (emphasis mine).

19. William Perkins, *Christian Oeconomie: or, A Short Survey of the Right Manner of Erecting and Ordering a Familie, according to the Scriptures* (London, 1609), 3.

20. Cleaver, *Godlie Forme*, 13. See also Gouge, *Of Domesticall Duties*, 17, 27, sig. 2v; and Rogers, *Matrimoniall Honour*, 17.

21. In her study on the importance of household work to English identity, *Staging Domesticity: Household Work and English Identity in Early Modern Drama* (Cambridge: Cambridge University Press, 2002), Wendy Wall explains that "the early modern family bore the tremendous burden of inculcating citizenship and virtue in a patriarchal and hierarchical world by structuring the proper dependencies that founded church, state and body politic" (2). Scholars have argued whether the hierarchies outlined in the conduct books were actually tenable or representative of actual practice. See Lena Cowen Orlin, *Private Matters and Public Culture in Post Reformation England* (Ithaca, NY: Cornell University Press, 1994), 125–130; and Susan Dwyer Amussen, *An Ordered Society: Gender and Class in Early Modern England* (New York: Columbia University Press, 1988), 38–47.

22. For more detail on the average age at the time of marriage, see Richard M. Smith, "Population and Its Geography in England, 1500–1730," in *An Historical Geography of England and Wales*, ed. R. A. Dodgshon and R. A. Butlin (London: Academic Press, 1978), 199–237; and R. B. Outhwaite, "Age at Marriage in England from the Late Seventeenth to the Nineteenth Centuries," *Transactions of the Royal Historical Society* 23 (1973): 55–70.

23. Carlson, *Marriage and the English Reformation*, 106.

24. John Lumley, Baron Lumley, Nonsuch, to Richard Bagot, 1589 November 25, Papers of the Bagot Family of Blithfield, Staffordshire, 1428–1671, Folger MS L.a.628, Folger Shakespeare Library, Washington, DC. Abbreviated words have been silently expanded.

25. Lumley to Bagot, 1589 November 25, Papers of the Bagot Family.

26. John Donne, "John Donne to Sir George More, February 2, 1602," in *John Donne's Marriage Letters in the Folger Shakespeare Library*, ed. M. Thomas Hester, Robert Parker Sorlien, and Dennis Flynn (Washington, DC: Folger Shakespeare Library, 2005), 36.

27. Bullinger, *Christen State of Matrymonye*, fol. 11v. He also states that the commandment requiring children to honor their parents is at play in wedding negotiations: "The obedience or disobedienc of the children at no tyme declare itself more then in contracting of wedlocke. Greater honoure canst thou not shewe unto thy parentes, then when thou folowest them herin: neyther greater dishonour then when thou herin refuseth them" (fol. 12r). Abbreviated words have been silently expanded.

28. In *Earthly Necessities: Economic Lives in Early Modern Britain* (New Haven, CT: Yale University Press, 2000), Keith Wrightson explains that servants and apprentices (common fixtures in the early modern household) were understood as "full members of their master's 'family'—a word which contemporaries used to describe the entire household, rather than to refer only to relatives by blood or marriage in the modern sense" (33).

29. Carlson, *Marriage and the English Reformation*, 106.

30. Outhwaite, *Clandestine Marriage*, 58.

31. Donne's employer, Sir Thomas Egerton, refused to reemploy him even after Sir George relented and made the request.

32. William Cobbett and T. C. Hansard, eds., *The Parliamentary History of England: From the Earliest Period to the Year 1803* (London, 1813), 15, 71.

33. Cobbett and Hansard, 3.

34. Robert Crofts, for instance, emphasizes equality when choosing a marriage match: "Chuse such as are of equall yeares, birth, fortunes and degree . . . for inconsiderate and unequall marriages are commonly very pernitious, and a multitude of mischievous and miserable effects spring from such marriages." *The Way to Happinesse on Earth: Concerning Riches, Honour, Conjugall Love, Eating, Drinking* (London, 1641), 180.

35. Carolyn Sale, "The 'Roman Hand': Women, Writing and the Law in the *Att.-Gen. v. Chatterton* and the Letters of the Lady Arbella Stuart," *ELH* 70, no. 4 (2003): 931.

36. Emma Hawkes, "Preliminary Notes on Consent in the 1382 Rape and Ravishment Laws of Richard II," *Legal History* 11, no. 1 (2007): 118–119. Hawkes explores how the legislation of 6 Richard II affected actual trials in the medieval period.

37. William Cecil, *Advice to a Son*, ed. Louis B. Wright (Ithaca, NY: Cornell University Press, 1962), 11.

38. For Stone's seminal, yet outdated, work on early modern family life, see *Family, Sex and Marriage*.

39. Outhwaite, *Clandestine Marriage*, 108.

40. Adelman, *Blood Relations*, 95.

41. See "The 32 Historie" in Richard Robinson, ed. and trans., *A record of auncient histories, entituled in Latin: Gesta Romanorum Discoursing vpon sundry examples for the aduauncement of vertue, and the abandoning of vice. No Less pleasant in reading then profitable in practice* (London, 1595), 96–105.

42. Carlson, *Marriage and the English Reformation*, 106.

43. Douglas Trevor, *The Poetics of Melancholy in Early Modern England* (Cambridge: Cambridge University Press, 2004), 72.

44. For scholarship that idealizes the casket test as ensuring Portia's happiness, see Joan Ozark Holmer, *"The Merchant of Venice": Choice, Hazard and Consequence* (New York: St. Martin's Press, 1995).

45. Gouge, *Of Domesticall Duties*, 605.

46. See Jean E. Howard, "Crossdressing, the Theatre, and Gender Struggle in Early Modern England," *Shakespeare Quarterly* 39, no. 4 (1988): 418–440; Lisa Jardine, "Cultural Confusion and Shakespeare's Learned Heroines: 'These Are Old Paradoxes,'" *Shakespeare Quarterly* 38, no. 1 (1987): 1–18; and Newman, "Portia's Ring."

47. Howard, "Crossdressing," 433.

48. Laurie Shannon has argued that Portia appropriates the language of husbandry in the courtroom scene to elevate her relationship with Bassanio from simply a wife to a husband, and thus to a friend worthy of the same status enjoyed by Antonio. See "Likenings: Rhetorical Husbandries and Portia's 'True Conceit' of Friendship," *Renaissance Drama* 31 (2002): 3–26.

49. See Adelman, *Blood Relations*, 91–98. On the importance of blood to race in the early modern period, see also Jean E. Feerick, *Strangers in Blood: Relocating Race in the Renaissance* (Toronto: University of Toronto Press, 2010).

50. Richard Helgerson, *Forms of Nationhood: The Elizabethan Writing of England* (Chicago: University of Chicago Press, 1992), 120. For Helgerson's account of this transition, see his chapter "The Land Speaks," 105–148.

51. Shapiro, *Shakespeare and the Jews*, 14.

52. John Foxe, *A Sermon preached at the Christening of a Certaine Jew by Iohn Foxe. Conteining an exposition of the xi chapter of S. Paul to the Romanes. Translated out of Latine into English by Iames Bell* (London, 1578), sig. A1v.

53. For the ways in which "Judaizing" could occur, see Shapiro, *Shakespeare and the Jews*.

54. For his outline of faulty speech acts, see J. L. Austin, *How to Do Things with Words: The William James Lectures Delivered in Harvard University in 1955*, ed. J. O. Urmson and Marina Sbisa (Oxford: Clarendon Press, 1975). A baptism, like a wedding, for instance, is a "procedure . . . designed for use by persons having certain thoughts or feelings, or for the inauguration of certain consequential conduct on the part of any participant. . . . A person participating in and so invoking the procedure must in fact have those thoughts or feelings, and the participants must intend so to conduct themselves" (Austin, 15). The fact that Shylock will not have the "thoughts or feelings" typically expected at a baptism will thus make his conversion "infelicitous" at best.

55. Gouge, *Of Domesticall Duties*, 205.

56. For the harsh treatment of those who had children out of wedlock, see Cressy, *Birth, Marriage, and Death*, 73–79.

57. Camille Slights, "In Defense of Jessica: The Runaway Daughter in *The Merchant of Venice*," *Shakespeare Quarterly* 31, no. 3 (1980): 363.

58. Kathy Lavezzo, *The Accommodated Jew: English Antisemitism from Bede to Milton* (Ithaca, NY: Cornell University Press, 2016).

59. Thanks to Joan Ozark Holmer for pointing out to me that Lorenzo's lateness suggests that he is a conscientious lover who wants to make sure the events of the night go smoothly.

60. Jessica and Lorenzo's prodigal behavior after their marriage has been disputed by scholars as either an example of their immoral thievery or harmless extravagance. My argument is that Jessica's clandestine marriage, which places her outside of typical social boundaries like spending, causes the other characters to hesitate to include her in the Christian community. For arguments that criticize the couple's extravagance, see Sigurd Burckhardt, *Shakespearean Meanings* (Princeton, NJ: Princeton University Press, 1968), esp. 224; and Raymond B. Waddington, "Blind Gods: Fortune, Justice, and Cupid in *The Merchant of Venice*," *ELH* 44, no. 3 (1977): 458–477, esp. 474–475. For the extravagance as harmless, although problematic, see Herbert S. Donow, "Shakespeare's Caskets: Unity in *The Merchant of Venice*," *Shakespeare Studies* 4 (1968): 86–93.

61. Holmer, *Merchant of Venice*, 126.

62. Adelman observes that Portia appears to speak only to Lorenzo. See *Blood Relations*, 73.

63. For Hutson's full argument, see *The Usurer's Daughter: Male Friendship and Fictions of Women in Sixteenth-Century England* (London: Routledge, 1994), esp. 224–238.

64. On Antonio as a father figure in this scene, see Cook, *Making a Match*, 138.

5. "Are You Fast Married?"

1. Julia Reinhard Lupton, *Citizen-Saints: Shakespeare and Political Theology* (Chicago: University of Chicago Press, 2005), 105. On *Othello* as a rewriting of *The Merchant of Venice*, see also Leslie A. Fiedler, *The Stranger in Shakespeare* (New York: Stein and Day, 1972), 139–145.

2. Stephen Rogers, "*Othello*: Comedy in Reverse," *Shakespeare Quarterly* 24, no. 2 (1973): 210. On *Othello* and comedy, see also Susan Snyder, "*Othello* and the Conventions of Romantic Comedy," *Renaissance Drama* 5 (1972): 123–141. Snyder argues, "The tragedy is generated and heightened *through* the relation to comedy rather than in spite of it" (124). On the carnivalesque elements of *Othello*, see Michael D. Bristol, "Charivari and the Comedy of Abjection in *Othello*," *Renaissance Drama* 21 (1990): 3–21.

3. See Martin Orkin, "Othello and the 'Plain Face' of Racism," *Shakespeare Quarterly* 38, no. 2 (1987): 166–188; Karen Newman, "'And Wash the Ethiop White': Femininity and the Monstrous in *Othello*," in *Shakespeare Reproduced: The Text in History and Ideology*, ed. Jean E. Howard and Marion F. O'Connor (London: Methuen, 1987), 143–162. For early modern discourses of race more generally, see Hall, *Things of Darkness*; Iyengar, *Shades of Difference*; and Floyd-Wilson, *English Ethnicity*. It is impossible to document all of the scholarship on the role of race in *Othello* here. For a more comprehensive discussion of scholarship on race in the play, see Michael Neill, introduction to *Othello*, by William Shakespeare (Oxford: Oxford University Press, 2006), 113–130.

4. Michael Neill, "'Mulattos,' 'Blacks,' and 'Indian Moors': *Othello* and Early Modern Constructions of Human Difference," *Shakespeare Quarterly* 49, no. 4 (1998): 361–374, esp. 364.

5. Emily C. Bartels, *Speaking of the Moor: From Alcazar to "Othello"* (Philadelphia: University of Pennsylvania Press, 2008), 155–194.

6. Daniel J. Vitkus, *Turning Turk: English Theater and the Multicultural Mediterranean, 1570–1630* (New York: Palgrave Macmillan, 2003). On racial difference serving as an indicator of religious difference, see Jonathan Burton, *Traffic and Turning: Islam and English Drama, 1579–1624* (Newark: University of Delaware Press, 2005), 252.

7. Neill, introduction to *Othello*, 115.

8. Lupton, *Citizen-Saints*, 106.

9. Dennis Austin Britton, *Becoming Christian: Race, Reformation, and Early Modern English Romance* (New York: Fordham University Press, 2014), 112–142.

10. See Stanley Cavell, *Disowning Knowledge: In Six Plays of Shakespeare* (Cambridge: Cambridge University Press, 1987), esp. 125–142. On the relationship between tragedy and skepticism on the early modern stage more generally, see William M. Hamlin, *Tragedy and Skepticism in Shakespeare's England* (New York: Palgrave Macmillan, 2005).

11. Britton, *Becoming Christian*, 121. On Othello's conversion through baptism, see also Jane Hwang Degenhardt, *Islamic Conversion and Christian Resistance on the Early Modern Stage* (Edinburgh: Edinburgh University Press, 2010), 50–51.

12. Meredith Hanmer, *The Baptizing of a Turke, A sermon preached at the Hospitall of Saint Katherin* (London, 1586), sig. 2v.

13. John Whitgift further insists that converts from Islam and Judaism be examined before being baptized. See John Whitgift, *The Defense of the Aunswere to the Admonition, against the Replie of T.C.* (London, 1574).

14. Bartels, *Speaking of the Moor*, 118. On Othello as a converted Morisco, like the historical Leo Africanus, see Barbara Everett, "'Spanish' *Othello*: The Making of Shakespeare's Moor," *Shakespeare Survey: An Annual Survey of Shakespearian Study and Production* 35 (1982): 101–112; and Eric Griffin, "Un-sainting James: Or, *Othello* and the 'Spanish Spirits' of Shakespeare's Globe," *Representations* 62 (1998): 58–99.

15. Vitkus, *Turning Turk*, 77.

16. Vitkus, 77.

17. Lupton, *Citizen-Saints*, 105 (emphasis mine).

18. Britton, *Becoming Christian*, 130 (emphasis mine).

19. Giovanni Battista Giraldi Cinthio, "*Gli Hecatommithi*," in *Narrative and Dramatic Sources of Shakespeare*, ed. and trans. Geoffrey Bullough (London: Routledge and Kegan Paul, 1973), 7:242.

20. Cinthio, 242.

21. E. A. J. Honigmann, ed., *Othello* (London: Arden Shakespeare, 2006), 371; Michael Neill, "Changing Places in *Othello*," in *Putting History to the Question: Power, Politics, and Society in English Renaissance Drama* (New York: Columbia University Press, 2000), 215.

22. Neill, 215.

23. Honigmann, *Othello*, 124.

24. Honigmann suggests that Desdemona is quite young, even a child. Her father, however, does not make her youth a factor when trying to annul the marriage. In my own analysis, therefore, I follow Brabantio's lead. Desdemona, at the very least, is old enough to marry legally without first obtaining parental consent. See Honigmann, introduction to *Othello*, 41–43.

25. On Cassio as feigning innocence here, see Harry Berger Jr., *A Fury in the Words: Love and Embarrassment in Shakespeare's Venice* (New York: Fordham University Press, 2012), 94. Even if Cassio does know about the elopement, he clearly does not assist Othello (or Desdemona) on his wedding night.

26. See T. G. A. Nelson and Charles Haines, "Othello's Unconsummated Marriage," *Essays in Criticism* 33, no. 1 (1983): 1–18. On the match as being unconsummated, see also Graham Bradshaw, *Misrepresentations: Shakespeare and the Materialists* (Ithaca, NY: Cornell University Press, 1993), 128; and R. N. Hallstead, "Idolatrous Love: A New Approach to *Othello*," *Shakespeare Quarterly* 19, no. 2 (1968): 107–124. On the marriage as being consummated, see Norman Nathan, "Othello's Marriage Is Consummated," *Cahiers Élisabéthains* 34, no. 1 (1988): 79–82.

27. Rogers, *Matrimoniall Honour*, 116.

28. Edward Kellett, *A Returne from Argier. A Sermon Preached at Minhead in the County of Somerset the 16. Of March, 1627, at the re-admission of a relapsed Christian into our Church* (London, 1628), 23.

29. Edward Aston, *The Manners, Lawes, and Customes of all Nations* (London, 1610), 137.

30. Vitkus, *Turning Turk*, 86–87.

31. *Oxford English Dictionary*, s.v. "fast (adv.)," 1a., 2a.

32. Shakespeare's relatively sparse use of the word, occurring only twenty-two times throughout his works, speaks to the practice's rarity, making Iago's use of it even more significant. Brabantio must have a lot of sway indeed for Iago to deploy the term.

33. On early modern divorce, see Sokol and Sokol, *Shakespeare, Law, and Marriage*, 139–143; and Lawrence Stone, *Road to Divorce: England 1530–1987* (Oxford: Oxford University Press, 1990).

34. See Helmholz, *Roman Canon Law*, 73–77; Houlbrooke, *Church Courts*, 67–75; Ingram, *Church Courts*, 146; and Carlson, *Marriage and the English Reformation*, 22.

35. On Brabantio's conflation of Desdemona with wealth as part of Venice's mercantilism, see Neill, "Changing Places," 209–211. On Brabantio as a Jewish Christian, see Lupton, *Citizen-Saints*, 107–109. The reference to women as property in early modern law makes Shylock's and Brabantio's own references not uniquely Christian or Jewish—women constitute property, it seems, in both the Christian and Jewish cultures.

36. Diane Purkiss, *The Witch in History: Early Modern and Twentieth-Century Representations* (London: Routledge, 1996), 263. On this scene as a witchcraft trial, see also Millicent Bell, *Shakespeare's Tragic Skepticism* (New Haven, CT: Yale University Press, 2002), 122–127.

37. On the crime of witchcraft and its punishments in early modern England, see Garthine Walker, "The Strangeness of the Familiar: Witchcraft and the Law in Early Modern England," in *The Extraordinary and the Everyday in Early Modern England: Essays in Celebration of the Work of Bernard Capp*, ed. Angela McShane and Garthine Walker (London: Palgrave Macmillan, 2010), 105–124.

38. Purkiss, *Witch in History*, 263.

39. Cook, *Making a Match*, 104–119.

40. Berger comments on this bizarre omission in his argument that Cassio becomes a "placeholder" for Othello during the courtship with Desdemona. See Berger, *Fury in the Words*, 97–100.

41. Berger, *Fury in the Words*, 208.

42. Rogers, *Matrimoniall Honour*, 116.

43. Rogers, 116.

44. Neill, "Changing Places," 230–235.

45. Neill, 234.

46. Natasha Korda, *Shakespeare's Domestic Economies: Gender and Property in Early Modern England* (Philadelphia: University of Pennsylvania Press, 2002), 148.

47. Berger, *Fury in the Words*, 111.

48. Lynda E. Boose, "Othello's Handkerchief: 'The Recognizance and Pledge of Love,'" *English Literary Renaissance* 5, no. 3 (1975): 360–374, esp. 360–361.

49. Thomas Rymer, *A Short View of Tragedy* (London, 1693), 139–140.

50. Korda, *Shakespeare's Domestic Economies*, 113.

51. On the relationship between Othello's fetishization of the handkerchief and his blackness, see Michael C. Andrews, "Honest Othello: The Handkerchief Once More," *Studies in English Literature, 1500–1900* 13, no. 2 (1973): 273–284; Abraham Bronson Feldman, "Othello's Obsessions," *American Imago* 9, no. 2 (1952): 147–164; and Peter G. Mudford, "*Othello* and the 'Tragedy of Situation,'" *English: Journal of the English Association* 20, no. 106 (1971): 1–6.

52. Harry Berger Jr., "Impertinent Trifling: Desdemona's Handkerchief," *Shakespeare Quarterly* 47, no. 3 (1996): 238.

53. Diana O'Hara, "The Language of Tokens and the Making of Marriage," *Rural History* 3, no. 1 (1992): 10.

54. O'Hara, 10.

55. O'Hara, 27.

56. Andrew Sisson, "Othello and the Unweaponed City," *Shakespeare Quarterly* 66, no. 2 (2015): 157.

57. Cavell, *Disowning Knowledge*, 138.

Conclusion

1. Of course, Shakespeare also used his own source, Arthur Brooke's *Romeus and Juliet* (1562), which is a translation of the story from an Italian nouvelle. On the many early modern adaptations of Shakespeare's *Romeo and Juliet*, see Arthur M. Sampley, "Sixteenth Century Imitation of *Romeo and Juliet*," *Studies in English* 9 (1929): 103–105.

2. Sonia Massai laments that much scholarship "overlooks the originality of *'Tis Pity* and perpetuates old-fashioned views about Caroline drama as derivative and decadent." Massai, introduction to *'Tis Pity She's a Whore*, by John Ford, ed. Sonia Massai (London: Arden Shakespeare, 2011), 3. I believe that Ford's appropriation of Shakespeare's play reveals a continued fascination with clandestine marriage and a need to grapple with the practice and its consequences through literature decades after *Romeo and Juliet* was written.

3. See R. L. Smallwood, "*'Tis Pity She's a Whore* and *Romeo and Juliet*," *Cahiers Élisabéthains* 20 (1981): 49–70; Sidney R. Homan, "Shakespeare and Dekker as Keys to Ford's *'Tis Pity She's a Whore*," *Studies in English Literature, 1500–1900* 7, no. 2 (1967): 269–276; and Larry S. Champion, "Ford's *'Tis Pity She's a Whore* and the Jacobean Tragic Perspective," *PMLA* 90, no. 1 (1975): 78–87; and Irving Ribner, "'By Nature's Light': The Morality of *'Tis Pity She's a Whore*," *Tulane Studies in English* 10 (1960): 39–50. On the relationship between *'Tis Pity She's a Whore* and Shakespeare's *Othello*, see Raymond Powell, "The Adaptation of a Shakespearean Genre: *Othello* and Ford's *'Tis Pity She's a Whore*," *Renaissance Quarterly* 48, no. 3 (1995): 582–592.

4. Bruce Thomas Boehrer, *Monarchy and Incest in Renaissance England: Literature, Culture, Kinship, and Kingship* (Philadelphia: University of Pennsylvania Press, 1992), 125. For a refutation of this argument, see Susannah B. Mintz, "The Power of 'Parity' in Ford's *'Tis Pity She's a Whore*," *Journal of English and Germanic Philology* 102, no. 2 (2003): 269–291.

5. Emily C. Bartels, "*'Tis Pity She's a Whore*: The Play of Intertextuality," in *The Cambridge Companion to English Renaissance Tragedy*, ed. Emma Smith and Garrett A. Sullivan Jr. (Cambridge: Cambridge University Press, 2010), 251.

6. Outhwaite, *Clandestine Marriage*, 9.

7. Gee and Hardy, *Documents Illustrative of English Church History*, 537–545.

8. "House of Commons Journal Volume 3: 25 October 1643," in *Journal of the House of Commons: Volume 3, 1643–1644* (London: His Majesty's Stationary Office, 1802), 288.

9. These arguments played a pivotal role in the English Reformation when Henry VIII argued for the invalidation of his marriage to Catherine of Aragon on the basis of incest (since Catherine had been previously married to his deceased brother). While the Catholic Church refused to overturn its papal dispensation that allowed Henry VIII to marry Catherine in the first place, this historical moment underscores how the topic of incest, like clandestine marriage, often became a political issue. See Boehrer, *Mon-*

archy and Incest, 19–35; and Henry Ansgar Kelly, *The Matrimonial Trials of Henry VIII* (Stanford, CA: Stanford University Press, 1976).

10. See Matthew Parker, *An Admonition: To all such as shall intend heereafter to enter the state of matrimonie godly, and agreeable to Lawes* (London, 1605). The pamphlet, for example, warns that a woman may not marry her grandfather, husband's grandfather, brother, or sister's husband.

11. Dympna Callaghan, *Romeo and Juliet: Texts and Contexts* (Boston: Bedford/ St. Martin's Press, 2003), 247.

12. Stone, *Family, Sex and Marriage*, 87.

13. John Ford, *'Tis Pity She's a Whore*, ed. Sonia Massai (London: Arden Shakespeare, 2011). All in-text citations are from this edition.

14. Richard A. McCabe, "*'Tis Pity She's a Whore* and Incest," in *Early Modern English Drama: A Critical Companion*, ed. Garrett A. Sullivan Jr., Patrick Cheney, and Andrew Hadfield (New York: Oxford University Press, 2006), 309.

15. Michael Neill also observes how the scenes resemble each other. See Michael Neill, "What Strange Riddle's This? Deciphering *'Tis Pity She's a Whore*," in *John Ford: Critical Re-visions*, ed. Michael Neill (Cambridge: Cambridge University Press, 1988), 153–180. On how the language of Ford's play verbally echoes Webster's *Duchess of Malfi*, see Dorothy M. Farr, *John Ford and the Caroline Theatre* (London: Macmillan, 1979), 50, 55, 171.

16. McCabe, "*'Tis Pity She's a Whore* and Incest," 314.

17. Here I disagree with the scholars who view the play as ultimately affording a sympathetic reading of Annabella and Giovanni. Unlike Juliet, who willfully commits suicide, Annabella is not happy to die when calling Giovanni "unkind" at the moment of her death (5.6.93). In this way, I follow Annabella's lead. The text ultimately invites us to condemn Giovanni and the incestuous clandestine marriage.

18. On incest as violating nature's law, see Richard A. McCabe, *Incest, Drama, and Nature's Law, 1550–1700* (Cambridge: Cambridge University Press, 1993).

Bibliography

Acts of the Privy Council Volume 26, 1596–1597. Edited by John Roche Dasent. London: Her Majesty's Stationery Office, 1902.

Adelman, Janet. *Blood Relations: Christian and Jew in "The Merchant of Venice."* Chicago: University of Chicago Press, 2008.

Alpers, Paul J. *The Poetry of "The Faerie Queene."* Princeton, NJ: Princeton University Press, 1967.

Altieri, Joanne. *"Hero and Leander*: Sensible Myth and Lyric Subjectivity." *John Donne Journal* 8, nos. 1–2 (1989): 151–166.

Amussen, Susan Dwyer. *An Ordered Society: Gender and Class in Early Modern England.* New York: Columbia University Press, 1988.

Anderson, Douglas. "'Vnto My Selfe Alone': Spenser's Plenary Epithalamion." *Spenser Studies* 5 (1985): 149–166.

Andrews, Michael C. "Honest Othello: The Handkerchief Once More." *Studies in English Literature, 1500–1900* 13, no. 2 (1973): 273–284.

Aston, Edward. *The Manners, Lawes, and Customes of all Nations.* London, 1610.

Austin, J. L. *How to Do Things with Words: The William James Lectures Delivered in Harvard University in 1955.* Edited by J. O. Urmson and Marina Sbisa. Oxford: Clarendon Press, 1975.

Aveling, Dom Hugh. "The Marriages of Catholic Recusants, 1559–1642." *Journal of Ecclesiastical History* 14, no. 1 (1963): 68–83.

Barber, C. L. *Shakespeare's Festive Comedy: A Study of Dramatic Form and Its Relation to Social Custom.* Princeton, NJ: Princeton University Press, 1959.

Bartels, Emily C. *Speaking of the Moor: From Alcazar to "Othello."* Philadelphia: University of Pennsylvania Press, 2008.

——. "'Tis Pity She's a Whore: The Play of Intertextuality." In *The Cambridge Companion to English Renaissance Tragedy*, edited by Emma Smith and Garrett A. Sullivan, Jr., 249–260. Cambridge: Cambridge University Press, 2010.

Bates, Catherine. "The Enigma of *A Lover's Complaint.*" In *A Companion to Shakespeare's Sonnets*, edited by Michael Schoenfeldt, 426–440. Malden, MA: Blackwell, 2007.

——. *The Rhetoric of Courtship in Elizabethan Language and Literature.* Cambridge: Cambridge University Press, 1992.

Bell, Ilona. *Elizabethan Women and the Poetry of Courtship.* Cambridge: Cambridge University Press, 1998.

——. "Rethinking Shakespeare's Dark Lady." In *A Companion to Shakespeare's Sonnets*, edited by Michael Schoenfeldt, 293–313. Malden, MA: Blackwell, 2007.

Bell, Millicent. *Shakespeare's Tragic Skepticism*. New Haven, CT: Yale University Press, 2002.

Berger, Harry, Jr. *The Absence of Grace: Sprezzatura and Suspicion in Two Renaissance Courtesy Book*. Stanford, CA: Stanford University Press, 2000.

———. *A Fury in the Words: Love and Embarrassment in Shakespeare's Venice*. New York: Fordham University Press, 2012.

———. "Impertinent Trifling: Desdemona's Handkerchief." *Shakespeare Quarterly* 47, no. 3 (1996): 235–250.

Bevington, David. *Action Is Eloquence: Shakespeare's Language of Gesture*. Cambridge, MA: Harvard University Press, 1984.

Boehrer, Bruce Thomas. *Monarchy and Incest in Renaissance England: Literature, Culture, Kinship, and Kingship*. Philadelphia: University of Pennsylvania Press, 1992.

The Book of Common Prayer: The Texts of 1549, 1559, and 1662. Edited by Brian Cummings. Oxford: Oxford University Press, 2011.

Boose, Lynda E. "Othello's Handkerchief: 'The Recognizance and Pledge of Love.'" *English Literary Renaissance* 5, no. 3 (1975): 360–374.

Boulton, Jeremy. "Itching after Private Marryings? Marriage Customs in Seventeenth-Century London." *London Journal* 16, no. 1 (1991): 15–34.

Bradbook, M. C. *Shakespeare and Elizabethan Poetry: A Study of His Earlier Work in Relation to the Poetry of the Time*. London: Chatto and Windus, 1965.

Braden, Gordon. *The Classics and English Renaissance Poetry: Three Case Studies*. New Haven, CT: Yale University Press, 1978.

———. "Hero and Leander in Bed (and the Morning After)." *English Literary Renaissance* 45, no. 2 (2015): 205–230.

Bradshaw, Graham. *Misrepresentations: Shakespeare and the Materialists*. Ithaca, NY: Cornell University Press, 1993.

Brandt, Bruce. "Marlowe's Amplification of Musaeus in *Hero and Leander*." *Early Modern Literary Studies* 17, no. 23 (2014): 1–15.

Bredbeck, Gregory W. *Sodomy and Interpretation: Marlowe to Milton*. Ithaca, NY: Cornell University Press, 1991.

Breitenberg, Mark. *Anxious Masculinity in Early Modern England*. Cambridge: Cambridge University Press, 1996.

Brink, J. R. "The Masque of the Nine Muses: Sir John Davies's Unpublished 'Epithalamion' and the 'Belphoebe-Ruby' Episode in *The Faerie Queene*." *Review of English Studies* 23, no. 92 (1972): 445–447.

Bristol, Michael D. "Charivari and the Comedy of Abjection in *Othello*." *Renaissance Drama* 21 (1990): 3–21.

Britton, Dennis Austin. *Becoming Christian: Race, Reformation, and Early Modern English Romance*. New York: Fordham University Press, 2014.

Broaddus, James W. *Spenser's Allegory of Love: Social Vision in Books III, IV, and V of "The Faerie Queene."* Madison, NJ: Fairleigh Dickinson University Press, 1995.

Brooks-Davies, Douglas. "Una." In *The Spenser Encyclopedia*, edited by A. C. Hamilton, Donald Cheney, W. F. Blissett, David A. Richardson, and William W. Barker, 704–705. Toronto: University of Toronto Press, 1990.

Brown, Georgia E. "Breaking the Canon: Marlowe's Challenge to the Literary Status Quo in *Hero and Leander*." In *Marlowe, History, and Sexuality: New Critical Essays on Christopher Marlowe*, edited by Paul Whitfield White, 59–76. New York: AMS Press, 1998.

——. "Gender and Voice in *Hero and Leander*." In *Constructing Christopher Marlowe*, edited by J. A. Downie and J. T. Parnell, 148–163. Cambridge: Cambridge University Press, 2000.

Brown, John Russell. Introduction to *The Merchant of Venice*, by William Shakespeare, xi-lviii. Edited by John Russell Brown. London: Arden Shakespeare, 2006.

Brown, Roger Lee. "The Rise and Fall of the Fleet Marriages." In *Marriage and Society: Studies in the Social History of Marriage*, edited by R. B. Outhwaite, 117–136. London: Europa Publications, 1981.

Bucer, Martin. *Melanchthon and Bucer*. Edited and Translated by Wilhelm Pauck. Philadelphia: Westminster Press, 1969.

Bullinger, Heinrich. *The Christen State of Matrymonye*. London, 1552.

Burckhardt, Sigurd. *Shakespearean Meanings*. Princeton, NJ: Princeton University Press, 1968.

Burn, John Southerden. *The Fleet Registers: Comprising the History of Fleet Marriages and Some Account of the Parsons and Marriage-House Keepers*. London: Rivingtons, 1833.

Burrow, Colin. *Epic Romance: Homer to Milton*. Oxford: Clarendon Press, 1993.

——. Introduction to *The Complete Sonnets and Poems*, by William Shakespeare, 1–158. Oxford: Oxford University Press, 2002.

Burton, Jonathan. *Traffic and Turning: Islam and English Drama, 1579–1624*. Newark: University of Delaware Press, 2005.

Burton, Robert. *The Anatomy of Melancholy*. Edited by Thomas C. Faulkner, Nicolas K. Kiessling, and Rhonda L. Blair. 6 vols. Oxford: Clarendon Press, 1994.

Bush, Douglas. *Mythology and the Renaissance Tradition in English Poetry*. New revised edition. New York: W. W. Norton, 1963.

Callaghan, Dympna. *Romeo and Juliet: Texts and Contexts*. Boston: Bedford / St. Martin's Press, 2003.

Calvin, John. *Commentaries on the Epistles to Timothy, Titus, and Philemon*. Translated by William Pringle. Edinburgh: T. Constable, 1856.

——. *Institutes of the Christian Religion*. Edited by John T. McNeill. Translated by Ford Lewis Battles. Volumes 1 and 2. Philadelphia: Westminster Press, 1960.

——. *Calvin's New Testament Commentaries: A Harmony of the Gospels*. Translated by A. W. Morrison. Edited by David W. Torrance and Thomas F. Torrance. Volume 3. Grand Rapids, MI: William B. Eerdmans, 1972.

Campbell, Marion. "'*Desunt Nonnulla*': The Construction of Marlowe's *Hero and Leander* as an Unfinished Poem." *English Literary History* 51, no. 2 (1984): 241–268.

Capp, Bernard. "Bigamous Marriage in Early Modern England." *Historical Journal* 52, no. 3 (2009): 537–556.

Carey, John. *John Donne: Life, Mind and Art*. London: Faber and Faber, 1981.

Carlson, Eric Josef. *Marriage and the English Reformation: Family, Sexuality and Social Relations in Past Times*. Oxford: Blackwell, 1994.

——. "Marriage Reform and the Elizabethan High Commission." *Sixteenth Century Journal* 21, no. 3 (1990): 437–452.

Castiglione, Baldassarre. *The Book of the Courtier*. Edited by W. E. Henley. Translated by Thomas Hoby. London, 1900.

Cavell, Stanley. *Disowning Knowledge: In Six Plays of Shakespeare*. Cambridge: Cambridge University Press, 1987.

Cecil, William. *Advice to a Son*. Edited by Louis B. Wright. Ithaca, NY: Cornell University Press, 1962.

Celovsky, Lisa. "Early Modern Masculinities and *The Faerie Queene*." *English Literary Renaissance* 35, no. 2 (2005): 210–247.

Champion, Larry S. "Ford's *'Tis Pity She's a Whore* and the Jacobean Tragic Perspective," *PMLA* 90, no. 1 (1975): 78–87.

Chapman, George. "Continuation of Hero and Leander." In *The Collected Poems of Christopher Marlowe*, edited by Patrick Cheney and Brian J. Striar, 220–267. New York: Oxford University Press, 2006.

——. "Musaeus: Of Hero and Leander." In *The Works of George Chapman: Poems and Minor Translations*, 93–102. London: Chatto and Windus, 1875.

Cheney, Patrick. Introduction to *The Collected Poems of Christopher Marlowe*, 1–25. Edited by Patrick Cheney and Brian J. Striar. New York: Oxford University Press, 2006.

——. *Marlowe's Counterfeit Profession: Ovid, Spenser, Counter-Nationhood*. Toronto: Toronto University Press, 1997.

——. *Marlowe's Republican Authorship: Lucan, Liberty, and the Sublime*. London: Palgrave Macmillan, 2009.

——. "'The Passionate Shepherd to His Love' and *Hero and Leander*." In *Christopher Marlowe at 450*, edited by Sara Munson Deats and Robert A. Logan, 163–200. New York: Routledge, 2016.

——. *Shakespeare, National Poet-Playwright*. Cambridge: Cambridge University Press, 2004.

——. *Spenser's Famous Flight: A Renaissance Idea of a Literary Career*. Toronto: University of Toronto Press, 1993.

Chintz, David. "The Poem as Sacrament: Spenser's *Epithalamion* and the Golden Section." *Journal of Medieval and Renaissance Studies* 21, no. 2 (1991): 251–268.

Cinthio, Giovanni Battista Giraldi. "From *Gli Hecatommithi*." Vol. 7, *Narrative and Dramatic Sources of Shakespeare*, edited and translated by Geoffrey Bullough, 239–265. London: Routledge and Kegan Paul, 1973.

Cleaver, Robert. *A Godlie Forme of Hovsholde Government*. London, 1598.

Cleland, Katharine. "Rota Virgiliana." In *The Princeton Encyclopedia of Poetry and Poetics*, edited by Roland Greene and Stephen Cushman, 1226–1227. 4th ed. Princeton, NJ: Princeton University Press, 2012.

Cobbett, William, and T. C. Hansard, eds. *The Parliamentary History of England: From the Earliest Period to the Year 1803*. London, 1813.

Colclough, David. "Donne, John (1572–1631)." In *Oxford Dictionary of National Biography*, edited by David Cannadine. Oxford: Oxford University Press, 2004.

Constitutions and Canons Ecclesiastical. London, 1604.

Cook, Ann Jennalie. *Making a Match: Courtship in Shakespeare and His Society.* Princeton, NJ: Princeton University Press, 1991.

Craik, Katharine A. "Shakespeare's *A Lover's Complaint* and Early Modern Criminal Confession." *Shakespeare Quarterly* 53, no. 4 (2002): 437–459.

Cressy, David. *Birth, Marriage, and Death: Ritual, Religion, and the Life Cycle in Tudor and Stuart England.* Oxford: Oxford University Press, 1997.

Crofts, Robert. *The Way to Happinesse on Earth: Concerning Riches, Honour, Conjugall Love, Eating, Drinking.* London, 1641.

Cummings, Brian. Introduction to *The Book of Common Prayer: The Texts of 1549, 1559, and 1662,* ix–lii. Edited by Brian Cummings. Oxford: Oxford University Press, 2011.

———. "Notes to Matrimony 1549." In *The Book of Common Prayer: The Texts of 1549, 1559, and 1662,* edited by Brian Cummings, 711–714. Oxford: Oxford University Press, 2011.

Degenhardt, Jane Hwang. *Islamic Conversion and Christian Resistance on the Early Modern Stage.* Edinburgh: Edinburgh University Press, 2010.

Deitch, Judith. "The Girl He Left Behind: Ovidian *imitatio* and the Body of Echo in Spenser's *Epithalamion.*" In *Ovid and the Renaissance Body,* edited by Goran V. Stanivukovic, 224–238. Toronto: University of Toronto Press, 2001.

Dolan, Frances E. *Marriage and Violence: The Early Modern Legacy.* Philadelphia: University of Pennsylvania Press, 2008.

Donne, John. *John Donne's Marriage Letters in the Folger Shakespeare Library.* Edited by M. Thomas Hester, Robert Parker Sorlien, and Dennis Flynn. Washington, DC: Folger Shakespeare Library, 2005.

———. "Sermon Preached at a Mariage (the marriage of Mistress Margaret Washington at the church of St. Clement Danes, May 30, 1621)." In *The Sermons of John Donne,* vol. 3. no. 11, edited by Evelyn Mary Spearing Simpson and George Rueben Potter, 1-15. Berkeley: University of California Press, 1957.

Donow, Herbert S. "Shakespeare's Caskets: Unity in *The Merchant of Venice.*" *Shakespeare Studies* 4 (1969): 86–93.

Doran, Susan. "Keys [*née* Grey], Lady Mary: (1545?–1578)." In *Oxford Dictionary of National Biography,* edited by David Cannadine. Oxford: Oxford University Press, 2004.

———. "Seymour [*née* Grey], Katherine, Countess of Hertford: (1540?–1568)." In *Oxford Dictionary of National Biography,* edited by David Cannadine. Oxford: Oxford University Press, 2004.

Dubrow, Heather. *Captive Victors: Shakespeare's Narrative Poems and Sonnets.* Ithaca, NY: Cornell University Press, 1987.

———. *Echoes of Desire: English Petrarchism and Its Counterdiscourses.* Ithaca, NY: Cornell University Press, 1995.

Duncan, Helga. "'Headdie Ryots' as Reformations: Marlowe's Libertine Poetics." *Early Modern Literary Studies* 12, no. 2 (2006): 1–38.

Duncan-Jones, Katherine. "Was the 1609 Shake-Speares Sonnets Really Unauthorized?" *Review of English Studies* 34, no. 134 (1982): 151–171.

Dunlop, Alexander. "The Unity of Spenser's *Amoretti*." In *Silent Poetry: Essays in Numerological Analysis*, edited by Alistair Fowler, 153–169. New York: Barnes and Noble, 1970.

Edwards, Robert R. *The Flight from Desire: Augustine and Ovid to Chaucer*. New York: Palgrave Macmillan, 2006.

Emsley, Sarah. "'By Evene Acord': Marriage and Genre in the 'Parliament of Fowls.'" *Chaucer Review* 34, no. 2 (1999): 139–149.

Everett, Barbara. "'Spanish' *Othello*: The Making of Shakespeare's Moor." *Shakespeare Survey: An Annual Survey of Shakespearian Study and Production* 35 (1982): 101–112.

Farr, Dorothy M. *John Ford and the Caroline Theatre*. London: Macmillan, 1979.

Feerick, Jean E. *Strangers in Blood: Relocating Race in the Renaissance*. Toronto: University of Toronto Press, 2010.

Feldman, Abraham Bronson. "Othello's Obsessions." *American Imago* 9, no. 2 (1952): 147–164.

Fiedler, Leslie A. *The Stranger in Shakespeare*. New York: Stein and Day, 1972.

Floyd-Wilson, Mary. *English Ethnicity and Race in Early Modern Drama*. Cambridge: Cambridge University Press, 2003.

Ford, John. *'Tis Pity She's a Whore*. Edited by Sonia Massai. London: Arden Shakespeare, 2011.

Foxe, John. *A Sermon preached at the Christening of a Certaine Jew by Iohn Foxe. Conteining an exposition of the xi chapter of S. Paul to the Romanes. Translated out of Latine into English by Iames Bell*. London, 1578.

Frye, Northrop. *Fables of Identity: Studies in Poetic Mythology*. New York: Harcourt, Brace & World, 1963.

——. *A Natural Perspective: The Development of Shakespearean Comedy and Romance*. New York: Columbia University Press, 1965.

Fuchs, Barbara. *Romance*. New York: Routledge, 2004.

Furnivall, Frederick James, ed. *Child-Marriages, Divorces, and Ratifications &c. in the Diocese of Chester, A.D. 1561–6*. London: Early English Text Society, 1897.

Gaskell, Elizabeth. *Wives and Daughters: An Every Day Story*. London, 1866.

Gee, Henry, and William Hardy. *Documents Illustrative of English Church History*. London: Macmillan, 1896.

Gerard, John. *The Autobiography of an Elizabethan*. Translated by Philip Caraman. London: Longmans, Green, 1956.

Gibbons, Brian. Introduction to *Romeo and Juliet*, by William Shakespeare, 1–77. Edited by Brian Gibbons. London: Arden Shakespeare, 2008.

Gibson, Jonathan. "The Legal Context of Spenser's *Daphnaïda*." *Review of English Studies*, n.s., 55, no. 218 (2004): 24–44.

Giese, Loreen L. *Courtships, Marriage Customs, and Shakespeare's Comedies*. New York: Palgrave Macmillan, 2006.

——. *London Consistory Court Depositions, 1586–1611*. London: London Record Society, 1995.

Gless, Darryl J. *Interpretation and Theology in Spenser*. Cambridge: Cambridge University Press, 1994.

Go, Kenji. "Samuel Daniel's *The Complaint of Rosamond* and an Emblematic Reconsideration of *A Lover's Complaint.*" *Studies in Philology* 104, no. 1 (2007): 82–122.

Godshalk, W. L. "*Hero and Leander*: The Sense of an Ending." In *"A Poet and a Filthy Play-Maker": New Essays on Christopher Marlowe*, edited by Kenneth Friedenreich, Roma Gill, and Constance B. Kuriyama, 293–314. New York: AMS Press, 1988.

Goldberg, Jonathan. *Sodometries: Renaissance Texts, Modern Sexualities.* Stanford, CA: Stanford University Press, 1992.

Gouge, William. *Of Domesticall Duties.* London, 1622.

Graves, Michael A. R. "Howard, Thomas, Fourth Duke of Norfolk (1538–1572)." In *Oxford Dictionary of National Biography*, edited by David Cannadine. Oxford: Oxford University Press, 2004.

Greene, Roland. "*Amoretti* and *Epithalamion* (1595)." In *The Oxford Handbook of Edmund Spenser*, edited by Richard A. McCabe, 256–270. Oxford: Oxford University Press, 2010.

Griffin, Eric. "Un-sainting James: Or, *Othello* and the 'Spanish Spirits' of Shakespeare's Globe." *Representations* 62 (1998): 58–99.

Haber, Judith. "'True-Loves Blood': Narrative and Desire in *Hero and Leander.*" *English Literary Renaissance* 28, no. 3 (1998): 372–386.

Hadfield, Andrew. "Duessa's Trial and Elizabeth's Error: Judging Elizabeth in Spenser's *Faerie Queene.*" In *The Myth of Elizabeth*, edited by Susan Doran and Thomas S. Freeman, 56–76. London: Palgrave Macmillan, 2003.

——. *Edmund Spenser: A Life.* Oxford: Oxford University Press, 2012.

——. *Literature, Politics, and National Identity: Reformation to Renaissance.* Cambridge: Cambridge University Press, 1994.

——. "Spenser and Religion—yet Again." *Studies in English Literature, 1500–1900* 51, no. 1 (2011): 21–46.

Hall, Kim F. "Guess Who's Coming to Dinner? Colonization and Miscegenation in *The Merchant of Venice.*" *Renaissance Drama* 23 (1992): 87–111.

——. *Things of Darkness: Economies of Race and Gender in Early Modern England.* Ithaca, NY: Cornell University Press, 1995.

Hallstead, R. N. "Idolatrous Love: A New Approach to *Othello.*" *Shakespeare Quarterly* 19, no. 2 (1968): 107–124.

Hamilton, A. C. *The Structure of Allegory in "The Faerie Queene."* Oxford: Clarendon Press, 1961.

Hamilton, A. C., Hiroshi Yamashita, and Toshiyuki Suzuki. Introduction to *The Faerie Queene*, by Edmund Spenser, 1–20. 2nd ed. Harlow: Longman, 2001.

Hamlin, William M. *Tragedy and Skepticism in Shakespeare's England.* New York: Palgrave Macmillan, 2005.

Hanmer, Meredith. *The Baptizing of a Turke, A sermon preached at the Hospitall of Saint Katherin.* London, 1586.

Harned, Jon. "Rhetoric and Perverse Desire in *A Lover's Complaint.*" In *Critical Essays on Shakespeare's "A Lover's Complaint": Suffering Ecstasy*, edited by Shirley Sharon-Zisser, 149–164. Burlington, VT: Ashgate, 2006.

Hawkes, Emma. "Preliminary Notes on Consent in the 1382 Rape and Ravishment Laws of Richard II." *Legal History* 11, no. 1 (2007): 117–132.

Head, David M. "'Beyng Ledde and Seduced by the Devyll': The Attainder of Lord Thomas Howard and the Tudor Law of Treason." *Sixteenth Century Journal* 13, no. 4 (1982): 3–16.

Helgerson, Richard. *Forms of Nationhood: The Elizabethan Writing of England*. Chicago: University of Chicago Press, 1992.

Helmholz, R. H. *Marriage Litigation in Medieval England*. Cambridge: Cambridge University Press, 1974.

——. *Roman Canon Law in Reformation England*. Cambridge: Cambridge University Press, 1990.

Hero and Leander: begun by Christopher Marloe; and finished by George Chapman. London: Paul Linley, 1598.

Hester, Thomas M., Robert Parker Sorlien, and Dennis Flynn, eds. *John Donne's Marriage Letters in the Folger Shakespeare Library*. Washington, DC: Folger Shakespeare Library, 2005.

Hieatt, A. Kent. "A Numerical Key for Spenser's *Amoretti* and Guyon in the House of Mammon." *Yearbook of English Studies* 3 (1973): 14–27.

Hieatt, A. Kent, Charles W. Hieatt, and Anne Lake Prescott. "When Did Shakespeare Write *Sonnets* 1609." *Studies in Philology* 88, no. 1 (1991): 69–109.

Hile, Rachel E. "The Limitations of Concord in the Thames-Medway Marriage Canto of *The Faerie Queene*." *Studies in Philology* 108, no. 1 (2011): 70–85.

——. *Spenserian Satire: A Tradition of Indirection*. Manchester: Manchester University Press, 2017.

Hirsch, Brett D. "'A Gentle and No Jew': The Difference Marriage Makes in *The Merchant of Venice*." *Parergon* 23, no. 1 (2006): 119–129.

Holland, Peter. "Shakespeare, William (1564–1616)." In *Oxford Dictionary of National Biography*, edited by David Cannadine. Oxford: Oxford University Press, 2004.

Holmer, Joan Ozark. *"The Merchant of Venice": Choice, Hazard, and Consequence*. New York: St. Martin's Press, 1995.

Homan, Sidney R. "Shakespeare and Dekker as Keys to Ford's *'Tis Pity She's a Whore*." *Studies in English Literature, 1500–1900* 7, no. 2 (1967): 269–276.

Honigmann, E. A. J., Introduction to *Othello*, by William Shakespeare, 1–111. Edited by E. A. J. Honigmann. London: Arden Shakespeare, 2006.

Hopkins, Lisa. *The Shakespearean Marriage: Merry Wives and Heavy Husbands*. New York: St. Martin's Press, 1998.

Houlbrooke, Ralph. *Church Courts and the People during the English Reformation, 1520–1570*. Oxford: Oxford University Press, 1979.

"House of Commons Journal Volume 3: 25 October 1643." In *Journal of the House of Commons: Volume 3, 1643–1644*. London: His Majesty's Stationery Office, 1802.

Howard, Jean E. "Crossdressing, the Theatre, and Gender Struggle in Early Modern England." *Shakespeare Quarterly* 39, no. 4 (1988): 418–440.

Hug, Tobias B. *Impostures in Early Modern England: Representations and Perceptions of Fraudulent Identities*. Manchester: Manchester University Press, 2010.

Hulse, Clark. *Metamorphic Verse: The Elizabethan Minor Epic*. Princeton, NJ: Princeton University Press, 1981.

Hume, Anthea. "Duessa." In *The Spenser Encyclopedia*, edited by A. C. Hamilton, Donald Cheney, W. F. Blissett, David A. Richardson, and William W. Barker, 229–230. Toronto: University of Toronto Press, 1990.

Hunter, G. K. "The Theology of Marlowe's *The Jew of Malta*." *Journal of the Warburg and Courtauld Institutes* 27 (1964): 211–240.

——. "Unity and Numbers in Spenser's *Amoretti*." *Yearbook of English Studies* 5 (1975): 39–45.

Hutson, Lorna. *The Usurer's Daughter: Male Friendship and Fictions of Women in Sixteenth-Century England*. London: Routledge, 1994.

Ingram, Martin. *Church Courts, Sex and Marriage in England, 1570–1640*. Cambridge: Cambridge University Press, 1987.

Ives, E. W. "Henry VIII (1491–1547)." In *Oxford Dictionary of National Biography*. Edited by David Cannadine. Oxford: Oxford University Press, 2004.

Iyengar, Sujata. *Shades of Difference: Mythologies of Skin Color in Early Modern England*. Philadelphia: University of Pennsylvania Press, 2005.

Jackson, MacDonald P. "Dating Shakespeare's Sonnets: Some Old Evidence Revisited." *Notes and Queries* 49, no. 2 (2002): 237–241.

——. *Determining the Shakespeare Canon: "Arden of Faversham" and "A Lover's Complaint."* Oxford: Oxford University Press, 2014.

——. "Echoes of Spenser's *Prothalamion* as Evidence against an Early Date for Shakespeare's *A Lover's Complaint*." *Notes and Queries* 37, no. 2 (1990): 180–182.

——. "*A Lover's Complaint, Cymbeline*, and the Shakespeare Canon: Interpreting Shared Vocabulary." *Modern Language Review* 103, no. 3 (2008): 621–638.

——. "Rhymes in Shakespeare's *Sonnets*: Evidence of Date of Composition." *Notes and Queries* 46, no. 2 (1999): 213–219.

——. "Vocabulary and Chronology: The Case of Shakespeare's Sonnets." *Review of English Studies* 52, no. 205 (2001): 59–76.

James, Heather. "Ovid and the Question of Politics in Early Modern England." *ELH* 70, no. 2 (2003): 343–373.

——. "The Poet's Toys: Christopher Marlowe and the Liberties of Erotic Elegy." *Modern Language Quarterly* 67, no. 1 (2006): 103–128.

Jardine, Lisa. "Cultural Confusion and Shakespeare's Learned Heroines: 'These Are Old Paradoxes.'" *Shakespeare Quarterly* 38, no. 1 (1987): 1–18.

Jensen, Ejner J. *Shakespeare and the Ends of Comedy*. Bloomington: Indiana University Press, 1991.

Johnson, William C. "'Sacred Rites' and Prayer-Book Echoes in Spenser's 'Epithalamion,'" *Renaissance and Reformation* 12, no. 1 (1976): 49–54.

——. "Spenser's *Amoretti* and the Art of the Liturgy." *Studies in English Literature, 1500–1900* 14, no. 1 (1974): 47–61.

Kaplan, M. Lindsay. *The Culture of Slander in Early Modern England*. Cambridge: Cambridge University Press, 1997.

——. "Jessica's Mother: Medieval Constructions of Jewish Race and Gender in *The Merchant of Venice*." *Shakespeare Quarterly* 58, no. 1 (2007): 1–30.

Kaske, Carol V. "Spenser's *Amoretti* and *Epithalamion* of 1595: Structure, Genre and Numerology." *English Literary Renaissance* 8, no. 3 (1978): 271–295.

Keach, William. *Elizabethan Erotic Narratives: Irony and Pathos in the Ovidian Poetry of Shakespeare, Marlowe, and Their Contemporaries.* New Brunswick, NJ: Rutgers University Press, 1977.

Kellett, Edward. *A Returne from Argier. A Sermon Preached at Minhead in the County of Somerset the 16. Of March, 1627, at the re-admission of a relapsed Christian into our Church.* London, 1628.

Kelly, Henry Ansgar. *Love and Marriage in the Age of Chaucer.* Ithaca, NY: Cornell University Press, 1975.

——. *The Matrimonial Trials of Henry VIII.* Stanford, CA: Stanford University Press, 1976.

Kermode, Lloyd Edward. *Aliens and Englishness in Elizabethan Drama.* Cambridge: Cambridge University Press, 2009.

Kerrigan, John. Introduction to *The Sonnets and A Lover's Complaint,* by William Shakespeare, 7–64. New York: Viking, 1986.

——. *Motives of Woe: Shakespeare and 'Female Complaint': A Critical Anthology.* Oxford: Clarendon Press, 1991.

King, John N. *Spenser's Poetry and the Reformation Tradition.* Princeton, NJ: Princeton University Press, 1990.

——. *Tudor Royal Iconography: Literature and Art in an Age of Religious Crisis.* Princeton, NJ: Princeton University Press, 1989.

Korda, Natasha. *Shakespeare's Domestic Economies: Gender and Property in Early Modern England.* Philadelphia: University of Pennsylvania Press, 2002.

Krier, Theresa. "*The Faerie Queene* (1596)." In *A Critical Companion to Spenser Studies,* edited by Bart van Es, 188–209. New York: Palgrave Macmillan, 2006.

Lambert, James S. "Spenser's *Epithalamion* and the Protestant Expression of Joy." *Studies in English Literature 1500–1900* 54, no. 1 (2014): 81–103.

Lavezzo, Kathy. *The Accommodated Jew: English Antisemitism from Bede to Milton.* Ithaca, NY: Cornell University Press, 2016.

Lawrence, William Witherle. *Shakespeare's Problem Comedies.* New York: Frederick Ungar, 1960.

Leech, Clifford. "Venus and Her Nun: Portraits of Women in Love by Shakespeare and Marlowe." *Studies in English Literature, 1500–1900* 5, no. 2 (1965): 247–268.

Lethbridge, J. B., ed. *Shakespeare and Spenser: Attractive Opposites.* New York: Palgrave Macmillan, 2008.

Levin, Carole. *The Reign of Elizabeth I.* New York: Palgrave, 2002.

Levin, Carole, and John Watkins. *Shakespeare's Foreign Worlds: National and Transnational Identities in the Elizabethan Age.* Ithaca, NY: Cornell University Press, 2009.

Lewis, C. S. *The Allegory of Love: A Study in Medieval Tradition.* Oxford: Oxford University Press, 1936.

Loewenstein, Joseph. "Echo's Ring: Orpheus and Spenser's Career." *English Literary Renaissance* 16, no. 2 (1986): 287–302.

Lumley, John, Baron. Letter from John Lumley, Baron Lumley Nonsuch, to Richard Bagot, 1589 November 25. In *Papers of the Bagot Family of Blithfield, Staffordshire, 1428–1671 (bulk 1557–1671).* Folger MS L.a. 628, Folger Shakespeare Library, Washington, DC.

Lupton, Julia Reinhard. *Citizen-Saints: Shakespeare and Political Theology*. Chicago: University of Chicago Press, 2005.

Luther, Martin. "An Open Letter to the Christian Nobility." In *Works of Martin Luther*, vol. 2, translated by Charles M. Jacobs, 61–164. Philadelphia: A.J. Holman Company, 1915.

MacCaffrey, Isabel G. *Spenser's Allegory: The Anatomy of Imagination*. Princeton, NJ: Princeton University Press, 1976.

MacFarlane, Alan. *Marriage and Love in England: 1300–1840*. Hoboken, NJ: Blackwell, 1987.

Mallette, Richard. *Spenser and the Discourses of Reformation*. Lincoln: University of Nebraska Press, 1997.

Malone, Edmond. *The Plays and Poems of William Shakespeare: In Ten Volumes*. London, 1790.

Manuale ad vsum percelebris ecclesie Sarisburiensis. Rouen, 1543.

Marcus, Leah S. Introduction to *The Duchess of Malfi*, by John Webster, 1–113. Edited by Leah S. Marcus. London: Arden Early Modern Drama, 2009.

Marlowe, Christopher. *The Collected Poems of Christopher Marlowe*. Edited by Patrick Cheney and Brian J. Striar. New York: Oxford University Press, 2006.

Marotti, Arthur F. "'Love Is Not Love': Elizabethan Sonnet Sequences and the Social Order." *ELH* 49, no. 2 (1982): 396–428.

——. "Shakespeare's Sonnets as Literary Property." In *Soliciting Interpretation: Literary Theory and Seventeenth Century English Poetry*, edited by Elizabeth D. Harvey and Katharine Eisaman Maus, 143–173. Chicago: University of Chicago Press, 1990.

Massai, Sonia. Introduction to *'Tis Pity She's a Whore*, by John Ford, 1–87. Edited by Sonia Massai. London: Arden Shakespeare, 2011.

Matteo, Anthony Di. "Spenser's Venus-Virgo: The Poetics and Interpretive History of a Dissembling Figure." *Spenser Studies* 10 (1992): 37–70.

Mazzolla, Elizabeth. "Marrying Medusa: Spenser's *Epithalamion* and Renaissance Reconstructions of Female Privacy." *Genre* 25, nos. 2–3 (1992): 193–210.

McCabe, Richard A. *Incest, Drama, and Nature's Law, 1550–1700*. Cambridge: Cambridge University Press, 1993.

——. "The Masks of Duessa: Spenser, Mary Queen of Scots, and James VI." *English Literary Renaissance* 17, no. 2 (1987): 224–242.

——. "'Tis Pity She's a Whore and Incest." In *Early Modern English Drama: A Critical Companion*, edited by Garrett A. Sullivan Jr., Patrick Cheney, and Andrew Hadfield, 309–320. New York: Oxford University Press, 2006.

Miller, David Lee. "The Death of the Modern: Gender and Desire in Marlowe's *Hero and Leander*." *South Atlantic Quarterly* 88, nos. 3–4 (1989): 757–787.

Miller, Jacqueline T. "The Omission in Red Cross Knight's Story: Narrative Inconsistencies in *The Faerie Queene*." *ELH* 53, no. 2 (1986): 279–288.

Mintz, Susannah B. "The Power of 'Parity' in Ford's *'Tis Pity She's a Whore*." *Journal of English and Germanic Philology* 102, no. 2 (2003): 269–291.

Moulton, Ian Frederick. "Jacque Ferrand's *On Lovesickness*: Love and Medicine." In *Love in Print in the Sixteenth Century: The Popularization of Romance*, 145–182. New York: Palgrave, 2014.

Mudford, Peter G. "*Othello* and the 'Tragedy of Situation.'" *English: Journal of the English Association* 20, no. 106 (1971): 1–6.

Musaeus. *Hero and Leander,* edited by Thomas Gelzer and translated by Cedric Whitman. Loeb Classical Library 421. Cambridge, MA: Harvard University Press, 1975.

Nathan, Norman. "Othello's Marriage Is Consummated." *Cahiers Élisabéthains* 34, no. 1 (1988): 79–82.

Neill, Michael. "Changing Places in *Othello.*" In *Putting History to the Question: Power, Politics and Society in English Renaissance Drama*, 207–236. New York: Columbia University Press, 2000.

——. Introduction to *Othello*, by William Shakespeare, 113–130. Oxford: Oxford University Press, 2006.

——. "'Mulattos, 'Blacks,' and 'Indian Moors': *Othello* and Early Modern Constructions of Human Difference." *Shakespeare Quarterly* 49, no. 4 (1994): 361–374.

——. "What Strange Riddle's This? Deciphering *'Tis Pity She's a Whore.*" In *John Ford: Critical Re-visions*, edited by Michael Neill, 153–180. Cambridge: Cambridge University Press, 1988.

Nelson, T. G. A., and Charles Haines. "Othello's Unconsummated Marriage." *Essays in Criticism* 33, no. 1 (1983): 1–18.

Neuse, Richard. "Book VI as Conclusion to *The Faerie Queene.*" ELH 35, no. 3 (1968): 329–353.

Newman, Karen. "'And Wash the Ethiop White': Femininity and the Monstrous in *Othello.*" In *Shakespeare Reproduced: The Text in History and Ideology*, edited by Jean E. Howard and Marion F. O'Connor, 142–162. London: Methuen, 1987.

——. "Portia's Ring: Unruly Women and Structures of Exchange in *The Merchant of Venice.*" *Shakespeare Quarterly* 38, no. 1 (1987): 19–33.

Niebrzydowski, Sue. "Encouraging Marriage in facie ecclesiae: The Mary Play 'Betrothal' and the Sarum Ordo ad faciendum Sponsalia." *Medieval English Theatre* 24 (2002): 44–61.

Nohrnberg, James. *The Analogy of "The Faerie Queene."* Princeton, NJ: Princeton University Press, 1976.

Northrop, Douglas A. "The Uncertainty of Courtesy in Book VI of *The Faerie Queene.*" *Spenser Studies* 14 (2000): 215–232.

O'Hara, Diana. *Courtship and Constraint: Rethinking the Making of Marriage in Tudor England.* Manchester: Manchester University Press, 2000.

——. "The Language of Tokens and the Making of Marriage." *Rural History* 3, no. 1 (1992): 1–40.

Oram, William A. "Daphnaida and Spenser's Later Poetry." *Spenser Studies* 2 (1981): 141–158.

——. "Elizabethan Fact and Spenserian Fiction." *Spenser Studies* 4 (1983): 33–47.

——. "Raleigh, the Queen, and Elizabethan Court Poetry." In *Early Modern English Poetry: A Critical Companion*, edited by Patrick Cheney, Andrew Hadfield, and Garrett A. Sullivan Jr., 113–124. Oxford: Oxford University Press, 2007.

——. "Spenser's Raleghs." *Studies in Philology* 87, no. 3 (1990): 341–362.

Oram, William A., Einar Bjorvand, Ronald Bond, Thomas H. Cain, Alexander Dunlop, and Richard Schell, eds. *The Yale Edition of the Shorter Poems of Edmund Spenser*. New Haven, CT: Yale University Press, 1989.

Orgel, Stephen. "Musaeus in English." *George Herbert Journal* 29, nos. 1–2 (2005–2006): 67–75.

Orkin, Martin. "Othello and the 'Plain Face' of Racism." *Shakespeare Quarterly* 38, no. 2 (1987): 166–188.

Orlin, Lena Cowen. *Private Matters and Public Culture in Post Reformation England*. Ithaca, NY: Cornell University Press, 1994.

Outhwaite, R. B. "Age at Marriage in England from the Seventeenth to the Nineteenth Centuries." *Transactions of the Royal Historical Society* 23 (1973): 55–70.

———. *Clandestine Marriage in England, 1500–1850*. London: Hambledon Press, 1995.

Ovid. *Heroides*. 2nd ed. revised by G. P. Goold. Translated and edited by Grant Showerman. Loeb Classical Library 41. Cambridge, MA: Harvard University Press, 1977.

Owens, Judith. "The Poetics of Accommodation in Spenser's *Epithalamion*." *Studies in English Literature* 40, no. 1 (2000): 41–62.

Ozment, Steven. *When Fathers Ruled: Family Life in Reformation Europe*. Cambridge, MA: Harvard University Press, 1983.

Parker Matthew. *An Admonition: To all such as shall intend hereafter to enter the state of matrimonie godly, and agreeable to Lawes*. London, 1605.

Parker, Patricia A. *Inescapable Romance: Studies in the Poetics of a Mode*. Princeton, NJ: Princeton University Press, 1979.

Perkins, William. *Christain Oeconomie: or, A Short Survey of the Right Manner of Erecting and Ordering a Familie, according to the Scriptures*. London, 1609.

Powell, Raymond. "The Adaptation of a Shakespearean Genre: *Othello* and Ford's *'Tis Pity She's a Whore*." *Renaissance Quarterly* 48 (1995): 582–592.

Purkiss, Diane. *The Witch in History: Early Modern and Twentieth-Century Representations*. New York: Routledge, 1996.

Puttenham, George. *Arte of English Poesie*. London, 1589.

Quint, David. "The Boat of Romance and Renaissance Epic." In *Romance: Generic Transformation from Chrétien de Troyes to Cervantes*, edited by Kevin Brownlee and Marina Scordilis Brownlee, 178–202. Hanover, NH: University Press of England, 1985.

———. *Epic and Empire: Politics and Generic Form from Virgil to Milton*. Princeton, NJ: Princeton University Press, 1993.

Raleigh, Walter. "Introduction." In *The Book of the Courtier*, edited by W. E. Henley and translated by Thomas Hoby, vii–lxxxviii. London, 1900.

Ray, Sid. "'Rape I Fear, Was Root of They Annoy': The Politics of Consent in *Titus Andronicus*." *Shakespeare Quarterly* 49, no. 1 (1998): 22–39.

Ribner, Irving. "'By Nature's Light': The Morality of *'Tis Pity She's a Whore*." *Tulane Studies in English* 10 (1960): 39–50.

Rickman, Johanna. *Love, Lust, and License in Early Modern England: Illicit Sex and the Nobility*. Burlington, VT: Ashgate, 2008.

Robinson, Richard, ed. and trans. "The 32 Historie." In *A record of auncient histories, entituled in Latin: Gesta Romanorum Discoursing vpon sundry examples for the aduancement of vertue, and the abandoning of vice*, 96–105. London, 1595.

Roche, Thomas P., Jr. *The Kindly Flame: A Study of the Third and Fourth Books of Spenser's "Faerie Queene."* Princeton, NJ: Princeton University Press, 1964.

Rogers, Daniel. *Matrimoniall Honour.* London, 1542.

Rogers, Stephen. "*Othello*: Comedy in Reverse." *Shakespeare Quarterly* 24, no. 2 (1973): 210–222.

Rosendale, Timothy. *Liturgy and Literature in the Making of Protestant England.* Cambridge: Cambridge University Press, 2007.

Rymer, Thomas. *A Short View of Tragedy.* London, 1693.

Sale, Carolyn. "The 'Roman Hand': Women, Writing and the Law in the *Att.-Gen. v. Chatterton* and the Letters of the Lady Arbella Stuart." *ELH* 70, no. 4 (2003): 929–961.

Sampley, Arthur M. "Sixteenth Century Imitation of *Romeo and Juliet.*" *Studies in English* 9 (1929): 103–105.

Sanchez, Melissa E. "'Modesty or Comeliness': The Predicament of Reform Theology in Spenser's *Amoretti* and *Epithalamion.*" *Renascence* 65, no. 1 (2012): 5–24.

Schoenbaum, Samuel. *William Shakespeare: A Documentary Life.* Oxford: Oxford University Press, 1975.

Schoenfeldt, Michael. *The Cambridge Introduction to Shakespeare's Poetry.* Cambridge: Cambridge University Press, 2010.

Semler, L. E. "Marlovian Therapy: The Chastisement of Ovid in *Hero and Leander.*" *English Literary Renaissance* 35, no. 2 (2005): 159–186.

Shakespeare, William. *The Riverside Shakespeare.* Edited by G. Blakemore Evans et al. 2nd ed. Boston: Houghton Mifflin, 1997.

Shannon, Laurie. "Likenings: Rhetorical Husbandries and Portia's 'True Conceit' of Friendship." *Renaissance Drama* 31 (2002): 3–26.

Shapiro, James. *Shakespeare and the Jews.* New York: Columbia University Press, 1996.

Silberman, Lauren. *Transforming Desire: Erotic Knowledge in Books III and IV of "The Faerie Queene."* Berkeley: University of California Press, 1995.

Sinfield, Alan. "Marlowe's Erotic Verse." In *Early Modern English Poetry: A Critical Companion*, edited by Patrick Cheney, Andrew Hadfield, and Garrett A. Sullivan Jr., 125–135. Oxford: Oxford University Press, 2007.

Sisson, Andrew. "Othello and the Unweaponed City." *Shakespeare Quarterly* 66, no. 2 (2015): 137–166.

Slights, Camille. "In Defense of Jessica: The Runaway Daughter in *The Merchant of Venice.*" *Shakespeare Quarterly* 31, no. 3 (1980): 357–368.

Smallwood, R. L. "'Tis Pity She's a Whore and Romeo and Juliet." *Cahiers Élisabétains* 20 (1981): 49–70.

Smith, Bruce R. *Homosexual Desire in Shakespeare's England: A Cultural Poetics.* Chicago: University of Chicago Press, 1991.

Smith, Richard M. "Population and Its Geography in England 1500–1730." In *An Historical Geography of England and Wales*, edited by R. A. Dodgshon and R. A. Butlin, 199–237. London: Academic Press, 1978.

Snyder, Susan. "*Othello* and the Conventions of Romantic Comedy." *Renaissance Drama* 5 (1972): 123–141.

Sokol, B. J., and Mary Sokol. *Shakespeare, Law, and Marriage*. Cambridge: Cambridge University Press, 2003.

Sokolov, Danila. "'Love Gave the Wound, Which While I Breathe Will Bleed': Sidney's *Astrophil and Stella* and the Subject of Melancholy." *Sidney Journal* 30, no. 1 (2012): 27–50.

Spenser, Edmund. *The Faerie Queene*. Edited by A. C. Hamilton, Hiroshi Yamashita, and Toshiyuki Suzuki. 2nd ed. Harlow: Longman, 2001.

——. *The Shorter Poems*. Edited by Richard A. McCabe. London: Penguin, 1999.

Spiller, Elizabeth A. "From Imagination to Miscegenation: Race and Romance in Shakespeare's *The Merchant of Venice*." *Renaissance Drama* 29 (1998): 137–164.

Steen, Sara Jayne. "The Crime of Marriage: Arbella Stuart and *The Duchess of Malfi*." *Sixteenth Century Journal* 22, no. 1 (1991): 61–76.

Stegner, Paul D. *Confession and Memory in Early Modern English Literature: Penitential Remains*. New York: Palgrave Macmillan, 2016.

——. "A Reconciled Maid: *A Lover's Complaint* and Confessional Practices in Early Modern England." In *Critical Essays on Shakespeare's "A Lover's Complaint"*, edited by Shirley Sharon-Zisser, 79–90. Aldershot: Ashgate, 2006.

Stewart, Alan. *Shakespeare's Letters*. Oxford: Oxford University Press, 2008.

Stone, Lawrence. *The Family, Sex and Marriage in England, 1500–1800*. New York: Harper & Row, 1977.

——. *Road to Divorce: England 1530–1987*. Oxford: Oxford University Press, 1990.

——. *Uncertain Unions: Marriage in England 1660–1753*. Oxford: Oxford University Press, 1992.

Stretton, Tim. *Women Waging Law in Elizabethan England*. Cambridge: Cambridge University Press, 1998.

Strong, Roy. *Artists of the Tudor Court*. London: Victoria & Albert Museum, 1983.

Strype, John. *The Life and Acts of John Whitgift, D.D.: The Third and Last Lord Archbishop of Canterbury in the Reign of Queen Elizabeth*. Volume 2. Oxford: Clarendon Press, 1822.

Stubbs, John. *The Discoverie of a Gaping Gulf Whereinto England is Like to be Swallowed by an other French mariage, if the Lord forbid not the banes, by letting her Maiestie see the sin and punishment thereof*. London, 1579.

Summers, Claude J. "*Hero and Leander*: The Arbitrariness of Desire." In *Constructing Christopher Marlowe*, edited by J. A. Downie and J. T. Parnell, 133–147. Cambridge: Cambridge University Press, 2000.

Swift, Daniel. *Shakespeare's Common Prayers: The Book of Common Prayer and the Elizabethan Age*. Oxford: Oxford University Press, 2013.

Swinburne, Henry. *A Treatise of Spousals, or Matrimonial Contracts*. London, 1686.

Targoff, Ramie. *Common Prayer: The Language of Public Devotion in Early Modern England*. Chicago: University of Chicago Press, 2001.

——. *Posthumous Love: Eros and the Afterlife in Renaissance England*. Chicago: University of Chicago Press, 2001.

Transcript of the proceedings, with depositions, etc., of a royal commission to enquire into an alleged marriage between Edward Seymour, Earl of Hertford, and the Lady Catherine Grey. 7 Feb 1562–12 May 1562. British Library Add. MS 33749.

Traub, Valerie. *The Renaissance of Lesbianism in Early Modern England*. Cambridge: Cambridge University Press, 2002.

Trevor, Douglas. *The Poetics of Melancholy in Early Modern England*. Cambridge: Cambridge University Press, 2004.

Tromly, Fred B. *Playing with Desire: Christopher Marlowe and the Art of Tantalization*. Toronto: University of Toronto Press, 1998.

Tufte, Virginia. *The Poetry of Marriage: The Epithalamium in Europe and Its Development in England*. Los Angeles: Tinnon-Brown, 1970.

Vickers, Brian. *Shakespeare, "A Lover's Complaint," and John Davies of Hereford*. Cambridge: Cambridge University Press, 2007.

Virgil. *Aeneid*. Translated by H. Rushton Fairclough. Loeb Classical Library 63. Cambridge, MA: Harvard University Press, 1967.

Vitkus, Daniel J. *Turning Turk: English Theater and the Multicultural Mediterranean, 1570–1630*. New York: Palgrave Macmillan, 2003.

Waddington, Raymond B. "Blind Gods: Fortune, Justice and Cupid in *The Merchant of Venice*." *ELH* 44 (1977): 458–477.

Walker, Garthine. "The Strangeness of the Familiar: Witchcraft and the Law in Early Modern England." In *The Extraordinary and the Everyday in Early Modern England: Essays in Celebration of the Work of Bernard Capps*, edited by Angela McShane and Garthine Walker, 105–124. London: Palgrave Macmillan, 2010.

Wall, Wendy. *Staging Domesticity: Household Work and English Identity in Early Modern Drama*. Cambridge: Cambridge University Press, 2002.

Walsh, William P. "Sexual Discovery and Renaissance Morality in Marlowe's *Hero and Leander*." *Studies in English Literature, 1500–1900* 12, no. 1 (1972): 33–54.

Ward, E. Y. Elliott, and Robert J. Valenza. "Glass Slippers and Seven-League Boots: C-prompted Doubts about Ascribing *A Funeral Elegy* and *A Lover's Complaint* to Shakespeare." *Shakespeare Quarterly* 48, no. 2 (1997): 177–207.

Waters, D. Douglas. *Duessa as Theological Satire*. Columbia: University of Missouri Press, 1970.

Watkins, John. *The Specter of Dido: Spenser and Virgilian Epic*. New Haven, CT: Yale University Press, 1995.

Weatherby, Harold L. *Mirrors of Celestial Grace: Patristic Theology in Spenser's Allegory*. Toronto: University of Toronto Press, 1994.

Weaver, William P. "Marlowe's Fable: *Hero and Leander* and the Rudiments of Eloquence." *Studies in Philology* 105, no. 3 (2008): 388–408.

——. *Untutored Lines: The Making of the English Epyllion*. Edinburgh: Edinburgh University Press, 2012.

Webster, John. *The Duchess of Malfi*. Edited by Leah S. Marcus. London: Arden Early Modern Drama, 2009.

Weston, William. *The Autobiography of an Elizabethan*. Translated by Philip Caraman. London: Longmans, Green, 1955.

Whately, William. *A Bride-Bvsh, or a Wedding Sermon*. London, 1617.

Wheeler, Richard P. *Shakespeare's Development and the Problem Comedies: Turn and Counter-Turn*. Berkeley: University of California Press, 1981.

Whitgift, John. *The Defense of the Aunswere to the Admonition, against the Replie of T.C.* London, 1574.

Wilson-Okamura, David Scott. "Problems in the Virgilian Career." *Spenser Studies* 26 (2011): 1–30.

Wrightson, Keith. *Earthly Necessities: Economic Lives in Early Modern Britain.* New Haven, CT: Yale University Press, 2000.

Zocca, Louis R. *Elizabethan Narrative Poetry.* New York: Octagon Books, 1970.

Zurcher, Andrew. *Spenser's Legal Language: Law and Poetry in Early Modern England.* Cambridge: D. S. Brewer, 2007.

Index

canon law: calling of banns and, 65;
Calvinist rejection of, 55; on celibacy,
49–50; on consent as sole requirement for
legal marriage, 5–6; *Corpus of Canon Law*,
143n8; *Decretals of Gregory IX*, 143n8;
enforcement of, 12; Gratian, *Concordance
of Discordant Canons*, 11, 143n8; legality
of marriage under, 137; sources for,
143n8. *See also* legality of clandestine
marriage; Roman canon law
Carlson, Eric Josef, 22, 91, 92
Caroline period, 134–35, 139
casket test (*Merchant of Venice*), 95–100, 104,
106
Castiglione, Baldassarre, *The Book of the
Courtier*, 46
Catherine of Aragon, 19, 168n9
Catholicism: clandestine marriage and, 26,
135–36, 141; English national identity
and, 19–22; Henry VIII and, 168n9; Jesuit
monks, 22; marriage to Protestants and,
15; sacraments and, 72; sympathies for,
79–80. *See also* Roman canon law
Catholic recusants, 22, 103, 147n29
Cavell, Stanley, 132–33
Cecil, Robert, 94
Cecil, William, Lord Burghley, 94
celebration of nuptials, 6, 52, 66, 70, 73–74,
76–77, 127
Celovsky, Lisa, 34
Chapman, George: clandestine marriage
plots, 3; continuation of Marlowe's *Hero
and Leander*, 4, 40, 56–62, 74, 81;
"Epithalamion Teratos," 57; Musaeus's
Hero and Leander and, 62; *Ovid's Banquet
of Sense*, 62, 152n9
Charles I, 135
chastity, 36, 42; iconography and, 46; marital
monogamy and, 48–50, 82; value of, 59.
See also virginity; virtue
Chaucer, Geoffrey, 158n28; *Legend of Good
Women*, 30; *Troilus and Criseyde*, 11
Cheney, Patrick, 64, 153n22
Christian community: Jewish integration into,
15, 87–88, 101–9; Muslim/Turk integration
into, 110–26. *See also Book of Common
Prayer*; Catholicism; conversion to
Christianity; English Reformation;
Protestant Reformation; religious outsiders
church courts. *See* ecclesiastical courts
Church of England, 147n17; dismantling of,
136. *See also* Catholicism; English
Reformation

Cinthio, *Gli Hecatommithi*, 112, 113
clandestine marriage: as deceptive practice,
5, 19, 26, 34, 76, 79, 125–26, 133, 136;
definitions of, 4–12; in early modern
English literature, 1–3, 11, 15–16 (*see also*
Chapman; Marlowe; Shakespeare;
Spenser); ease of, 106; evidence as proof
of, 31, 83–84, 118, 120–21, 131, 138–39;
financial consequences of, 10–11; legality
of, 1–2, 5–6, 9–10, 127; legitimacy of,
108–9, 112, 126–33; levels of, 6; by license,
80–81; political discourses and, 3, 14–15,
22–23, 27, 134 (*see also* English national
identity); religious discourses and, 3,
17–24, 26–27, 31–34, 42, 76, 88, 134
(*see also* English Reformation; Protestant
Reformation); scholarship on, 3–6;
seduction and, 81; sexual desire and, 8,
25–27 (*see also* sexual desire); social
discourses and, 12, 56, 76, 86, 134;
transformation of identity and
(*see* identity); as transgressive
(*see* transgression). *See also* elopement;
handfasting; private marital contracts;
trothplight
Cleaver, Robert, 7, 91
clerics. *See* ministers; priests
comedies, 87–88, 99
community approval of marriages: consent
and, 70–71, 97; elopement and, 94, 104–6;
impediments and, 28; importance of, 122,
132; lack of, 127, 132; prevention of
abandonment and, 81. *See also* public
surveillance of courtship and marriage
companionship, marital, 7, 62, 66
confession, 80
consent: age of, 137; of community
(*see* community approval of marriages);
elopement and, 120, 122–23; expressions
of mutual, 13; intersubjectivity and, 83;
parental, 91–100, 104, 132, 138; as sole
requirement for legal marriage, 5–6, 9,
19–21, 55; tokens as sign of, 83 (*see also*
love tokens)
consummation: absence of, 132–33;
"bed-vow," 78; public surveillance of,
73–74, 86; as validating marriage
contract, 5, 33, 52, 56, 63, 73, 85, 115;
violence and, 54, 60, 76
conversion to Christianity, 16, 87–90,
101–13, 117–19, 122–23, 125, 131, 133;
through baptism, 102, 112–13, 164n54,
165n13